Siri Hustvedt

Siri Hustvedt is the author of the novels *The Blindfold*, *The Enchantment of Lily Dahl*, *What I Loved*, *The Sorrows of an American* and *The Summer Without Men*. She has also published the essay collections *Yonder*, *Mysteries of the Rectangle* and *A Plea for Eros*, a book of poetry, and the autobiographical *The Shaking Woman or A History of My Nerves*. Born in Minnesota, she lives in Brooklyn, New York.

'Her interests in neuroscience and philosophy might at first seem unusual in a novelist, but these subjects throw light on phenomena – memory, imagination, our sense of self – that cannot fail to fascinate a writer of fiction . . . she is an inspiring guide to territory where both the humanities and the sciences can throw light on the ways in which we construct meaning in our lives.'

Nick Rennison, *The Sunday Times*

'Her erudition, the sharp clarity of her thinking, the variety of her sources and the supple ways in which she weaves them into personal narrative, coupled with her fearlessness in the face of those aspects of the human condition which are of necessity ambiguous, infuse her work with a rare kind of quiet intellectual confidence. "In the best art something always escapes us and bewilders us. If it didn't, we wouldn't return to it," she says. For the same reason, I'll be returning to these essays.'

Melanie McGrath, *Sunday Telegraph*

'Exquisitely eloquent . . . You'll be by turns inspired, provoked, educated and enchanted. Her writing is scientifically precise and poetically elegant, and this intense compilation merits careful attention. It's a book you can return to time and time again.'

Beatrice Hodgkin, *Easy Living*

'Richly intelligent insights on every page'

George Pendle, *Financial Times*

'Hustvedt is wholly present and compelling in her iridescent essays . . . Mystery, fact, intelligence, and enchantment flourish here.'

Booklist

'While there is nothing simple about Hustvedt's subject matter – it ranges from migraine to Goya via existential philosophy and psychoanalysis – there is something refreshingly straightforward about her style. It has the confidence born of complex but well digested thoughts and thus lacks the tendency to obfuscate that is the hallmark of the inferior thinker's style.'

Salley Vickers, *Observer*

'Like a good poem, *Living, Thinking, Looking* is by turns concrete and abstract, illuminating hidden corners of experience and feeling.'

Abigail Meisel, *New York Times Book Review*

'Hustvedt addresses a broad public without dumbing down her material . . . At once stimulating and warm-hearted, with sentences of drop-dead beauty and acuity on nearly every page.'

Kirkus Reviews

Siri Hustvedt

LIVING, THINKING, LOOKING

SCEPTRE

First published in Great Britain in 2012 by Sceptre
An imprint of Hodder & Stoughton
An Hachette UK company

First published in paperback in 2013

1

A CIP catalogue record for this title is available from the British Library

ISBN 9781444732658

Printed and bound by Clays Ltd, St Ives plc

Hodder & Stoughton policy is to use papers that are natural, renewable
and recyclable products and made from wood grown in sustainable
forests. The logging and manufacturing processes are expected to
conform to the environmental regulations of the country of origin.

Hodder & Stoughton Ltd
338 Euston Road
London NW1 3BH

www.sceptrebooks.com

For Frances Coady

CONTENTS

AUTHOR'S NOTE

AFTER REREADING THE ESSAYS COLLECTED in this book, I understood that although they take on a number of subjects, they are linked by an abiding curiosity about what it means to be human. How do we see, remember, feel, and interact with other people? What does it mean to sleep, to dream, and to speak? When we use the word *self,* what are we talking about? Every age has had its own platitudes, truisms, folk wisdom, and dogmas of varying kinds that purport to answer such questions. Ours is no different. In fact, we are drowning in answers. From simplistic self-help manuals on sale in every bookstore to the just-pull-yourself-together advice offered by talk-show therapists to the more sophisticated arguments made in evolutionary sociobiology, analytical and continental philosophy, psychiatry, and neuroscience, theories abound in our culture. It is important to remember that despite the plethora of solutions, *who we are and how we got that way* remain open queries, not only in the humanities but in the sciences as well.

Written over the course of six years, these essays reflect my desire to use insights from many disciplines for the simple reason that

I have come to believe that no single theoretical model can contain the complexity of human reality. The reader will find references to philosophy, neuroscience, psychology, psychoanalysis, neurology, and literature. Some thinkers make repeated appearances: Edmund Husserl, Maurice Merleau-Ponty, Martin Buber, Sigmund Freud, William James, D. W. Winnicott, A. R. Luria, Mary Douglas, and Lev Vygotsky. The findings of neuroscience research run throughout the book, especially the work that has been done on perception, memory, emotion, and the relationship between self and other.

I am deeply committed to the use of ordinary language in my work. Esoteric jargons, however, do not come about because those in the know are snobs. Specialized languages make certain conversations possible because the speakers have refined their definitions and can then share and work with them. The problem is that the circle of speakers is closed unto itself, and the expertise of one field is not available to those in another, not to mention to laypersons who comprehend nothing. I believe that to some degree, at least, genuine talk among disciplines is possible and that distinct discourses can be unified through a lucid exposition of ideas. Nevertheless, it is fair to point out that these essays first appeared in a wide range of publications, from literary magazines such as *Granta, Conjunctions, Salmagundi,* and *The Yale Review,* to newspapers and magazines such as *The Guardian* of London, *The New York Times,* and the *Nouvel Observateur,* to more specialized journals including *Contemporary Psychoanalysis* and the peer-reviewed *Neuropsychoanalysis.* Some of the pieces therefore have extensive notes, while others have none. Some of the texts were originally delivered as lectures. The Morandi essay was one in a series of talks at the Metropolitan Museum: Sunday Lectures at the Met. "Why Goya?" was delivered at the Prado. "Embodied Visions: What Does It Mean to Look at a Work of Art?" was given as the third annual Schelling Lecture at the Academy of Fine Arts in Munich, and "Freud's Playground" was written for the thirty-ninth annual Sigmund Freud Lecture, which I gave in Vienna in May of 2011. In some of these cases, I was able to assume certain kinds of knowledge among the members of my audience, while in others I was not. Nevertheless, every text in this collection is an essay—from the French *essayer,* to try—and they are all written in the first person.

The personal essay began with Montaigne in the sixteenth century and continues to thrive today. Like the novel, its form is elastic and accommodating. It makes use of both stories and arguments. It can proceed with rigorous precision or meander into surprising terrain. Its shape is determined exclusively by the movements of the writer's thoughts and, unlike papers published in science journals, or articles in academic journals or in newspapers, the first-person point of view is not banished but embraced. For me, this is more than a question of genre. My use of the first person represents a philosophical position, which maintains that the idea of third-person objectivity is, at best, a working fiction. Third-person, "objective" research and writing is the result of a collective consensus—an agreement about method, as well as shared underlying assumptions about how the world works, be it in neuroscience or journalism. No one can truly escape her or his subjectivity. There is always an *I* or a *we* hiding somewhere in a text, even when it does not appear as a pronoun.

But who is the I on the page? Why use it? Some of the essays in this book are anecdotal, explicitly about my own experience; others make arguments I could easily elaborate without bringing myself into the text. I *want* to implicate myself. I do not want to hide behind the conventions of an academic paper, because recourse to my own subjective experience can and, I think, does illuminate the problems I hope to untangle. In an age of the confessional memoir, it is perhaps not surprising that there are those who expect a torrent of intimate material whenever they pick up a nonfiction book written in the first person. I'm afraid this is alien to my character. My essays are a form of mind travel, of walking toward answers with an acute awareness that I will never come to the end of the road. I use my own experiences the way I use the experiences of others—as insights to further an idea. In the following essays, I appear and disappear as a character. My presence and absence depends on the argument I am making,

There is nothing new about such an approach. We find out a great deal about Augustine in his *Confessions*, but what he tells us about the agonizing struggles he wages with himself is never gratuitous. It is illustrative of a profound philosophical investigation meant to bring the reader to his own spiritual awakening. A modern and far more circumspect example of the self as vehicle for ideas is found in Freud's *The Interpretation of Dreams*. By analyzing his own dreams, the neurologist reveals enough of himself to make his points stick, to sway his reader toward his new theory of sleep and dreams. Admittedly monumental, these two writers stand as exemplary nevertheless.

I received my Ph.D. in English literature at Columbia University in 1986, but I did not become a professor. I have been free to pursue my education as I have seen fit, and I feel blessed that I do not have to "keep up" in my field. Because my reading is self-directed, I have been able to spend countless hours studying neuroscience papers, aesthetics, psychoanalysis, the history of medicine, and philosophy, among other fields that interest me. I have attended many lectures and conferences and, in these last years, have also been giving lectures at conferences. There is no question that I am an outsider, an unaffiliated intellectual roamer who follows her nose and has found herself on unexpected ground, surveying landscapes I knew very little about before I arrived on site. These mental travels have been a joy for me, as have my encounters with the inhabitants of what were once foreign worlds, the scientists and doctors and thinkers of varying kinds I have met during my adventures.

The book is divided into three sections: "Living," "Thinking," "Looking." As with most categories in this world, they are not absolute, but they aren't arbitrary either. It would be difficult to do much thinking or looking if you weren't living, for example. Still, I chose "Living" for the most personal essays, those that were, in one way or another, generated directly out of my life. The "Thinking" texts, on the other hand, were all driven by an intellectual puzzle. What is the difference between writing fiction and writing a memoir? What role does memory play in the imagination? Are they the same faculty or two different ones? How can we frame what happens between one person and another? Do two people create a third reality between them? The essays in the "Looking" section are all about art and artists. I have been writing about visual art for close to twenty years now. Over and over, I find myself lured in by some mysterious or disturbing work I can't resist pondering for a while, and I am prompted to say something about it. Since my last book on painting, *Mysteries of the Rectangle,* was published in 2005, I have continued to try to write about artworks in a language that does not violate, reduce, or betray perceptual experience. This is not easy. An image is not a text. The difficulties inherent in the undertaking, however, have pushed me to examine further what it means to look at works of art and to develop an embodied, intersubjective approach to the question, one articulated most fully in the last essay in this collection.

Every book is *for* someone. The act of writing may be solitary, but it is always a reach toward another person—a single person—since every book is read alone. The writer does not know for whom she writes. The reader's face is invisible, and yet, every sentence inscribed on a page represents a bid for contact and a hope for understanding. The essays in *Living, Thinking, Looking* were written in this spirit. They were written for you.

—*S.H.*

LIVING

VARIATIONS ON DESIRE
A Mouse, a Dog, Buber, and Bovary

DESIRE APPEARS AS A FEELING, a flicker or a bomb in the body, but it's always a hunger for something, and it always propels us somewhere else, toward the thing that is missing. Even when this motion takes place on the inner terrain of fantasy, it has a quickening effect on the daydreamer. The object of desire—whether it's a good meal, a beautiful dress or car, another person, or something abstract, such as fame, learning, or happiness—exists outside of us and at a distance. Whatever it is, we don't have it now. Although they often overlap, desires and needs are semantically distinct. I need to eat, but I may not have much desire for what is placed in front of me. While a need is urgent for bodily comfort or even survival, a desire exists at another level of experience. It may be sensible or irrational, healthy or dangerous, fleeting or obsessive, weak or strong, but it isn't essential to life and limb. The difference between need and desire may be behind the fact that I've never heard anyone talk of a rat's "desire"—instincts, drives, behaviors, yes, but never desires. The word seems to imply an imaginative subject, someone who thinks and speaks. In *Webster's,* the second definition for the noun *desire* is: "an expressed wish, a request." One could argue about whether animals have "desires." They certainly have preferences. Dogs bark to signal they wish to go outside, ravenously consume one food but leave another untouched, and make it known that the vet's door is anathema. Monkeys express their wishes in forms sophisticated enough to rival those of their cousins, the Homo sapiens. Nevertheless, human desire is shaped and articulated in symbolic terms not available to animals.

When my sister Asti was three years old, her heart's desire, repeatedly expressed, was a Mickey Mouse telephone, a Christmas wish that sent my parents on a multi-city search for a toy that had sold out everywhere. As the holiday approached, the tension in the family grew. My sister Liv, then seven, and I, nine, had been brought into the emotional drama of the elusive toy and began to fear that the object our younger sister craved would not be found. As I remember it, my father tracked the thing down in the neighboring city of Fairbault, late in the afternoon that Christmas Eve, only hours before the presents were to be opened. I recall his triumphant arrival through the garage door, stamping snow from his boots, large garish box in hand—and our joy. My youngest sister, Ingrid, is missing from the memory, probably because she was too young to have participated in what had become a vicarious wish for the rest of us. Asti knows the story, because it took on mythical proportions in the family, and she remembers the telephone, which remained part of the toy collection for some time, but the great unwrapping on the living room floor that I watched with breathless anticipation isn't part of her memory.

This little narrative of the Mickey Mouse telephone opens an avenue into the peculiarities of human desire. Surely the telephone's luminous and no doubt aggrandized image on the television screen whetted Asti's desire and triggered fantasies of possession. The Disney rodent himself must have played a role. She may have imagined having conversations with the real mouse.

I don't know, but the object took on the shine of glamour, first for her, and then for the rest of us, because it wasn't gained easily. It had to be fought for, always an augmenting factor in desire. Think of the troubadours. Think of Gatsby. Think of literature's great, addled Knight Errant on Rocinante. A three-year-old's desire infected four other family members who loved her because her wish became ours through intense identification, not unlike the sports fan's hope that his team will win. Desire can be contagious. Indeed, the churning wheels of capitalism depend upon it.

Asti's "Mickey Mouse" desire presupposes an ability to hold an object in the mind and then imagine its acquisition at some other time, a trick the great Russian neurologist A. R. Luria (1902–1977) explicitly connected to language with its roaming *I* and the labile quality of linguistic tenses: was, is, will be. Narrative is a mental movement in time, and longing for an object very often takes on at least a crude narrative: P is lonely and longs for company. He dreams of meeting Q. He imagines that he is talking to Q in a bar, her head nestled on his shoulder. She smiles. He smiles. They stand up. He imagines her lying in his bed naked, and so on. I have always felt intuitively that conscious remembering and imagining are powerfully connected, that they are, in fact, so similar as to be at times difficult to disentangle from each other, and that they both are bound to places. It's important to anchor the people or objects you remember or imagine in a mental space—or they begin to float away, or worse, disappear. The idea that memory is rooted in location goes back to the Greeks and exerted a powerful influence on medieval thought. The scholastic philosopher Albertus Magnus wrote, "Place is something the soul itself makes for laying up images."[1]

Scientists have recently given new force to this ancient knowledge in a study of amnesia patients with bilateral hippocampal damage. The hippocampus, in connection with other medial temporal lobe areas of the brain, is known to be vital to the processing and storage of memory, but it also appears to be essential to *imagining*. When asked to visualize a specific scene, the brain-damaged patients found it difficult to provide a coherent spatial context for their fantasies. Their reports were far more fragmented than those of their healthy counterparts (or "controls," as scientists like to call them). This insight does not, of course, affect desire itself. People with hippocampal damage don't lack desire—but fully imagining what they long for is impaired. Other forms of amnesia, however, would make it impossible to keep the image of a Mickey Mouse telephone or the phantom Ms. Q in the mind for more than seconds. This form of desire lives only in the moment, outside narrative, an untraceable eruption of feeling that could be acted upon only if a desirable object popped up in the same instant and the amnesiac reached out and grabbed it.

But desire can be aimless, too. It happens to me from time to time that I wonder what it is I am wanting. A vague desire makes itself felt before I can name the object—a restlessness in my body, possibly hunger, possibly the faintest stirring of erotic appetite, possibly a need to write again or read again or read something else, but there it is—a push in me toward a satisfaction I can't identify. What *is* that? Jaak Panksepp, a neuroscientist, writes in his book, *Affective Neuroscience: The Foundations of Human and Animal Emotions,* about what he calls "the SEEKING system." Other scientists have given drabber names to the same circuit: "behavioral activation system" or "behavioral facilitation system." Panksepp writes:

> Although the details of human hopes are surely beyond the imagination of other creatures, the evidence now clearly indicates that certain intrinsic aspirations of all mammalian minds, those of mice as well as men, are driven by the same ancient neurochemistries. These chemistries lead our companion creatures to set out energetically to investigate and explore their

worlds, to seek available resources and make sense of the contingencies in their environments. These same systems give us the impulse to become actively engaged with the world and to extract meaning from our various circumstances.[2]

Curiosity, that need to go out into the world, appears to be hardwired in all mammals. As Panksepp articulates it: it's "a goad without a goal."[3] The "extraction of meaning" from those investigations, however, requires higher cortical areas of the brain unique to human beings. My dear departed dog Jack, when unleashed in the Minnesota countryside, would move eagerly from stump to thistle to cow pie, nostrils quivering, inhaling each natural marvel, and then, once he had mastered the lay of the land, he would burst into a run and race back and forth across the territory like a demented conquering hero. Through his superlative nose, he remembered and recognized the place, but I don't think that when he was back home in Brooklyn he carried about with him a mental image of the wide flat land where he could romp freely or that he actively longed to return to it. Nor do I think he lay on his bed and imagined an ideal playground of myriad odors. And yet, he missed his human beings when we were gone. He grieved, in fact. Attachment and separation anxiety are primitive evolutionary mechanisms shared by all mammals. Once, when my sister Ingrid cared for Jack in our absence, she was sitting in a room of the house and, feeling a chill, went to the closet and put on a sweater of mine. When she returned, the poor dog was seized with a fit of joy, jumping up on her, turning circles in the air, and licking whatever part of her he could reach. Jack's nose was spot-on; what he lacked was a human sense of time and context, which might have prevented him from believing in my sudden materialization out of nowhere.

There is a beautiful passage in Martin Buber's book *Between Man and Man*, in which he describes stroking a beloved horse on

his grandparents' estate when he was eleven years old. He tells of
the immense pleasure it gave him, his tactile experience of the
animal's vitality beneath its skin, and his happiness when the
horse greeted him by lifting its head.

But once—I do not know what came over the child, at any rate
it was childlike enough—it struck me about the stroking, what
fun it gave me, and suddenly I became conscious of my hand.
The game went on as before, but something had changed, it
was no longer the same thing. And the next day, after giving
him a rich feed, when I stroked my friend's head he did not raise
his head. A few years later, when I thought back to the incident,
I no longer supposed that the animal had noticed my defection.
But at the time I considered myself judged.[4]

Buber's story is meant to illustrate the withdrawal from a life
of dialogue with the Other into a life of monologue or "reflexion." For Buber, this self-reflective or mirroring quality disrupts
true knowledge of the Other because he then exists as "only part
of myself." It's notable that Buber shifts to the third person in the
early part of the passage and then resumes in the first, because his
experience is of a sudden, intrusive self-consciousness that alters
the character of his desire. He has become another to himself, a
third person he sees in his mind's eye petting the horse and en-
joying it, rather than an active "I" with a "you." This self-theater
of the third person is, I think, uniquely human and is forever invading our desires and fantasies. Celebrity culture demonstrates
the extreme possibilities of this position because it runs on the
idea of a person seen from the outside as spectacle, and the possibility that lesser mortals, with some luck, can rise to the ranks of
the continually photographed and filmed. With the Internet and
sites like Facebook, the intense longing to live life in the third
person seems to have found its perfect realization. But all of us,

whether we are Internet voyeurs of our own dramas or not, are infected by Buber's "reflexion," his description of narcissism, in which the self is trapped in an airless hall of mirrors.

Buber's condemnation of the monologue position is profound, and yet self-consciousness itself is born in "mirroring" and the acquisition of symbols through which we are able to represent ourselves as an "I," a "he," or a "she." It is this distance from the self that makes narrative movement and autobiographical memory possible. Without it, we couldn't tell ourselves the story of ourselves. Living solely in reflection, however, creates a terrible machinery of insatiable desire, the endless pursuit of the thing that will fill the emptiness and feed a starved self-image. Emma Bovary dreams of Paris: "She knew all the latest fashions, where to find the best tailors, the days for going to the Bois or the Opera. She studied descriptions of furniture in Eugene Sue, and sought in Balzac and George Sand a vicarious gratification of her own desires."[5]

It is no secret that, once gained, the objects of desire often lose their sweetness. The real Paris cannot live up to the dream city. The high-heeled pumps displayed in a shop window that glow with the promise of beauty, urbanity, and wealth are just shoes once they find their way into the closet. After a big wedding, which in all its pomp and circumstance announces marriage as a state of ultimate arrival, there is life with a real human being, who is inevitably myopic, weak, and idiosyncratic. The revolutionary eats and sleeps the revolution, the grand cleansing moment when a new order will triumph, and then, once it has happened, he finds himself wandering among corpses and ruins. Only human beings destroy themselves by ideas. Emma Bovary comes to despair: "And once again the deep hopelessness of her plight came back to her. Her lungs heaved as though they would burst. Then in a transport of heroism which made her almost gay, she ran down the hill and across the cow-plank, hurried along the path, up the lane, through the market-place and arrived in front of the chemist's shop."[6] It is the phrase "a transport of heroism" that is most poignant to me, the absurd but all too human desire to inflate the story of oneself, to see it reflected back as heroic, beautiful, or martyred.

Desire is the engine of life, the yearning that goads us forward with stops along the way, but it has no destination, no final stop, except death. The wondrous fullness after a meal or sex or a great book or conversation is inevitably short-lived. By nature, we want and we wish, and we assign content to that emptiness as we narrate our inner lives. For better and for worse, we bring meaning to it, one inevitably shaped by the language and culture in which we live. Meaning itself may be the ultimate human seduction. Dogs don't need it, but for us to go on, it is essential, and this is true despite the fact that most of what happens to us is beneath our awareness. The signifying, speech-making, willful, consciously perceiving circuits of our brains are minute compared to the vast unconscious processes that lie beneath.

Almost twenty years ago, I gave birth to my daughter. Actually, "I" did nothing. My water broke. Labor happened. After thirteen hours of it, I pushed. I liked this time of pushing. It was active, not passive, and I finally expelled from between my legs a bloody, wet, awe-inspiring stranger. My husband held her, and I must have, too, but I don't remember her in my arms until later. What I do recall is that as soon as I knew the baby was healthy, I lapsed into a state of unprecedented satisfaction. A paradisaical torpor seemed to flood my body, and I went limp and still. I was wheeled away to a dim room, and after some minutes, my obstetrician appeared, looked down at me, and said, "I'm just checking on you. How are you?" It was an effort to speak, not because I had any pain or even a feeling of exhaustion, but because speech seemed unnecessary. I did manage to breathe out the words that described my condition: "I'm fine, fine. I've never felt like this. I have no desire, no desire of any kind." I remember that she grinned and patted my arm, but after she left, I lay there for some time, luxuriating in the sated quiet of my body, accompanied only by the awed repetition of the same words: I have no desire, none, no desire of any kind. I am sure that I was under the sway of the hormone oxytocin, released in quantities I had never experienced before, and which had turned me into a happy lump of flesh. Birth was a wholly animal experience; its brutal corporeal paroxysms left reflection behind. The executive, thinking, narrative "I" lost itself entirely in the ultimate creative act: one body being born of another. After the birth, it returned as a stunned commentator, similar to a voice-over in a movie that noted the novelty of my situation to an audience of one: me. Of course, the stupefaction didn't last. It couldn't last. I had to take care of my child, had to hold her, feed her, look at her, want her with my whole being. There is nothing more ordinary than this desire, and yet to be gripped by it feels miraculous.

Martin Buber doesn't treat mothers and infants in his I/Thou dialectic, but the ideal dialogue he describes of openness to the other, of communication that is not dependent on speech, but which can happen in silence "sacramentally," is perhaps most perfectly realized in the mother/child couple. Especially in the first year, a mother opens herself up to her baby. As D. W. Winnicott writes in *The Family and Individual Development,* she is able to "drain interest from her self onto the baby." A mother, he adds, in his characteristically lucid way, has "a special ability to do the right thing. She knows what the baby could be feeling like. No one else knows. Doctors and nurses know a lot about psychology, and of course they know a lot about body health and disease. But they do not know what a baby feels like from minute to minute because they are outside this area of experience."[7] Imagining what your baby feels like by reading her carefully and responding to her is a mother's work; it is a first/second-person business, and it brings with it ongoing gratification for both sides of the dyad. It is also, as Allan Schore makes clear in his book *Affect Regulation and the Origin of the Self,* essential to the neurobiological development of the infant.

Maternal desire is a subject fraught with ideology. From the screaming advocates of "family values" to those whose agenda makes it necessary to replace the word "mother" with "caregiver" at every opportunity, popular culture trumpets its competing narratives. In a country where human relationships are seen as entities to be "worked on," as if they were thousand-piece puzzles that only take time to complete, the pleasure to be found in one's children, the desire we have for them falls outside the discussion. It is not my intention to be a Romantic. Parenthood can be grueling, boring, and painful, but most people want their children and love them. As parents, they are, as Winnicott said about mothers: "good enough." This "good enough" is not perfection but a form of dialogue, a receptiveness that doesn't impose on the child the monologic desires of the parents, but recognizes his autonomy, his real separateness.

Every week, I teach a writing class to inpatients at the Payne Whitney psychiatric clinic. My students are all people who find themselves in the hospital because life outside it had become unbearable, either to themselves or to other people. It is there that I've witnessed what it looks like to have no desire or very little desire for anything. Psychotic patients can be electrifying and filled with manic, creative energy, but severely depressed patients are strangely immobile. The people who come to my class have already put one foot in front of the other and found their way into a chair, which is far more than some of the others can do—the ones who remain in their rooms, inert on their beds like the living dead. Some people come to class but do not speak. Some come but do not write. They look at the paper and pencil and are able to say they cannot do it, but will stay and listen. One woman who sat rigidly in her chair, hardly moving except for the hand that composed her piece, wrote of a morgue where the bodies were laid out on slabs, their mouths opened to reveal black, cankerous tongues. "That's why we're here," she said after she had finished reading it aloud, "because we're dead. We're all dead." As I listened to her words, I felt cut and hurt. This was more than sadness, more than grief. Grief, after all, is desire for the dead or for what's been lost and can never come again. Grief is longing. This was stasis without fulfillment. This was the world stopped, meaning extinguished. And yet, she had written it, had bothered to record this bleak image, which I told her frightened me. I said I had pictured it in my mind the way I might remember some awful image in a movie, and I tried to hold her with my eyes, keep her looking at me, which I did for several seconds. When I think of it now, bringing up film might have been defensive on my part, a way of keeping some distance between me and that morgue (where I'll end up sooner or later). Nevertheless, I've come to understand that what I say is often less important to the students than my embodied attention, my rapt interest in what is happening among us, that they know I am listening, concentrated, and open. I have to imagine what it feels like to be in such a state without coming unglued myself.

I don't know what that woman's particular story was or why she landed in the hospital. Some people come wearing the bandages of their suicide attempts, but she didn't. Everybody has a story, and each one is unique, and yet now that I've been going to the hospital for a year, I've seen many variations of a single narrative. One man encompassed it beautifully in a short poem. I can't remember his exact wording but have retained the images it brought to mind. He is a child again, wandering alone in an apartment, longing for "someone" to be there. He finds a door. It swings open, and the room is empty. I can't think of a better metaphor for unrequited longing than that vacant room. My student understood the essence of what he was missing: the responsive presence of another, and he knew that this absence had both formed and damaged him.

I seem to have come far from the Mickey Mouse telephone, but like so many objects of desire, the telephone was more than a telephone, and the story of searching for it and finding it at last to fulfill a child's wish is a small parable of genuine dialogue: I have heard you and I'm coming with my answer.

2007

MY MOTHER, PHINEAS, MORALITY, AND FEELING

"DON'T DO ANYTHING YOU DON'T really want to do," my mother said as she drove me home from some class, meeting, or friend's house I have long forgotten. I don't remember anything else my mother said during our conversation, and I can't say why she offered me this piece of advice just then. I do remember the stretch of Highway 19 just outside my hometown, Northfield, Minnesota, that is now forever associated with those words. It must have been summer, because the grass was green and the trees were in full leaf. I also distinctly recall that as soon as she had spoken, I felt guilty. Was I doing things I didn't really *want* to do? I was fifteen years old, in the middle of my adolescence, a young person filled with private longings, confusions, and torments. My mother's words gave me pause, and I have never stopped thinking about them.

Hers is a curious sentence when you look at it closely, with its two *don't*s framing the highly positive phrase "anything you really want to do." I knew my mother wasn't offering me a prescription for hedonism or selfishness, and I received this bit of wisdom as a moral imperative about desire. The *don't*s in the sentence were a warning against coercion, probably sexual. Notably, my mother did not say, "Don't have sex, take drugs, or go wild." She cautioned me to listen to my moral feelings—but what exactly are they? Feeling, empathy in particular, inevitably plays a crucial role in our moral behavior.

That day she spoke to me as if I were an adult, a person beyond looking to her parents for direction. This both flattered and scared me a little. Hiding behind the sentence was the clear implication that she would *not tell me what to do* anymore. Because my own daughter is now twenty, I understand my mother's position more vividly. As a toddler, Sophie wanted to stick her fingers into outlets, grab toys from other children, and take off her clothes at every opportunity. When her father and I interfered with these desires, she howled, but our six-year-old girl was another person altogether. Even a mild reprimand from either her father or me would make her eyes well up with tears. Guilt, an essential social emotion, had emerged in her and become part of a codified moral world of rights and wrongs, dos and don'ts.

The journey from naked savage to modest, empathetic little person to independent adult is also a story of brain development. From birth to around the age of six, a child's prefrontal cortex develops enormously, and how it develops depends on her environment—which includes everything from poisons in the atmosphere to how her parents care for her. It is now clear from research that an adolescent's brain also undergoes crucial changes and that emotional trauma and deprivation, especially when repeated, can leave lasting, detrimental imprints on the developing brain. The prefrontal cortex is far more developed in human beings than in other animals and is often referred to as the "executive" area of the brain, a region involved in evaluating and controlling our feelings and behavior.

Twenty years ago, I stumbled across the story of Phineas

Gage in a neurology textbook. In 1849, the railroad foreman suffered a bizarre accident. A four-foot iron rod rammed into his left cheek, blasted through his brain, and flew out through the top of his head. Miraculously, Gage recovered. He could walk, talk, and think, but along with a few cubic centimeters of the ventromedial region of his frontal lobe, he lost his old self. The once considerate, highly competent foreman became impulsive, aggressive, and callous with other people. He made plans, but could never carry them out. Fired from one job after another, his life deteriorated, and he wandered aimlessly until he died in San Francisco in 1861. This story haunted me because it suggested an awful thing: moral life could be reduced to a chunk of brain meat.

I remember asking a psychoanalyst about this story not long after I had read it. She shook her head: It wasn't possible. From her point of view, the psyche had nothing to do with the brain—ethics simply don't vanish with gray matter. But I now think of the Phineas story differently. Gage lost what he had gained earlier in his life—the capacity to feel the higher emotions of empathy and guilt, both of which inhibit our actions in the world. After his injury he turned into a kind of moral infant. He could no longer imagine how his actions would affect others or himself, no longer feel compassion, and without this feeling, he was fundamentally handicapped, even though his cognitive capacities remained untouched. He behaved like the classic psychopath who acts on impulse and feels no remorse.

In *Decartes' Error,* the neurologist Antonio Damasio retells the story of Phineas Gage and compares his case to that of one of his patients, Elliot, who, after surgery for a malignant brain tumor, suffered damage to his frontal lobes. Like Gage before him, Elliot could no longer plan ahead and his life fell apart. He also became strangely cold. Although his intellectual faculties appeared to work well, he lacked feeling, both for himself and for others. Damasio writes: "I found myself suffering more when listening to Elliot's stories than Elliot himself seemed to be suffering."[1] After doing a series of experiments on his patient, Damasio theorizes about what my mother took for granted: emotion not only enhances decision-making in life, it is essential to it.

Sometimes, however, I don't know what I really want. I have to search myself, and that search involves both a visceral sense of what I feel and a projection of myself into the future. Will I regret having accepted that invitation? Am I succumbing to pressure from another person that will fill me with resentment later? I feel furious after reading this e-mail now, but haven't I learned that waiting a couple of days before I respond is far wiser than sending off a splenetic answer right now? The future is, of course, imaginary—an unreal place that I create from my expectations, which are made from my remembered experiences, especially repeated experiences. Patients with prefrontal lesions exhibit the same curious deficits. They can pass all kinds of mental cognition tests, but something crucial is still missing. As A. R. Luria notes in *Higher Cortical Functions in Man* (1962), ". . . clinicians have invariably observed that, although the 'formal intellect' is intact, these patients show marked changes in behavior."[2] They lose the critical faculty to judge their own behaviors, and lapse into a bizarre indifference about themselves and others. I would argue that something has gone awry with their emotional imaginations.

A couple of years after that conversation with my mother in the car, I was skiing with my cousin at a resort in Aspen, Colorado. Early one evening, I found myself alone at the top of a steep slope made more frightening by the mini-mountains on its surface known as moguls. I wasn't a good enough skier to take that hill, but I had boarded the wrong chairlift. There was only one way out for me and that was down. As I stood there at the summit looking longingly at the ski chalet far below, I had a revelation: I understood then and there that I didn't *like* skiing. It was too fast, too cold. It scared me. It had always scared me. One may wonder how it is possible for a young woman of seventeen not to have understood this simple fact about her existence until faced with a crisis. I come from a Norwegian family. My mother was born and raised in that northern country and my father's grandparents emigrated from Norway. In Norway, people say that children ski before they walk, an overstatement that nevertheless brings the point home. The idea that skiing might *not* be fun, might *not* be for everyone, had never occurred to me. Where I come from, the sport signified pleasure, nature, family happiness. As these thoughts passed through my mind, I noticed that the chairlifts were closing and the sky was darkening. I took a breath, gave myself a push with my poles, and went over the edge. About half an hour later, a patrol on a snowmobile discovered me lying in a heap under a mogul, minus a ski, but otherwise intact.

Ridiculous as the story is, its implications are far reaching. We sometimes imagine we want what we don't really want. A way of thinking about something can become so ingrained, we fail to question it, and that failure may involve more than a tumble on a ski slope. The friend who returns repeatedly to a man who mistreats her is in the grip of a familiar, self-defeating desire in which the imagined future has been forgotten. When I was an impoverished graduate student, I would sometimes spend twenty or thirty dollars on a T-shirt or accessory I didn't need or even particularly want. What I craved was the purchase, not the thing itself. Of course, a sense of not being deprived may fill an emotional void without ruinous consequences. On the other hand, if you can't pay your electric bill, you're stuck. I found myself in a bad spot on the ski slope because I was doing something I didn't really want to do. My poor judgment was the result of both an alienation from my feelings and a lack of sympathy for myself.

The latter observation is vital. Because, like all human beings, I can objectify myself—see myself as one person among others in the social world—I am able not only to plan ahead by imagining how what I do now will affect what happens to me later, I gain the distance needed to recognize myself as a being who deserves compassion.

During the first year of my marriage, I was nervous. I worried in an abstract way about losing my freedom, about domestic life in general, about how to be "a wife." When I confronted my new husband with these worries, he looked at me and said, "Why, Siri, do whatever you want to do." I hadn't told my husband what my mother said to me on Highway 19 twelve years earlier, but his words created an undeniable echo. I understood that he wasn't giving me license to hurl myself into the arms of another man. He released me to my desires because, like my mother, he trusted my moral feeling. The effect was one of immediate liberation. A burden fell off my shoulders, and I went about doing what I wanted to do, which included being married to the particular man I loved.

My marriage thinking wasn't all that different from my skiing thinking. I adopted an externalized, rigid, heartless view of both: skiing is supposed to be fun and marriage is an institution of constriction. I didn't ask myself what I *really* wanted, because I was in the grip of a received idea, one I had to interrogate and feel for myself before I could discard or embrace it. Unlike Phineas and Elliot, my frontal lobes are intact. I know, however, that the mysteries of my personal neurology are, like everybody else's, a synthetic combination of my innate genetic temperament and my life experience over time, a thought that takes me back to my mother, a person central to that story. When I told her that I was writing about the advice she gave me years ago, she said, "Well, you know, I couldn't have said that to just anyone."

Unlike some hackneyed phrase lifted from the pages of a parenting guide, my mother's sentence was addressed directly to me, and it was given with knowledge, empathy, and love. No doubt, that's why her words have stayed with me. I felt them.

2007

SEARCH FOR A DEFINITION

AMBIGUITY: NOT QUITE ONE THING, not quite the other. Ambiguity resists category. It won't fit into the pigeonhole, the neat box, the window frame, the encyclopedia. It is a formless object or a feeling that can't be placed. And there is no diagram for ambiguity, no stable alphabet, no arithmetic. Ambiguity asks: Where is the border between this and that?

There is comfort in saying the word *chair* and pointing into the room where the chair sits on the floor. There is comfort in seeing the chair and saying the word *chair* softly to one's self, as if that were the end of the matter, as if the world and the word have met. Naïve realism. In English, I can add a single letter to *word* and get *world*. I put a small *l* between the *r* and the *d* and close the chasm between the two, and the game gives me some satisfaction.

Ambiguity does not obey logic. The logician says, "To tolerate contradiction is to be indifferent to truth." Those particular philosophers like playing games of true and false. It is either one thing or the other, never both. But ambiguity is inherently contradictory and insoluble, a bewildering truth of fogs and mists and the unrecognizable figure or phantom or memory or dream that can't be contained or held in my hands or kept because it is always flying away, and I cannot tell what it is or if it is anything at all. I chase it with words even though it won't be captured, and every once in a while I come close to it.

That feeling of nearness to the shapeless ghost, Ambiguity, is what I want most, what I want to put inside a book, what I want the reader to sense. And because it is at once a thing and a nothing, the reader will have to find it, not only in what I have written, but also in what I have not written.

2009

MY STRANGE HEAD
Notes on Migraine

1. ARMS AT REST

I AM A MIGRAINEUR. I use the noun with care, because after a lifetime of headaches, I have come to think of migraines as a part of me, not as some force or plague that infects my body. Chronic headaches are my fate, and I have adopted a position of philosophical resignation. I am aware that such a view is resoundingly un-American. Our culture does not encourage anyone to *accept* adversity. On the contrary, we habitually declare war on the things that afflict us, whether it's drugs, terrorism, or cancer. Our media fetishizes the heartwarming stories of those who, against all odds, never lose hope and fight their way to triumph over poverty, addiction, disease. The person who lies back and says, "This is my lot. So be it," is a quitter, a passive, pessimistic, spineless loser who deserves only our contempt. And yet, the very moment I stopped thinking of my condition as "the enemy," I made a turn and began to get better. I wasn't cured, wasn't forever well, but I was better. Metaphors matter.

Although I wasn't diagnosed with migraine until I was

twenty, I can't remember a time when I didn't suffer from headaches. A German neurologist, Klaus Podoll, who has studied migraine auras and artists, contacted me a few years ago after he read
an interview I had given, in which I mentioned a hallucination
that preceded one of my headaches. In an e-mail conversation, he
questioned me carefully about my history and concluded that the
annual bouts of what my mother and I thought were stomach flu
were probably migraine attacks. I have come to agree with him.
My "flu" was always accompanied by a severe headache and violent vomiting. It didn't occur during the flu season, and the sick-
ness always followed exactly the same course. Two days of pain
and nausea that lightened on the third day. Throughout my childhood, the attacks came with ritual regularity. In high school, I
didn't have as many "flus," but after I returned from an intensely
exciting semester abroad, spent mostly in Thailand, during my
third year of college, I fell ill with what I thought was yet another
flu, a siege of excruciating head pain and retching that lasted six
days. On the seventh day, the pain lifted somewhat, but it didn't
go away. It didn't go away for a year. It was better, it was worse,
but my head always hurt and I was always nauseated. *I refused to
give in to it.* Like a dutiful automaton, I studied, wrote, received
the desired As, and suffered alone until I went to my family doctor, sobbed in his arms, and was diagnosed with migraine.

My young adulthood was punctuated by the headaches with
their auras and abdominal symptoms, nervous storms that came
and went. And then, after I married the man I was deeply in love
with when I was twenty-seven, I went to Paris on my honeymoon
and fell sick again. It began with a seizure: my left arm suddenly
shot up into the air, and I was thrown back against the wall in an
art gallery I was visiting. The seizure was momentary. The headache that followed went on and on for month after month. This
time I searched for a cure. I was determined to battle my symptoms. I visited neurologist after neurologist, took innumerable

drugs: Cafergot, Inderal, Mellaril, Tofranil, Elavil, and others I've forgotten. Nothing helped. My last neurologist, known as the Headache Czar of New York City, hospitalized me and prescribed Thorazine, a powerful antipsychotic. After eight days of stuporous sedation and an ongoing headache, I checked myself out. Panicked and desperate, I began to think that I would never be well. As a last resort, the Czar sent incurables like me to a biofeedback man. Dr. E. hooked me up to a machine via electrodes and taught me how to relax. The technique was simple. The more tense I was, the louder and faster the machine beeped. As I relaxed, the sounds grew slower until they finally stopped. For eight months, I went for a weekly visit and practiced letting go. Every day I practiced at home without the machine. I learned how to warm my cold hands and feet, to increase my circulation, to dampen the pain. I learned to stop fighting.

Migraine remains a poorly understood illness. Although new techniques, such as neuroimaging, have helped isolate some of the neural circuits involved, brain pictures won't provide a solution. The syndrome is too various, too complex, too mixed up with external stimuli and the personality of the sufferer— aspects of migraine that can't be seen on fMRI or PET scans with their colored highlights. I have come to understand that my headaches are cyclical and that they play a part in my emotional economy. As a child, life with my peers in school was always hard for me, and my yearly purges no doubt served a purpose. For two days a year, I suffered a cathartic dissolution, during which I was able to stay home and be close to my mother. But times of great happiness can also send me over the edge— the adventure in Thailand and falling in love and getting married. Both were followed by a collapse into pain, as if joy had strained my body to its breaking point. The migraine then became self-perpetuating. I am convinced that a state of fear, anxiety, and a continual readiness to do combat with the monster headache pushed my central nervous system into a state of continual alarm, which could only be stopped by a deep rest. I continue to cycle. Periods of obsessive and highly productive writing and reading that give me immense pleasure are often followed by a neurological crash—a headache. My swings from high to low resemble the rhythms of manic depression, or bipolar disorder, except that I fall into migraine, not depression, and my manias are less extreme than those of people who suffer from the psychiatric illness. The truth is that separating neurological from psychiatric problems is often artificial, as is the old and stubborn distinction between psyche and soma. All human states, including anger, fear, sadness, and joy, are of the body. They have neurobiological correlates, as researchers in the field would say. What we often think of as purely psychological, how we regard an illness, for example, is important. Our thoughts, attitudes, even our metaphors create physiological changes in us, which in the case of headaches can mean the difference between misery and managing. Research has shown that psychotherapy can create therapeutic brain changes, an increase of activity in the prefrontal cortex. Yes, just talking and listening can make you better.

No one ever died of a migraine. It isn't cancer, heart disease, or a stroke. With a life-threatening disease, your attitude—whether bellicose or Buddhist—cannot keep you alive. It may simply change *how* you die. But with my migraines that continue to arrive and no doubt always will, I have found that capitulation is preferable to struggle. When I feel one coming on, I go to bed, and now machineless, I do my relaxation exercises. My meditations aren't magical, but they keep the worst pain and nausea at bay. I do not welcome my headaches, but neither do I see them as alien. They may even serve a necessary regulatory function, by forcing me to lie low, a kind of penance, if you will, for those other days of flying high.

2. "CURIOUSER AND CURIOUSER"

Who in the world am I? Ah, that's the great puzzle!" says Lewis Carroll's Alice after experiencing a sudden, disorienting growth spurt. While she meditates on this philosophical conundrum, her body changes again. The girl shrinks. I have asked myself the same question many times, often in relation to the perceptual alterations, peculiar feelings, and exquisite sensitivities of the migraine state. *Who in the world am I?* Am "I" merely malfunctioning white and gray matter? In *The Astonishing Hypothesis* Francis Crick (famous for his discovery of the DNA double helix with James Watson) wrote, "You, your joys and your sorrows, your memories and ambitions, your sense of personal identity and free will, are, in fact, no more than the behavior of a vast assembly of nerve cells and their associated molecules."[1] Mind is matter, Crick argued. All of human life can be reduced to neurons.

There is a migraine aura phenomenon named after Charles Lutwidge Dodgson's (Lewis Carroll's) story of myriad transformations: Alice in Wonderland syndrome. The afflicted person feels that she or parts of her are ballooning or diminishing in size. The neurological terms for the peculiar sensations of growing and shrinking are *macroscopy* and *microscopy*. Dodgson was a migraineur. He was also known to take laudanum. It seems more than possible that he had experienced at least some of the somatic oddities that he visited upon his young heroine. These experiences are not unique to migraine. They are also seen in people who have suffered neurological damage. In *The Man with a Shattered World*, A. R. Luria recorded the case of a patient, Zazetsky, who suffered a terrible head injury during the Second World War. "Sometimes,"

Zazetsky wrote, "when I'm sitting down I suddenly feel as though my head is the size of a table—every bit as big—while my hands, feet, and torso become very small."[2] Body image is a complex, fragile phenomenon. The changes in the nervous system wrought by an oncoming headache, the lesions caused by a stroke or a bullet, can affect the brain's internal corporeal map, and we metamorphose.

Is *Alice in Wonderland* a pathological product, the result of a single man's "nerve cells and their associated molecules" run amok? The tendency to reduce artistic, religious, or philosophical achievements to bodily ailment was aptly named by William James in *The Varieties of Religious Experience*. "Medical materialism," he wrote, "finishes up Saint Paul by calling his vision on the road to Damascus a discharging lesion of the occipital cortex, he being an epileptic. It snuffs out Saint Teresa as an hysteric, Saint Francis of Assisi as a hereditary degenerate."[3] And, I might add, Lewis Carroll as an addict or migraineur. We continue to live in a world of medical materialism. People pay thousands of dollars to get a peek at their genetic map, hoping to ward off disease early. They rush to embrace the latest, often contradictory, news on longevity. One study reports it's good to be chubby. Another insists that when underfed, our close relatives the chimpanzees live longer, and we would do well to follow suit. Republicans and Democrats are subject to brain scans to see what neural networks are affected when they think about politics. The media announces that researchers have found the "God spot" in the brain. Before the genome was decoded and scientists discovered that human beings have only a few more genes than fruit flies, there were innumerable articles in the popular press speculating that a gene would be found for alcoholism, OCD, an affection for purple ties; in short, for everything.

It is human to clutch at simple answers and shunt aside ambiguous, shifting realities. The fact that genes are expressed through environment, that however vital they may be in determining vulnerability to an illness, they cannot predict it, except in rare cases, such as Huntington's disease; that the brain is not a static but a plastic organ, which forms itself long after birth through our interactions with others; that any passionate feeling, whether it's about politics or tuna fish, will appear on scans as activated emotional circuits in the brain; that scientific studies on weight and longevity tell us mostly about correlations, not causes; that the feelings evoked by the so-called "God spot" may be interpreted by the person having them as religious or as something entirely different—all this is forgotten or misunderstood.

The man who gave us *Alice in Wonderland* suffered from migraine. He was also a mathematician, a clergyman, a photographer, and a wit. He was self-conscious about a stammer and *may* have had sexual proclivities for young girls. It is impossible to know exactly what role migraine played in his creative work. My own experience of the illness—scotomas, euphorias, odd feelings of being pulled upward, a Lilliputian hallucination—figure in the story of myself, a story that in the end can't be divided into nature or nurture. Migraine runs in families, so I probably have a hereditary predisposition to headaches, but the way the illness developed, and its subsequent meaning for me, are dependent on countless factors, both internal and external, many of which I will never penetrate. *Who in the world am I?* is an unsolved question, but we do have some pieces to the puzzle.

As Freud argued over a century ago, most of what our brains do is unconscious, beneath or beyond our understanding. No one disputes this anymore. The human infant is born immature, and in the first six years of its life, the front part of its brain (the prefrontal cortex) develops enormously. It develops *through experience* and continues to do so, although less rapidly than before. Our early life, much of which never becomes part of our conscious memory because it's lost to infantile amnesia (our brains cannot consolidate conscious memories until later), is nevertheless vital to who we become. A child who has good parental care—is stimulated, talked to, held, whose needs are answered—is *materially* affected by that contact, as is, conversely, the child who suffers shocks and deprivations. What happens to you is decisive in determining which neural networks are activated and kept. The synaptic circuits that aren't used are "pruned"; they wither away. This explains why so-called wild children are unable to acquire anything but the most primitive form of language. It's too late. It also demonstrates how nurture *becomes* nature and why making simple distinctions between them is absurd. A baby with a hypersensitive genetic makeup that predisposes him to anxiety can end up as a reasonably calm adult if he grows up in a soothing environment.

So Crick was technically right. What seem to be the ineffable riches of human mental life do depend on "an assembly of nerve cells." And yet, Crick's reductionism does not provide an adequate answer to Alice's question. It's rather like saying that Vermeer's *Girl Pouring Milk* is a canvas with paint on it or that Alice herself is words on a page. These are facts, but they don't explain my subjective experience of either of them or what the two girls *mean* to me. Science proceeds by testing and retesting its findings. It relies on many people's work, not just a few. Its "objectivity" rests upon consensus, the shared presuppositions, principles, and methods from which it arrives at its "truths," truths which are then modified or even revolutionized over time. It should be noted that even the late Francis Crick wasn't able to leap out of his subjective mental apparatus and become a superhuman observer of BRAIN.

We are all prisoners of our mortal minds and bodies, vulnerable to various kinds of perceptual transfigurations. At the same time, as embodied beings we live in a world that we explore, absorb, and remember—partially, of course. We can only find the *out there* through the *in here*. And yet, what the philosopher Karl Popper called World 3, the knowledge we have inherited—the science, the philosophy, and the art—stored in our libraries and museums, the words, images, and music produced by people now dead, becomes part of us and may take on profound significance in our everyday lives. Our thinking, feeling minds are made not only by our genes but also through our language and culture. I have been fond of Lewis Carroll's Alice since childhood. She may have started out as words on a page, but now she inhabits my in ner life. (One could also say her story has been consolidated in my memory through important work done by my hippocampus.) It is possible that my headache episodes have made me particularly sympathetic to the girl's adventures and her metaphysical riddle, but I am hardly alone in my affection. I dare say countless people have lifted her from World 3, a kind of Wonderland in itself, and taken her into their own internal landscapes, where she continues to grow and shrink and muse over who in the world she is.

3. LIFTING, LIGHTS, AND LITTLE PEOPLE

Not every migraine has a prologue or "aura," and not every aura is followed by a headache. Nevertheless, these overtures to pain or isolated events are the most peculiar aspect of the illness and may offer insights into the nature of perception itself. As a child I had what I called "lifting feelings." Every once in a while, I had a powerful internal sensation of being pulled upward, as if my head were rising, even though I knew my feet hadn't left the ground. This lift was accompanied by what can only be called awe—a feeling of transcendence. I variously interpreted these elevations as divine (God was calling) or as an amazed connection to things in the world. Everything appeared strange and wondrous. The lights came later in my life—showers of stars that begin on one side, usually the right, sharp black points surrounded by shining light that cascade downward and then move toward the center of my vision, or brilliant lights surrounded by black rings or just tiny black spots swimming in air. I've had fogs and gray spots that make it hard to see what's in front of me, weird holes in my vision, and a sensation that there's a heavy cloud in my head. I've had feelings of euphoria that are indescribably wonderful and supernatural exhaustion—a weariness unlike any other I've experienced, a pull toward sleep that is irresistible. Sometimes I have fits of yawning that I can't stop. Also, often just before I wake up with a migraine, I have an aphasia dream. I am trying to speak, but my lips won't form the words and every utterance is terribly distorted. But my most remarkable premigraine event was hallucinatory. I was lying in bed reading a book by Italo Svevo, and for some reason looked down, and there they were: a small pink man and his pink ox, perhaps six or seven inches high. They were perfectly made creatures and, except for their color, they looked very *real*. They didn't speak to me, but they walked around, and I watched them with fascination and a kind of amiable tenderness. They stayed for some minutes and then disappeared. I have often wished they would return, but they never have.

Lilliputian hallucinations before migraine are rare. There are other documented cases, however. Klaus Podoll has written about a woman who during her migraine attacks sees amusing little beetles with faces run across her floor and ceiling. Another reported case involved tiny Indians, and yet another, a dwarf. It wasn't until after my duo had vanished that I understood I had seen a miniature version of two legendary, oversized characters from my childhood in Minnesota: Paul Bunyan and his blue ox, Babe. The giant man and his huge animal that I had read about in stories had shrunk dramatically and turned pink. It was then that I asked myself about the *content* of the hallucination. What did it mean that my aura took that form, rather than something else? Are these visions purely nonsensical? What memory traces are activated during these experiences? A man I met in the hospital, where I teach a writing class to psychiatric inpatients, told me that during a psychotic episode he had hallucinated little green men getting into a spaceship. This stereotypical vision of Martians appeared during his crisis, but unlike most of the migraineurs I've read about, he found his little aliens disturbing. Psychosis, alcoholism, dementia, epilepsy, and hallucinogens like LSD can all produce neurological disturbances that conjure tiny, life-size, or gigantic persons and animals, as can a disorder called Charles Bonnet syndrome, often but not always associated with deteriorating vision. In his book *Phantoms in the Brain,* V. S. Ramachandran reports that during a conversation he had with one of his patients, she told him that she saw little cartoon characters scooting up his arms. Why Paul Bunyan? Why Martians? Why cartoon characters? Oddly, all of these visions have a folkloric quality, more contemporary versions of the mythological little people around the world: leprechauns, brownies, fairies, gnomes, goblins, Nordic *nisse* and *tomten,* the Hawaiian *Menehune,* the Greek *kalikauzari,* the Cherokee *yumwi.* Where did all these wee folk come from? The content of hallucinations must surely be at once personal and cultural.

My dear little creatures were migrainous figments, aura products similar to other experiences of complex visual hallucinations, which although they may have various medical causes, bear a resemblance to one another and no doubt have some neurobiological connection. As Oliver Sacks points out in his book on migraine, we all hallucinate in our sleep. We generate dream images and stories that are often peculiar, violate the laws of physics, and are highly emotional. But why we dream remains a scientific mystery. Sigmund Freud proposed that dreams protect sleep. Mark Solms, a neurologist and sleep researcher, agrees: "Patients who lose the ability to dream due to brain damage suffer from sleep-maintenance insomnia—they have difficulty staying asleep."[4] We human beings may have a need to create stimulating imagery that keeps us busy while we're in that parallel state and the waking world has vanished.

Another ordinary form of spontaneous mental images are hypnagogic hallucinations, which appear on the threshold between sleeping and waking. I had always believed that the brilliant mutating images I see as I drift off every night are universal, but I have since discovered that while common, not everyone falls asleep to visions. I am deeply attached to my presleep cinema of ghouls and monsters, shifting faces and bodies that grow and shrink, to my own nameless cartoon characters who flee over mountaintops or jump into lakes, to the brilliant colors that explode or bleed into gorgeous geometries, to the gyrating dancers and erotic performers who entertain me while I am still conscious but falling toward Morpheus. Except as a spectator, I play no role in this lunatic borderland. It is a world distinct from that of my dreams, in which I am always an actor, and therefore it is more closely allied to my Lilliputian experience. I watched them, but I felt no need to interact with them. They were simply there for my viewing pleasure.

It is comforting to think that visual perception is a matter of taking in what's out there, that a clear line exists between "seeing things" and the everyday experience of looking. In fact, this is not how normal vision works. Our minds are not passive containers of external reality or experience. Evidence suggests that what we see is a combination of sensory information coming in from the outside, which has been *dynamically* translated or decoded in our brains through both our expectations of what it is we are looking at and our human ability to create coherent images. We don't just digest the world; we make it. For example, we all have a blind spot in each eye at the place where the optic nerve enters the retina, but we don't sense that hole, because our minds automatically fill it in. As V. S. Ramachandran and the philosopher Patricia Churchland have argued, "filling in" isn't always the covering over of a blank with more of the same; there are instances when the brain *provides* pictures—a normal form of hallucination. Very simply, for the mind, absence can be a catalyst for presence. In his beautiful memoir, *And There Was Light,* Jacques Lusseyran describes his experience of the world after he went blind at age eight: "Light threw its color on things and on people. My father and mother, the people I met or ran into in the street, all had their characteristic color which I had never seen before I went blind. Yet now this special attribute impressed itself on me as part of them as definitely as any impression created by a face."[5] For Lusseyran, losing his vision became an avenue to almost mystical insight. He found himself lifted up into a world of color and light drenched with meaning.

A lot of research has been done on visual perception. Scientists have isolated cells in particular areas of the *seeing* parts of the brain that serve special functions—the recognition of verticality, color, and motion, for example—but mysteries remain. Philosophers, neuroscientists, and cognitive scientists argue madly over "the binding problem"—how an object can appear whole and unified to us when each of its features is channeled through disparate networks in the brain. Qualia—the subjective experiences of things—are just as controversial. I don't see a consensus coming any time soon. Migraine auras of light, color, black holes and fogs, of high feeling and dread, and of peculiar little creatures that run or dance or just amble about, occupy a special place in the medical literature. They are anomalies, no doubt, tics of the nervous system that affect some, not all, but they could well help explain more general human qualities—who we are, what we feel, and how we see. I suspect that everyone has a few Lilliputians in hiding. It may be just a question of whether they pop out or not.

2008

PLAYING, WILD THOUGHTS, AND A NOVEL'S UNDERGROUND

PSYCHOANALYSIS PROPOSES THAT WE ARE strangers to ourselves. There were precursors to Freud's idea of a psychic unconscious in both philosophy and science. Schopenhauer and Nietzsche each had a version of it, as did the scientists William Benjamin Carpenter in nineteenth-century England and Gustav Fechner and Hermann von Helmholtz in Germany. All of them believed that much of what we are is hidden from us, not only our automatic biological processes but also memories, thoughts, and ideas. Pierre Janet, Jean-Martin Charcot's younger colleague at the Salpêtrière Hospital in Paris, pursued a psychobiological notion of the self. Ideas, he argued, can split off from consciousness, travel elsewhere, and appear as hysterical symptoms. Theories never bloom in nothingness. What is certain is that Sigmund Freud and his followers, both the faithful and the revisionist, have altered the way we think of ourselves. But the question here is about the novel. Has psychoanalysis changed the novel? Does putting a psychoanalyst in a novel affect its form, its sense of time, its essence?

The novel is a chameleon. That is its glory as a genre. It can be an enormous waddling monster or a fast, lean sprite. It can take everything in or leave most things out. It is Tolstoy and Beckett. There are no rules for writing novels. Those who believe there are rules are pedants and poseurs and do not deserve a minute of our time. Modes of writing and various schools come and go: Grub Street, Naturalism, the *nouveau roman,* magical realism. The novel remains. The modern novel was born a *hybrid,* to borrow the Russian theorist M. M. Bakhtin's word for the genre's mingling, contradictory voices that shout and murmur from every level and corner of society. When psychoanalysis appeared on the horizon, the novel welcomed it into itself as it welcomes all discourses.

When the "I" of the book is an analyst, does it fundamentally alter the way the novel works? Laurence Sterne's *Tristram Shandy* (1759) has a structure far more radical and, I would say, more akin to the associative workings of the human mind and memory, than Simone de Beauvoir's far more conventional book *The Mandarins* (1954), which has a narrating analyst, Anne. But to address this question, I cannot remain outside it, looking down at it from a third-person view. In life there is no omniscient narrator. Making a work of fiction is playing, playing in deadly earnest, perhaps, but playing nevertheless. D. W. Winnicott, the English psychoanalyst and pediatrician, argued that play is universal, part of every human being's creativity and the source of a meaningful life. Making art is a form of play.

In fact, I have discovered that a novel can be written only in play: an open, relaxed, responsive, permissive state of being that allows a work to grow freely. *The Sorrows of an American* was generated by an unbidden mental image that came to me while I was daydreaming. In a room that looked very much like the tiny living room in my grandparents' farmhouse, I saw a table. On the table was an open coffin, and in the coffin lay a girl. Then, as I watched, she sat up. My father was dying then, and despite the familiar setting—my father grew up in that house—and the un-disguised wish to wake the dead that must have been at the heart of the fantasy, I did not interpret it. Not long afterwards, my father died. There are no miracles in the book, but the farmhouse is there, and a girl child who wakes up, and all through it the dead return to the living. Sections of the book came directly from a memoir my father had written at the end of his life for his family and friends. I now know I used those passages as a way to revive him, if only as a ghost.

And where did my storyteller come from, my forty-seven-year-old, divorced, lonely, grieving psychiatrist/psychoanalyst, Erik Davidsen? Some time in the early eighties, I saw a drawing by Willem de Kooning called "Self-Portrait with Imaginary Brother" at the Whitney Museum in New York. I love de Kooning's work, but in this case it was the artist's title that hit me. As one of four sisters, I knew this was the only kind of brother I could ever have. After I finished my Ph.D. in 1986, I considered training to earn my living as a psychoanalyst, but I was too poor for more schooling. Nevertheless, when I began writing the story, my imaginary brother-analyst-self was waiting for me. And I began to play.

The truth about unconscious processes is that the book can know more than the writer knows, a knowing that comes in part from the body, rising up from a preverbal, rhythmic, motor place in the self, what Maurice Merleau-Ponty called *schéma corporel*. When I cannot find words, a walk helps. My feet jog the sentence loose from that secret underground. Images lurk in that cellar, too, along with half-formed phrases, and whole sentences that belong to no one. Wilfred Bion, an English psychoanalyst, said, "If a thought without a thinker comes along, it may be what is a stray thought, or it could be a thought with the owner's name and address upon it, or it could be a 'wild thought.'"[1] Sometimes when I'm writing, wild thoughts appear. They fly ahead of me. I have to run after them to understand what is happening.

I discovered the novel's music as I went along, as well as its gaps and silences. There are always things that are unsaid—significant holes. I was aware that I was writing about memory. Freud's notion of *Nachträglichkeit* haunted the book. We remember, and we tell ourselves a story, but the meanings of what we remember are reconfigured over time. Memory and imagination cannot be separated. Remembering is always also a form of imagining. And yet some memories remain outside sequence, story, and felt human time: the involuntary flashbacks of trauma. These timeless bits and pieces of images and sensory shocks subvert and interrupt narration. They resist plot. The real secrets of this particular novel are not revealed through the plot. Many of them never come to light at all.

Surely, what I have learned about psychoanalysis over the years has shaped my work, because it has altered my thoughts, both wild and tame. But so have philosophy, linguistics, neurobiology, paintings, poems, and other novels, not to speak of my lived experiences, both remembered and forgotten. As Winnicott knew, long before there was psychoanalysis, there was play.

2009

SLEEPING/NOT SLEEPING

1. FAILING TO FALL

THE NARRATOR OF CHAUCER'S POEM *The Book of the Duchess* cannot sleep. As his fitful thoughts come and go, he lies awake. He hasn't slept for so long, he fears he may die of insomnia. But what is the reason for his sleeplessness? "Myselven can not telle why,"[1] he says. The English expression "to fall asleep" is apt because the transition between waking and sleeping is a gradual drop from one state of being into another, a giving up of full self-consciousness for unconsciousness or for the altered consciousness of dreams. Except in cases of exhaustion or with the aid of drugs, the movement from one world to another is not instantaneous; it takes a little time. Full waking self-consciousness begins to loosen and unravel.

During this interval, I have often had the illusion that I am walking. I feel my foot slip off a curb and fall, but before I hit the pavement, I feel a jerk and am fully awake again. I also watch brilliant mutating spectacles on my closed eyelids, hypnagogic hallucinations, that usher me into sleep. Sometimes I hear voices speak a single word or a short emphatic sentence. In *Speak, Memory*, Vladimir Nabokov tells about his own visual and auditory semi-oneiric phenomena. "Just before falling asleep I often become aware of . . . a neutral, detached anonymous voice which I catch saying words of no importance to me whatever—an English or Russian sentence." He, too, had visions, often "grotesque," that preceded sleep. Although hypnagogic hallucinations are poorly studied except in relation to narcolepsy, many people without that affliction report seeing pictures or just colors and shadows when they linger at the threshold of sleep. What distinguishes these experiences from dreams proper is awareness, a kind of double reality. As Nabokov writes of his images, "They come and go without the drowsy observer's participation, but are essentially different from dream pictures for he is still master of his senses."[2]

When I have insomnia, I cannot drop into this peculiar zone between waking and sleeping—this half-dreaming, half-aware state of words and pictures does not arrive. As Jorge Luis Borges observes in his poem "Insomnia": "In vain do I await/ the disintegration, the symbols that come before sleep."[3] My internal narrator, the one who is speaking in my head all day long, refuses to shut up. The day-voice of the self-conscious thinker races along heedless of my desire to stop it and relax. Chaucer's narrator seems to have a similar problem: "Suche fantasies ben in myn hede, / So I not what is best to doo."[4] And so, like many insomniacs before and after him, he picks up a book and begins to read.

I was thirteen when I had my first bout of sleeplessness. My family was in Reykjavík, Iceland, for the summer, and day never really became night. I couldn't sleep, and so I read, but the novels I was reading only stimulated me more, and I would find myself wandering around the house with rushing fragments of Dickens, Austen, or the Brontës whirring in my head. It is tempting to think of this form of insomnia, the inability to *fall* asleep, as a disease of agency and control, the inability to relinquish high self-reflexive consciousness for the vulnerable, ignorant regions of slumber when we know not what we do. In *On the Generation of Animals,* Aristotle regards sleep as a between-world: ". . . the transition from being to not-being to being is effected through the intermediate state, and sleep would appear to be by its nature a state of this sort, being as it were a borderland between living and not-living: a person who is asleep would appear to be neither completely non-existent nor completely existent . . ."[5] Sleep as nearer to death than waking or, as Banquo calls it in *Macbeth,* death's counterfeit.

In sleep we leave behind the sensory stimulation of the outside world. A part of the brain called the thalamus, involved in the regulation of sleeping and waking, plays a crucial role in shutting out somatosensory stimuli and allowing the cortex to enter sleep. One theory offered to explain hypnagogic hallucinations is that the thalamus deactivates before the cortex in human beings, so the still active cortex manufactures images, but this is just a hypothesis. What is clear is that going to sleep involves making a psychobiological transition. Anxiety, guilt, excitement, a racing bedtime imagination, fear of dying, and pain or illness can keep us from toppling into the oneiric underworld. Depression often involves sleep disturbances, especially waking up early in the morning and not being able to get back to sleep. Weirdly enough, keeping a depressed patient awake for a couple of nights in the hospital can alleviate his symptoms temporarily. They return as soon as he begins to sleep normally again. On the rare occasion that I have had both a migraine headache and suffered from a whole night of insomnia, I have found that the insomnia appears to cure the migraine. No one understands how either depression or migraine are related to, or overlap with, the sleep cycle.

Chaucer's insomniac reads Ovid's *The Metamorphosis.* It does not put him to sleep. He gets very interested in it and spends many lines reporting on his reading. I read in the afternoons now, never at night, because books enliven the internal narrator to one vivid thought after another. No doubt my obsessive reading kept me up that summer long ago, but the permanent daylight of Reykjavík in June must have played havoc with my circadian rhythms, my normal twenty-four-hour wake/sleep cycle and, without darkness, my body never fell into the borderland that would carry me into slumber. When I look back on it, I think I was more anxious about not sleeping than about anything else I can name, and this is still often the case when I am seized with a fit of wakefulness. I am lucky it doesn't happen often. It is bitter to hear the birds.

2. WHY SLEEP?

Waking and sleeping are the two sides of being. Aristotle put it this way: "It is necessary that every creature which wakes must also be capable of sleeping, since it is impossible that it should be always actualizing its powers."[6] This makes sense. We know that we have to sleep. We know sleeplessness makes us cranky, stupid, and sad. And yet, why we sleep, why we dream, and even why we are wakeful—conscious—remain mysteries. In *The Meditations* René Descartes asked if he could be certain he was even awake. "How often, asleep at night, am I convinced that I am here in my dressing gown, sitting by the fire when in fact I am lying undressed in bed! . . . I see plainly that there are never any sure signs by means of which being awake can be distinguished from being asleep."[7] Dreamless sleep gave Descartes a further problem. It followed from his *cogito ergo sum* that the apparent thoughtlessness of deep imageless sleep would mean an end to human existence. He was forced to postulate that both waking and sleeping states are conscious, even those periods when we don't dream at all. John Locke found this ridiculous and came to the opposite conclusion: dreamless sleep is not part of the self, because there is nothing to remember, and personal identity is made of memories. Most of us accept the fact that although we may believe our dreams to be real events when asleep, upon waking in the morning in the same place, we can tell the difference between nocturnal hallucination and reality. But what is sleep and why do we need it? Who are we when we sleep? What exactly does the insomniac crave?

Until the middle of the twentieth century, most researchers agreed that fatigue led to reduced brain activity in sleep, that sleep was, by and large, a dormant state of mind. But this was proved wrong. In REM (rapid eye movement) sleep, brain activity compares to that of full wakefulness. Indeed, sometimes neural firing is more intense than when we're awake. The old answer was: that's because we're dreaming. But the hard and fast equation between REM sleep and dreaming has been overturned, although the debates go on about exactly what this means. There are dreams during the non-REM phase of sleep as well. What waking consciousness is and what it's for is also a mystery, although there are many competing theories. Does sleeping help consolidate our memories? Some scientists say yes. Some say no. Do dreams mean anything? There are people involved in dream research who say yes, Freud was essentially right, or right about some aspects of dreaming. Others who say no, dreams are mental refuse, and still others who say they have meanings but not as Freud thought they did. What is the evolutionary purpose of consciousness, of sleep, of dreams? There is no agreement.

If you keep rats awake, they die within two to four weeks. Of course, in order to prevent the poor creatures from sleeping, the scientists make it impossible for them to drop off, and whether they actually die of sleep deprivation or stress isn't clear. Fruit flies and cockroaches perish without sleep. The putative record for a human being intentionally staying awake belongs to Randy Gardner, a seventeen-year-old, who remained awake for eleven days in 1965 for a science fair. He survived just fine but was a cognitive wreck by the end of his ordeal. As a volunteer writing teacher at the Payne Whitney psychiatric clinic in New York, I had many bipolar patients in my classes who had been admitted to the hospital during bouts of mania. A number of them told me that they had stayed awake for days, flying high as they had sex, shopped, danced, and even wrote. One woman reported she had written thousands of pages during her most recent manic phase. A strange illness called Morvan's syndrome can cause people to remain essentially sleepless for long periods of time. In 1974, Michel Jouvet, a French researcher, studied a young man with the disorder who remained awake for several months. He was entirely cogent and suffered no memory impairment or anxiety. He did, however, have visual, auditory, tactile, and olfactory hallucinations every night for a couple of hours. He dreamed awake. Depending on their location, brain lesions can make people sleepy or prevent them from sleeping. They can also cause exceedingly vivid dreams or the cessation of dreaming altogether. Then again, people with no brain injury can experience all of these symptoms as well.

These admittedly random examples of sleeping and sleeplessness are all suggestive, and each one could feasibly become part of a larger argument about why we sleep and dream. Various understandings of both sleeping and waking consciousness depend on how the lines are drawn between and among the various states. Ernest Hartmann of Tufts University School of Medicine proposes a model he calls a "focused-waking-to-dreaming-continuum" which moves from the highly self-conscious, logical, category-bound, sequential wakefulness to daydreaming and reverie with their more fragmented, less logical, and more metaphorical thoughts to dreaming that is highly visual and much less self-conscious. This makes a lot of sense to me. The insomniac remains on the focused waking or daydreaming less-focused side of the continuum, unable for any number of reasons to let go. Hartmann shares with other researchers the conviction that dreaming is more emotional than waking life and that we make connections in dreams, often metaphorical ones, that are more creative than when we're wide awake and working at some task. He does not believe dreams are random nonsense. Dreaming is another form of mental activity.

There is no place for dreamless sleep on Hartmann's continuum, but that blankness might reside around the dreaming state. Gottfried Leibniz answered Descartes and Locke by arguing that not all thoughts are conscious. Some perceptions are too unfocused and confused to enter our self-reflective awareness. He argued for a continuum of perception from unconsciousness to full self-consciousness; therefore even deep, dreamless sleep is part of what and who we are. Leibniz died in 1716, but his insight remains startling. We still may not know why we sleep or wake up, but we know that both states are part of a dynamic, changing organism. Long after Descartes, Locke, and Leibniz, the French philosopher Maurice Merleau-Ponty wrote in *The Phenomenology of Perception* (1945): "The body's role is to ensure metamorphosis."[8] Surely, that is exactly what we do when we move through the various stages of being wide awake and concentrated to the piecemeal musings of reverie, to sinking drowsiness, to sleep and dreaming, or to sleep with no dreams at all.

3. GOING UNDER

I remember a lamp that stood on the floor in the opened doorway to the bedroom where my sister and I slept. My mother put it there every night so the darkness would never be total. This is an old memory and around it are the usual fogs that dim recollection, but the light offered the hope that blackness would not snuff out the visible world entirely during my anxious transition to sleep. Bedtime rituals for children ease the way to the elsewhere of slumber—teeth brushing and pajamas, the voice of a parent reading, the feel and smell of the old blanket or toy, the night-light glowing in a corner. For the child, bedtime means double separation, not only from wakefulness but also from Mother and Father. I wonder how many glasses of water have been fetched, how many extra stories have been read and lullabies sung, how many small backs and arms and heads have been rubbed in the past week alone in New York City.

In the "Metapsychological Supplement to the Theory of Dreams," Sigmund Freud wrote,

> We are not in the habit of devoting much thought to the fact that every night human beings lay aside the wrappings in which they have enveloped their skin as well as anything which they may use as a supplement to their bodily organs . . . for instance their spectacles, their false hair and teeth and so on. We may add that they carry on an entirely analogous un-dressing of their minds and lay aside most of their psychical acquisitions. Thus on both counts they approach remarkably close to the situation in which they began life.[9]

Children are even closer to that beginning than we adults are. Night looms larger because time moves more slowly—a child's day represents a much larger percentage of life lived than it does for the middle-aged parent. The mental capacities of little children do not include the rationalizations grown-ups use to explain to themselves that a fear is unjustified. The three-year-old does not yet live in a world of Newtonian physics. Not long ago,

I saw a film of a psychology experiment in which young children worked hard to get their oversized bodies into toy cars.

Sleep resistance, bouts of insomnia, nightmares and night terrors, crawling into bed with parents in the middle of the night are so common among children it seems fair to call them "normal." Infants, of course, are notorious for refusing to sleep and wake on command. The exasperated parent can now call a counselor who, for a fee, will come to your house and address your baby's "sleep issues." As far as I can tell, these interventions are directed more at exhausted parents than at the welfare of children. They consist of behaviorist techniques that "teach" the offspring to give up hope for comfort at times inconvenient for her progenitors. The message here is an early-life version of self-help. The truth is that a baby develops through the reflective exchanges he has with his mother (or what is now called the "primary caregiver"). Essential brain development that regulates emotion takes place after birth, and it happens through the back and forth of maternal-infant relations—looking, touching, comforting. But there is also an intrinsic alarm system in the brain that the neuroscientist Jaak Panksepp calls the PANIC system. All mammals exhibit "distress vocalizations" when they are separated from their caretakers. They cry when they're left alone. As Panksepp writes, "When these circuits are aroused [PANIC system] animals seek reunion with individuals who help create the feeling of a 'secure neurochemical base' in the brain."[10] Harry Harlow's famous experiments with rhesus monkeys demonstrated that isolated baby monkeys preferred inanimate "terry cloth mothers" to hard wire ones that provided them with food. The animals raised in isolation became anxious, timid, maladjusted adults.

I am not saying that "sleep training" creates psychiatric problems. No doubt many sleep-trained children grow up just fine, but I am saying that sleep training is *counterintuitive*. When your baby cries, you want to go to her, pick her up, and rock her back to sleep. If anything has become clear to me, it is how quickly advice about raising children changes. In the early twentieth century when the dictates of behaviorism reigned supreme, experts on child care advocated strict feeding and sleeping regimens and discouraged parents from *playing* with their children.

I couldn't bear to let my baby cry in the night, so I didn't. For years I read to my daughter while she drifted off to sleep, her fingers in my hair. As she grew older, I continued to read to her and, after I had said good night, she would lean over and switch on a tape of Stockard Channing reading one of the Ramona books by Beverly Cleary. The tape had become a *transitional object*—a bridge between me and sleep. D. W. Winnicott coined this term for the things children cling to—bits of blanket or stuffed animals or their own fingers or thumb—that occupy a space between the subjective inner world and the outside world. These objects are especially necessary at bedtime when, as Winnicott writes, "From waking to sleeping, the child jumps from a perceived world to a self-created world. In between there is need for all kinds of transitional phenomena—neutral territory."[11] I vividly remember my sister Asti's ragged blanket she called her "nemene." One of my nieces used three pacifiers— one to suck and two to twirl. How she loved her "fires."

There is no reason we should expect young children to enter the nocturnal darkness of sleep and dreams without help. Parental rituals and transitional objects serve as vehicles for making the passage and, indeed, to a child's ability eventually to comfort himself. Freud was surely right about the strangeness of preparing for bed and about the fact that the human mind is undressed in sleep. The so-called executive part of the brain—the bilateral prefrontal cortex—is largely quiet, which probably accounts for the disinhibition and high emotion of many dreams. It is not always easy to go to the region that lies beneath wakefulness, to relinquish the day and its vivid sensory reality. And for a small child the most vital part of that reality is Mother and Father, the beloveds she must leave behind as she drops into the very private land of sleep.

2010

OUTSIDE THE MIRROR

I T IS A PECULIAR TRUTH that I see far less of myself than other people do. I can see my fingers typing when I look down at them. I can examine my shoes, the details of a shirt cuff, or admire a pair of new tights on my legs while I am sitting down, but the mirror is the only place where I am whole to myself. Only then do I see my body as others see it. But does my mirror-self really represent my persona in the world? Is that woman who gives herself the once-over, who checks for parsley in incisors to avoid a green smile, who leans close to study new wrinkles or the red blotches that sometimes appear on her rapidly aging countenance a reasonable approximation of what others see? I do not witness myself as I talk and gesture emphatically to make absolutely sure my point has been made. I do not see myself as I stride down the street, dance, or stumble, nor do I know what I look like when I laugh, grimace, cry, or sneer. This is no doubt a blessing. Were I to see myself in medias res, my critical faculties might never shut down, and I would barely be able to lift a finger without crippling self-consciousness.

Instead of actually seeing ourselves, we walk around with an *idea* about ourselves. We have a *body image* or a *body identity*. This is the conscious notion of what we look like. I'm pretty or ugly, fat or thin, feminine or masculine, old or young. Everyone knows that we can be wrong about our body image. We have all met thin people who believe they are fat and old people who think they have the bodies of thirty-year-olds and dress accordingly. I confess I am sometimes surprised when I regard my own face in photographs. "Good heavens!" I say to myself. "Is that what you look like now? Are you really so *old*?" At other times, I find myself saying admirably "You're not so bad for fifty-six. You're hanging in there." But then photographs, those documents of an instant, don't capture a person in motion. They are static, and we are not. Nevertheless, I think my body image sometimes lags behind my real body.

If body image is what we think we look like, style is meant to express who we think we are, and since we spend most of our lives dressed, not naked, clothes can efficiently announce something about a person's character. Whether sober and sleek, humorous, sweet, modest, loud, or dangerous—they serve as an indication of personality. When I put on my clothes, I hope that the dresses and trousers and blouses and coats and shoes and boots and scarves and purses and all the rest of the sartorial paraphernalia I select will speak for me, will suggest to the world an idea I have about myself. It is interesting to ask how these ideas come about. I have learned after almost thirty years of marriage that my husband regards any shirt with a shiny fabric (even the barest sheen) as anathema to his true character. My sister Liv wears a lot of jewelry and she looks wonderful in it. I have sometimes tried to imitate her, but inevitably take it all off and leave on what I always wear—earrings. A lot of jewelry just isn't "me." But what is this me-ness about? Where does it come from?

If every person has an idea about garments that *are* him or her, most of us also have an ideally dressed self. When it comes to wearing clothes, *idea* and *ideal* intersect; the real and the imaginary inevitably come together. In my life, I have mostly found my ideal garments in the movies. I have a great weakness for those gleaming images of manufactured glamour and sophistication filmed on glorious Hollywood sets with monumental white staircases, billowing draperies, and sparkling chandeliers. How I have loved sitting in the dark and watching a world in which every suitcase is weightless and even poor shopgirls are as astutely attired as a chic Frenchwoman on the Champs-Élysées.

I believe it all started with a Walt Disney film, *Pollyanna,* starring Hayley Mills. Based on a revoltingly saccharine best-selling novel published in 1913, this movie captivated me entirely. I was only five when it was first released in 1960, so I think I must have seen it some time later, but not much later. In all events, I identified myself completely with Hayley Mills in her white sailor suit with navy blue trim. (I had no idea then that my mother had spent a good part of her childhood in southern Norway dressed in the very same fashion, de rigueur for middle-class children in the 1920s.) In my young mind, the sailor dress must have been emblematic of the story: a relentlessly cheerful girl sweetens up one sourpuss after another until she has won over an entire town. I pined for a dress like that. I must have believed in it as a vehicle of transformation: in that dress, I too might become like the heroine, adored, simply *adored,* by every single resident of my own small town.

My fixation on marine garb ended, but my cinematic identifications did not. When I first saw Marlene Dietrich slouching down a stairway in a tuxedo in the 1930 film *Morocco,* I thought I would never wear a dress again, only men's suits and smoking jackets. The sight of Lana Turner in a white turban in *The Postman Always Rings Twice* made me consider that form of headwear. Although turbans never worked, I do own a tuxedo. I am well aware that I look nothing like Dietrich in it, but I credit her for the inspiration. Perhaps my favorite films are Hollywood comedies of the thirties and forties. In those movies, the heroes and heroines are not only capable of finding their way to the end of an English sentence, they know how to banter. They know how to deliver a barb, fire off a witticism, and send a wry offhanded compliment. Their crackling dialogues are inseparable from their characters, characters that are also expressed, at least in part, by their clothes.

In the movies, I like to watch clothes in action—the flow of a dress as an actress moves across the floor, dances, or, better yet, runs. Near the end of *It Happened One Night*, Claudette Colbert, no longer a spoiled heiress, but leavened by her adventures on the road with that man of the people, Clark Gable, stands before the minister who is going to marry her to a frivolous playboy, the perfect movie sap, and, when asked if she will take this man to be her lawfully wedded husband, she vigorously shakes her head no-she-won't, hitches up her immense train, and runs, a mile-long veil streaming behind her on the grass. It's a great shot, one that has the punch of a vividly remembered image from a dream.

Like countless others before and after me, I fell for Katharine Hepburn. I fell for her style. It is hardly news that she was a woman who did not bow to conventional standards, and the way she dressed was a sign of rebellion. There was a masculine quality to whatever she wore, even when she was draped in an evening gown. I remember her in a pair of wide trousers, striding down a golf course with Spencer Tracy in *Pat and Mike*. And I remember her in *Holiday*, wearing a gloriously simple black dress with a high neck. No froufrou or silliness for her, no peekaboo blouses or big bows or ridiculous shoes.

I was nineteen when I first saw *Holiday*, the 1938 romantic comedy directed by George Cukor and based on the play by Philip Barry. As a freshman in college, I had my second moment of profound identification with a celluloid being: Hepburn's character

Linda. What did it matter that she was the offspring of a fantastically wealthy man of business and I the daughter of a not very well paid professor? What difference did it make that she inhabited a mansion on Park Avenue with an elevator, and I had grown up in a modest house with scenic views of corn and alfalfa fields? Wasn't she misunderstood just as I was? Didn't she wish desperately to escape all that luxury and superficial nonsense? And even if I had no luxury to flee from, didn't I, too, fantasize about another life? This kind of thinking, of course, is an essential aspect of what is referred to as "the magic of the movies."

As I watched entranced, I did not see myself sitting in my seat in my old jeans and sweater, both of which had undoubtedly been purchased on sale. I was not in Minnesota anymore. Some ideal self had been embodied onscreen, a character with whom I shared nothing except an emotional reality: a feeling of being trapped and unhappy. I participated in the fable unfolding before me, and as I participated, I imagined myself in those clothes, Linda's clothes, not the ones worn by her snooty, shallow sister, whose expensive wardrobe seemed so fussy in comparison. No, I was in that black evening dress, and I was wearing it just as Linda did, wearing it as if it made no difference to me that it was supremely elegant, because I had other more pressing, more important things on my mind. I was falling in love with another free spirit, played by Cary Grant.

Few people are immune to such enchantments, and they long predate the movies. We enter characters in novels, too, and imagine ourselves into their stories and into whatever habiliments they may have on during their adventures, and it is possible for us because we do not have to look at ourselves *while* we are doing it. When we are invisible to ourselves, every transformation is possible. Movies give visual form to our myriad waking dreams. The marvelous people on the screen take the place of the mirror for a while, and we see ourselves in them. Mirroring is a physiological and a social phenomenon. We are born with the ability to imitate the expressions of others, but we also become creatures of our culture with its countless images of what is chic and beautiful. When we choose what to wear we don't just choose particular pieces of clothing, we select them because they carry meanings about us, meanings we hope will be understood by other people.

These days, I often find myself buying clothes that look suspiciously like ones I already own. This may sound a little dull and perhaps it is. My body image has changed; I am not the girl of nineteen who sat in the movie theater and watched *Holiday* anymore. I did leave Minnesota only a few years after seeing that film, and moved to New York City. I broke away from my small town and the constraints of provincial life. It is fair to say that certain movie stars continue to haunt my wardrobe. Katharine Hepburn has been an ideal of tailored beauty whispering in my ear ever since I saw her all those years ago on the screen in that wonderful dress. I eschew frippery and excessive adornment of any kind. I like clothes with a masculine feeling that don't make me look like a man. I like shoes that I can move and dance and even run in if necessary. Towering heels, platforms, complex straps that resemble fetters are not "me." I like clothes that preserve and enhance my dignity, but are not so sober and serious that they make me look humorless. This is what I wish to convey when I get dressed. Whether I succeed or not in this endeavor, I honestly don't know. I don't see myself often enough. Before I leave the house for an evening out, I check myself in the mirror for just a moment and then I go off, happily ignorant of what I look like when I am living my life.

2011

SOME MUSINGS ON THE WORD
SCANDINAVIA

As a child, I'm not sure I even knew what *Scandinavia* meant. It was shrouded in a cultural mist that somehow wafted over me and mine, but why or how wasn't at all clear to me. I was already a person divided. A girl living in America with a Norwegian mother and a Norwegian-American father, I spoke Norwegian before I spoke English, but rural Minnesota was my everyday world; Norway was another world. As a four-year-old in 1959, I had spent five months with my mother and sister in Bergen. Until I returned for a year with my family in 1967, Norway lived inside me as a jumble of inchoate fragments—isolated memories (my hands in a gooseberry bush, an orange lying in the snow, the tears of my older cousin at the dinner table), household objects (chests and china, photographs and paintings on the wall), food (especially rice pudding, *bløtkake,* cream cake, and little chocolates called Twist), my parents' stories, and a few significant words. During the seven years between childhood visits, I mostly forgot Norwegian.

The advantage of not living in a place is that it becomes pure idea. Under the sway of a homesick mother and a father whose identification with the immigrant community in which he was raised led him to become a professor of Norwegian language and literature, I succumbed to an illusion of an ideal elsewhere, a magic kingdom of trolls and *nisse* and *fiskeboller,* of Ibsen, Hamsun, and Munch, a fantastic *over there,* where the children were happier and healthier, floors were cleaner, and the people kinder and more just. My parents weren't uncritical of Norway, but they were both prone to a form of nationalism that flourishes in tiny cultures that have been shaped by the humiliations of external control. In the case of Norway, that meant Denmark, and after that, it meant Sweden. At some point, I discovered that together these three comprised Scandinavia. Despite the maniacal flag-waving that took place every May 17 to trumpet *our* independence from Sweden, it turned out that we were somehow in the same family with *them,* and not only them, but the Danes, too. It took a while to grapple with this concept, but eventually it penetrated my young mind, and I came to accept it.

The binding principle of Scandinavia is not geography, but language. If you have one of the three languages, the other two can be easily managed with a little work—at least on the page. Danish, so comprehensible to me in print, can quickly become a series of indistinguishable noises in the mouth and throat of an actual speaker, and Swedish, though easier to understand, can also trail off into pleasant music when I'm not paying close attention. And yet so many words belong to all three languages, and more than anything else, it is language that shapes perception of the world, that draws the lines and creates the boundaries that make what is out there legible. It is a legacy of my childhood that I am a Norwegian-American who doesn't feel quite American but who doesn't feel quite Norwegian either. If I didn't speak Norwegian, I would most certainly feel alienated from that country's culture in a far more fundamental way. It is the language that lures me into *feeling* the connection to a past that extends backward to a time long before I was born. The vocabulary and cadences of Norwegian continue to live inside me, and moreover, they haunt my English. My prose is decidedly Protestant, and despite the fact that Scandinavia is no longer exclusively Protestant, its mores and culture were profoundly influenced by that iconoclastic, stark, and lonely version of Christianity.

Unlike English, the Scandinavian languages are word poor. With William the Conqueror in 1066 and the infusion of Latinate French into Anglo-Saxon, what we now know as English evolved. And yet, it's exactly their poverty of vocabulary that gives writers possibilities in the Scandinavian languages that English writers don't have. A word like *lys* in Norwegian—which means both light and candle—allows repetitions, ambiguities, and depths that aren't possible in English. *Lys* is a word heavy with the knowledge of darkness, of summer and winter, of precious long days of light opposed to long days of murk and clouds. In Bergen, where I went to gymnasium for a year, it rained so much that when the sun was shining, the authorities canceled school. Even after she had been living in Minnesota for years, my mother would turn her face to the sun and close her eyes as if the warm rays might disappear any moment. Perhaps the darkness lies behind the omnipresent candles in Scandinavian households, too, lit even during the day and shining in rooms at night. The northern experience of darkness and light is *untranslatable*. The contrast between them has to be lived in the body. I have often wondered what immigrants to Scandinavia must feel when they arrive from places where summer and winter aren't so radically defined by light and dark, how strange it must be to shop in afternoon gloom or see the sun late at night in summer. I have wondered how it changes the rhythms of their lives and the meaning of the words *light* and *dark* in their native languages. My paternal grandparents and my father, none of them born in Norway, all spoke English with Norwegian accents. Their Norwegian, however, was unlike the language spoken on the other side of the Atlantic. Their speech was dense with nineteenth-century locutions and sprinkled with hybrids—nouns borrowed from English and assigned a gender—words for things that had no Norwegian equivalent.

This is a certainty: like the rest of Europe, Scandinavia is no longer homogenous. The stereotype of the giant, pale-skinned, Lutheran blonde (the only stock character I embody perfectly) has become an anachronism and is being replaced by a variety of body types, complexions, and religions. I, for one, celebrate a changing image of Scandinavia, because migrations of people from one place always enliven the culture of *here*. Movements of people create new words, new ideas, and inspire new art. I am the product of an immigrant culture in the Midwest, and I now live in New York City, where forty percent of my fellow inhabitants were born in another country. On one of my last trips to Oslo, I climbed into a taxi, gave an address, and began a conversation with the driver. His father had been born in Pakistan, but he was born in Norway. He needn't have told me; his Oslo dialect was unmistakable.

While immigrants always revivify the country they enter, their presence also creates conflict. In the United States, where all of us, with the exception of Native Americans, came from somewhere else, superiority was measured in generations. The longer your family had lived in America, the better. In 1972–73, when I lived in Bergen, there were no immigrants in town, and yet with a regularity that never failed to surprise me, and despite the fact that I was a passionate supporter of civil rights, I was attacked for my country's racism. After the wave of Pakistani immigration to Norway, I returned to find people casually using racial slurs and prey to denigrating stereotypes. In short, they said things that would have been anathema in the United States. Like their cohorts all over the world, right-wing politicians in Scandinavia are guilty of thinking in terms of *us* and *them,* of exploiting ignorance and fear to maintain a fiction of "the nation," not as a shared geography or language, but nation as blood or background. This is always dangerous, and it inevitably stinks of the ugliest of ideas: racial purity. In the United States, one of the oddest legacies of our racist culture is that people who have very pale skin but some African ancestry, like Lena Horne or Colin Powell, are inevitably called "black" rather than "white." The Nazi racial laws created the most ludicrous hairsplitting over percentages of Jewishness in the population, a frankly absurd notion in a country where Jews had lived for hundreds of years and had been marrying Gentiles for just as long. In the tiny world of immigrants and their children and grandchildren in which my father spent his boyhood, the Swedes and Danes in neighboring communities were not regarded as linguistic cousins with important historical and cultural links to Norwegians. They were *foreigners*. And yet, there is no story without change. That world my father knew as a child is gone forever. In college, I knew a person with a background he described as "part Swedish, part German, and part Sioux Indian." My daughter refers to herself as "half Norwegian" and "half Jewish." She likes to call herself a "Jewegian." *Scandinavia* is a word whose meanings are in flux. Its myriad references and significations are being determined, and we can only hope that it will stand as a sign of inclusion, not exclusion.

2005

MY INGER CHRISTENSEN

INGER CHRISTENSEN IS DEAD. A great writer has died. I know that *great* is a word we often use to decorate a venerable cultural figure and then put him or her on a high shelf with the other moldering greats, but this is not my intention. Great books are the ones that are urgent, life changing, the ones that crack open the reader's skull and heart. I was in my early twenties when I first read *Det,* and I felt I had been sent a revelation. This work was like no other I had ever read—its rhythms and repetitions were of my own body, my heartbeat, my breath, the motion of my legs and the swing of my arms as I walk. As I read it, I moved with its music. But inseparable from that corporeal music, embedded in the cadences themselves, was a mind as rigorous, as tough, as steely as any philosopher's. Christensen did not compromise. Paradox upon paradox accumulated in a game of embodied thought. Logic, systems, numbers came alive and danced for me, but they did so hand in hand with ordinary things, which her voice enchanted and made strange. She made me see differently. She made me feel anew the power of incantation. I read more of her work then. I love especially her poems.

I met her twice, first at a festival in New York City. I rushed up to her, shook her hand, and babbled some words in an effort to articulate my intense admiration. She was kind. The second occasion was in Copenhagen at a dinner where I sat beside my idol, who was charming, funny, and told me she wouldn't return to New York because nobody let you smoke there. The merry, unpretentious woman at the table and the great poet were one, and yet there is always some split at such moments between the person in the room and the person on the page. I didn't know the woman, but the poet altered my inner world. She whispers to me in my own writing, a brilliant, fierce literary mother whom I will read and reread again and again. The last words belong to Christensen: the music of life and death. They are the last three lines of *Det*.

En eller annen er død og bæres ud av sit hus ved mørkets frembrud.
En eller annen er død og betragtes af nogen der omsider er blinde.
En eller annen står stille og er omsider alene med den anden døde.

Someone or other is dead and is carried out of the house as night falls.
Someone or other is dead and is seen by someone who is blind at last.
Someone or other stands still and is alone at last with the other dead
   person.
(my translation)

                                                                    2009

MY FATHER/MYSELF

THERE IS A DISTANCE TO fatherhood that isn't part of motherhood. In our earliest days, fathers are necessarily a step away. We don't have an interuterine life with our fathers, aren't expelled from their bodies in birth, don't nurse at their breasts. Even though our infancies are forgotten, the stamp of those days remains in us, the first exchanges between mother and baby, the back-and-forth, the rocking, the soothing, the holding and looking. Fathers, on the other hand, enter the stage from elsewhere. As the psychoanalyst Jessica Benjamin points out, fathers are *exciting,* and their play is usually different from that of mothers and more arousing to the infant. Fathers are often the ones who introduce "jiggling, bouncing, whooping."[1] I vividly recall my own baby's joyous face as she straddled her father's jumping knee. He regularly turned her into "Sophie Cowgirl," and the two took wild rides together as my husband provided the shoot-'em-up sound effects. I cannot remember bouncing on my father's knee, but I can recall the noise of the door opening, his footsteps in the hall, and the intense happiness that accompanied his homecoming. Every day for years, my three sisters and I greeted our father as if he were a returning hero, running to the door, shrieking, "Daddy's home!" We were only daughters in my family. The boy never arrived, and I have often thought that in the end, his absence served us all, including my father, whose relationship with a son would have been colored by an intense identification he didn't have with his daughters. I think that was oddly liberating. My sisters and I were born into a culture that didn't expect great ambition from girls. The irony is that because we didn't have to share our father with a brother, our interests were able to bloom. A boy would inevitably have felt more pressure from both his parents to *become* someone, but I feel sure we would have envied that pressure, nevertheless.

God the father, land of our fathers, forefathers, Founding Fathers all refer to an origin or source, to what generated us, to an *authority*. We fall into the paternal line. Patronymic as identity. I have my father's name, not my mother's. I didn't take my husband's name when I married, but the symbolic mark of paternity is inscribed into the signs for me: Siri Hustvedt. We were called "the Hustvedt girls" or "the Hustvedt sisters" when we were growing up, four apples from the same tree. The father's name is the stamp of genealogy, legitimacy, and coherence. Although we know when a woman gives birth that she is the child's mother, the father's identity can't be *seen*. It's hidden from us in the mysteries of the bedroom where potentially clandestine unions with *other* men might have taken place. In Judaism, this difficulty is circumvented by establishing Jewish identity through the mother, the known origin, not through the far less certain one: the father. Doubt or confusion about paternal identity and the scourge of illegitimacy have been the stuff of literature in the West since the Greeks. In the Oedipus story, the hero commits patricide and incest *accidentally,* but once the crimes are known, the world's foundations shake. The virgin birth in Christianity is the ultimate evocation of paternal mystery, for here the progenitor is God himself, the Holy Spirit, who by means beyond human understanding has impregnated a mortal woman. Edmund in *King Lear* bemoans his fate as illegitimate son, "Why brand they us with base? With baseness? bastardy?" But Edmund's treachery is part and parcel of his position as an outsider, a child born from the right father but the wrong mother—a crooked line. Charles Dickens populated his books with illegitimate children and articulated and rearticulated the drama of fatherlessness as a nullity to the self and to others. The illegitimate Arthur Clennam in *Little Dorrit* is repeatedly referred to as "Nobody." In another pointed passage in the same novel, when asked about the mysterious Miss Wade, Mr. Pancks answers, "I know as much about her as she knows about herself. She is somebody's child—anybody's—nobody's."[2] Without an identifiable past, the route to self-knowledge has been closed. The father's power to name fixes and defines us in a relation that allows us to become somebody, not nobody. This is the source of Jacques Lacan's famous pun on the dual symbolic role of the father. He names and he sanctions: *le nom de père* and *le non de père*.

When I was a child, *Father Knows Best* was on television. This benign series evoked an orderly family, which is to say everyone in it knew his or her place in the hierarchy. Every week, the structure was rattled by a minor storm, which then passed over. I am sure that the mythical dads of that postwar era mingled with my internal fantasies about my own father. They weren't despots, but they were in charge, and they had the last word, the ideal fathers of a period that was invested in reestablishing a familial order that had been dismantled during the war when the fathers of many American children were overseas. My father wasn't a disciplinarian, but he had an unchallenged, unspoken authority. Even a hint of anger or irritation from him was enough to mortify me. Those occasions were rare, but the power of paternal sanction ran deep. I wanted so much to please him. I wanted to be good.

It has been said, and it is true—

And this is real pain,
Moreover. It is terrible to see the children,

I he righteous little girls;
They expect to be so good . . .[3]

That is how George Oppen ends his poem "Street," and for me the last two lines have always had the force of a blow. I was a righteous little girl.

They are so delicate, these attachments of ours, these first great passions for our parents, and I have often wondered what would have become of me had my father used his power differently. In the hospital where I teach a weekly writing class to psychiatric patients, I have listened to many stories about fathers—violent fathers, runaway fathers, seductive fathers, negligent fathers, cruel fathers, fathers who are in prison or dead of drink or drugs or suicide. Shameful fathers. These are the paternal characters that fuel the stark narratives of "abuse" that people in our culture gulp down so eagerly. It is simple then to create cause and effect, to eliminate all ambiguity, to ignore the particulars of each case, to march down the road of moral outrage. There are brutal stories. We have all heard them, but there are also subtler forms of paternal power that create misshapen lives. I think of a man like the father in Henry James's *Washington Square,* Dr. Sloper. He intervenes when he understands that the young man courting his daughter, Catherine, is a fortune hunter. His assessment is by no means wrong, and his desire to protect his child is eminently reasonable, but beneath his acumen lurks not only coldness to his offspring but an ironic distance that borders on sadism. In a remarkable exchange between Sloper and his sister, they discuss Catherine's decision not to marry her beau immediately but to wait in the hope that her intractable father will change his mind.

"I don't see that it should be such a joke that your daughter adores you."

"It is the point where the adoration stops that I find interesting to fix."

"It stops where the other sentiment begins."

"Not at all—that would be simple enough. The two things are extremely mixed up, and the mixture is extremely odd. It will produce some third element, and that's what I'm waiting to see. I wait with suspense—with positive excitement; and that is a sort of emotion that I didn't suppose Catherine would ever provide for me. I am really very much obliged to her."[4]

Sloper's comment that Catherine's emotions for him and her lover are "extremely mixed up" is irrefutable as an insight, and it carries far beyond the boundaries of James's novel. Our deepest adult attachments are all colored by our first loves. They are extremely mixed up. But it is Catherine's love for and fear of her father that give him power. Her desire to please him holds her captive to his will. In James's story, however, there is a further irony, the third element, which is that the struggle over the bounder, Morris Townsend, uncovers what might have remained hidden: the father's contempt for his daughter. The revelation gives Catherine an iron will, and when Sloper insists she promise that after his death she will not marry Townsend, she refuses, not because she has any intention of marrying him, but because it is her only avenue of resistance.

My father was gentle, kind, often interested in what we did and proud of our accomplishments. The man basked in his young daughters' love. I have understood this only in hindsight. During my childhood, I wasn't able to put myself in his position, to imagine what that adulation must have felt like. He was a magical being then, enchanted, I think, by excitement, by the glamour of his otherness. He seemed to know the answer to every question. He was tall and strong, a carpenter, woodchopper, and builder of fires, friend to all mammals and insects, a storyteller, a smoke-ring-blower, and of course, a man who went to work, where he taught college students and engaged in various other cerebral activities, the nature of which were a little dim to me. It is ordinary for children to idealize their fathers. It is also ordinary for children to grow up and recognize that same father's humanity, including his weaknesses and blind spots. As Winnicott said, it is good for children to have "the experience of being let down gently by a real father."[5] The transition from ideal to real isn't always so easy, however, not for the children or for the father.

Identities, identifications, and desires cannot be untangled from one another. We become ourselves through others, and the self is a porous thing, not a sealed container. If it begins as a genetic map, it is one that is expressed over time and only in *relation* to the world. Americans cling desperately to their myths of self-creation, to rugged individualism, now more free-market than pioneer, and to self-help, that strange twist on do it yourself, which turns a human being into an object that can be repaired with a toolbox and some instructions. We do not author ourselves, which is not to say that we have no agency or responsibility, but rather that becoming doesn't escape relation. "You do not stop hungering for your father's love,"[6] my husband, Paul Auster, wrote in the first part of *The Invention of Solitude*, "Portrait of an Invisible Man," "even after you are grown up." The second part, "The Book of Memory," is told in the third person. The *I* becomes *he*:

When the father dies, he writes, the son becomes his own father and his own son. He looks at his own son and sees himself in the face of the boy. He imagines what the boy sees
when he looks at him and finds himself becoming his own
father. Inexplicably, he is moved by this. It is not just the sight
of the boy that moves him, nor even the thought of standing
inside his own father, but what he sees in the boy of his own
vanished past. It is a nostalgia for his own life that he feels,
perhaps, a memory of his own boyhood as a son to his father.
Inexplicably, he finds himself shaking at that moment between both happiness and sorrow, if this is possible, as if he
were going both forward and backward, into the future and
into the past. And there are times, often there are times, when
these feelings are so strong that his life no longer seems to dwell
in the present.[7]

Here the identifications are seamless. Three generations mingle
and time collapses in *likeness*. I am you. I have become you. But
we cannot write, *When the father dies, the daughter becomes her own
father and then her own son*. The daughter never becomes a father.
The sex threshold is a thick seam, not easily crossed. It complicates identification and desire. Paul didn't have a daughter, our
daughter, when he wrote those words. She came later. Once, when
she was very small, she asked us if she would grow a penis when
she got older. No, we told her, that would never come to be. It
wasn't the moment to introduce the subject of sex-change operations, but one may wonder in all seriousness about Freud's much
maligned comment that "anatomy is destiny." To what degree are
we prisoners of our sex?

I, too, have felt the continuities among generations of
women in my family, the maternal as an unbroken chain of feeling. I loved my maternal grandmother, whom I knew well, my

mormor, mother's mother in Norwegian. She adored my own mother, her youngest child, and she adored me. I remember her hand on my face when I said good-bye after a visit, the affection in her eyes, her mildness. My own mother's face, her hands, her touch and voice, have resonated in me all my life and have be-came part of a legacy I carried with me to my own daughter, an inheritance, which is like music in my body, a wordless knowl-edge given and received over time. In this, I was lucky. There is little dissonance in that tune that was passed from one woman to the next. Mother love is everyone's beginning, and its potency is overwhelming. I remember once finding myself with a group of women—it may have been at a baby shower—when one of them proposed a ghoulish choice: If your husband and child were drowning, which would you save? Every woman, one after another, said the child, and as the confessions accumulated, there were also several jokes (told by more than one woman) that fell into the *no contest* category, which were greeted by peals of laughter. I remember this because it spoke to the ferocity of the love most women have for their children, but also to an un-disguised hostility, at least among those particular women, to-ward the men whom they had left to die in an imaginary deep, a feeling I honestly didn't share.

It is impossible then to talk about fathers without talking about mothers. For both boys and girls, the mother begins as a towering figure, source of life, food, and feeling. The sentimentality that has lain thickly over motherhood in Western culture, at least since the nineteenth century, strikes me as a way to tame a two-way passion that has a threatening quality, if only by dint of its strength. Chil-dren must escape their mothers, and mothers must let them go, and separation can be a long tug-of-war. Every culture seeks to orga-nize the mysteries of maternity—menstruation, pregnancy, birth, and separation, the initiation into adulthood. Taboos, rituals, and stories create the frames for understanding human experience by distinguishing one thing from another and creating a comprehensible order. In her discussion of various kinds of social organization, Mary Douglas makes an interesting comment in her book *Purity and Danger,* "I would like to suggest that those holding office in the explicit part of the [social] structure tend to be credited with consciously controlled powers, in contrast with those whose role is less explicit and who tend to be credited with unconscious, uncontrollable powers, menacing those in better defined positions."[8] Her point is that ambiguity is dangerous, and that "articulate, conscious powers" seek to protect the system as a whole "from inarticulate and unstructured areas." She cites the witch as an example of "nonstructure." "Witches are social equivalents of beetles and spiders who live in cracks of the walls and wainscoting." But then she mentions another kind of ambiguous character, the *legitimate intruder.* "Of these Joan of Arc can be taken as a splendid prototype: a peasant at court, a woman in armour, an outsider in the councils of war; the accusation that she was a witch puts her fully in this category."[9]

In classical psychoanalysis, the conscious articulate power is the father, who comes between mother and son as a kind of savior from unarticulated nonstructure, maternal engulfment, but he also thwarts the son's desire for his mother and inspires rivalry: the Oedipal drama. Once it is resolved, the father's law is internalized, and the boy can go on to occupy the father's place. Using Douglas's model, the mother in psychoanalysis comes very close to being a witch. Moreover, exactly where all this left little girls in relation to their fathers has been something of a muddle in the field. Turning the story around doesn't work, because little girls also want to leave their mothers. In *The Dissolution of the Oedipus Complex,* Freud continues his observation on anatomy and destiny: "The little girl's clitoris behaves just like a penis to begin with, but when she makes a comparison with a playfellow of the opposite sex, she perceives that she has come off badly and she feels this as a wrong done to her and a ground for inferiority. For a while she consoles herself with the expectation that later on, when she grows older, she will acquire just as big an appendage as the boy's . . ."[10] It isn't strange that feminists have found the idea of penis envy uncompelling. In its place, Jessica Benjamin proposes another reading: "What Freud called penis envy, the little girl's masculine orientation really reflects the wish of the toddler—of either sex—to identify with the father, who is perceived as representing the outside world."[11]

Girls can certainly identify with their fathers. Many do. In fact, it is far more usual for a girl to admit to *being like* her father than for a boy to say, "I'm just like my mother," which would impinge on his masculinity by summoning his dependency on her. What the girl cannot do is take her father's place, which remains the articulated position of power and authority in the culture. Benjamin is not alone in her critique. The Oedipal conflict has been criticized inside psychoanalysis for some time, and it is widely recognized that Freud's focus on the father underestimated the mother and her vital role in a child's early life. The importance of mothers, however, doesn't change the fact that it is still harder for girls to find a place in the sexual divide, to embrace an articulated position of power. The witch is always hiding in the background.

Of course, life never corresponds exactly to any myth. The sharp divisions erected to explain sexual *difference* elude the ambiguities of what it means to be a person growing up in the world with real parents. I was not a tomboy. As a small child, I liked girls' games, and I liked dolls, and I can't remember a time when I didn't have love feelings for boys. I cried easily. I was extremely alert to my parents' expectations, rather passive, and empathetic to a fault. My animistic tendencies lasted longer than most people's. I remember personifying just about everything. My greatest happinesses were drawing, reading, and daydreaming.

Most of the action in my life took place internally. This is still true. In my neck of the woods, the expression for such a person was "femmy" or "wimpy." Virginia Woolf's "Angel in the House," the person she had to defeat to write, exemplifies the wimpy feminine ideal of the Victorian era:

> She was intensely sympathetic. She was immensely charming. She was utterly unselfish. She excelled in the difficult arts of family life. She sacrificed herself daily. If there was a chicken, she took the leg. If there was a draught, she sat on it—In short she was so constituted that she never had a mind or a wish of her own, but preferred to sympathize always with the minds and wishes of others.[12]

The Angel is a person without subjectivity, a mirror held up to the desires of others. Arguably, she no longer exists as a paragon of womanhood, but there is something about her that isn't easily dismissed, because her "sympathy with the minds and wishes of others" is part of maternal reality. What Winnicott called "good enough mothering" includes the ability to be in harmony with an infant's needs, to answer, mirror, and calm. Allan Schore calls this the "psychobiological attunement"[13] of the mother/child duo, and it is crucial to the growth of every human being. Neurobiological studies have made it clear that the interaction between mother and baby are essential to the child's brain development. Attunement is not a selfless process on the part of the mother but rather an immersion in betweenness, into a dialectical movement that connects two organisms but which is, in fact, a single process. Woolf's Angel is like a mother during her baby's first year of life, when her child's vulnerability and needs are intense and draining. The Victorian trap for women was multiple. It idealized maternal qualities, isolated them as the distinctive, rigid features of womanliness entirely separate from the qualities of the paternal, and linked feminine traits to childish ones, thereby infantilizing women. The good-enough mother is not the perfect mother. The good-enough mother is a subject with interests, thoughts, needs, and desires beyond her child. Nevertheless, the lure of the desire of others is strong, not just for women, but for men, too, and yet it may be that for many reasons—psychic, biological, social—most women have found the pressure of "the minds and wishes of others" more difficult to resist than men. The continual suppression of the self for another will inevitably produce resentment, if not rage.

Accommodation, squeezing oneself into the expectations of others, however, is part of every childhood. Children of both sexes are dwarfed by their parents in every way. Small and powerless, they are easily crushed by parental authority. Obedience to mother's and father's wishes is hardly enslavement, but all children are in thrall to the people they've been born to, and the desire to please can easily become a form of internal tyranny. In the letter he wrote to his father, which never reached its destined reader, Franz Kafka presented a stark picture of childhood puniness:

> I was, after all, weighed down by your mere physical presence. I remember, for instance, how we often undressed in the same bathing hut. There was I, skinny, weakly, slight; you, strong, tall, broad. Even inside the hut I felt a miserable specimen, and what's more, not only in your eyes but in the eyes of the whole world, for you were for me the measure of all things. But then when we stepped out of the bathing hut before the people, you holding my hand, a little skeleton, unsteady, barefoot on the boards, frightened of the water, incapable of copying your swimming strokes, which you, with the best of intentions, but actually to my profound humiliation, always kept on showing me, then I was frantic with desperation

and at such moments all my bad experiences in all spheres fitted magnificently together.[14]

Here the father's body is huge, and before it the child becomes a
shrinking "little skeleton." It is a boy's experience because a woman's body would not be "the measure of all things" for a male
child. I distinctly remember the feeling of awe and alienation I
felt when I saw naked adult bodies as a child, but here Kafka's
experience of his naked father is terrifying, an impossible standard, which humiliates him and very quickly becomes bound to
all his "bad experiences." Desire, fear, and shame are extremely
mixed up. The letter as a whole is one of only intermittently sup
pressed rage, an overt bid for dialogue that is in reality a statement of grievance. Why is it so hard to *talk* to fathers? Montaigne
argues in his essay "Of Friendship" that there cannot be friendship between children and fathers.

> From children toward fathers, it is rather respect. Friendship
> feeds on communication, which cannot exist between them
> because of their too great inequality, and might therefore in-
> terfere with the duties of nature. For neither can all the secret
> thoughts of fathers be communicated to children lest this be-
> get an unbecoming intimacy, nor could the admonitions and
> corrections, which are one of the chief duties of friendship, be
> administered by children to fathers.[15]

Montaigne is right. Inequality engenders necessary silences.
Young children don't really want friendship from a father, but a
heroic figure to look up to. Is there something in fatherhood as
we know it that by its very nature blocks communication?

My father liked instructing us, liked working in the garden
with us, liked to explain just about anything to us, and he listened

to us, but there were distances in him that were difficult to breach, and unlike my mother, he found it hard to speak directly to his daughters about anything personal, especially as we got older and matured sexually. Sometimes he would communicate his worries about his children through his wife, which generally meant that his comments had been screened or edited by her judgments about the situation, so exactly what had alarmed him had become rather foggy once it reached us. The older I became, the more hidden I felt he was, and there were moments when he seemed unavailable to a degree that startled me. It could be difficult for him to *say*, so sometimes he would *do*. My father drove me home after I had been fitted with braces for my teeth, painful and grueling hours made worse by the fact that the orthodontist was a truly unpleasant man who gruffly told me to stop moving my feet when I squirmed in discomfort, to open my mouth wider, and to stop flinching when he hit a tender spot. I left the ordeal with tears in my eyes. My father didn't say much, but then he stopped at a gas station, left the car, and returned with a box, which he handed to me. I looked down: chocolate-covered cherries. My father's favorite. I was eleven years old, and even then, I felt poignancy mingle with comedy. I didn't like chocolate-covered cherries and was in no shape to eat them even if I had liked them, but the mute gesture has stayed with me as one of infinite if somewhat wrongheaded kindness, as a token of his love.

By all accounts, my father was a good boy. He was the oldest of four as I am, upright, sensitive, intelligent, with a perfectionist streak that showed up strongly in me. My father's sister once told me that some of the boys who attended their one-room schoolhouse in rural Minnesota teased my father for reading too much. Apparently, it was a pursuit that lacked manliness. In my father's childhood, masculine and feminine roles were strictly defined by the kinds of labor done on the farm. My grandfather and grandmother both worked hard, but at different jobs. In his memoir, my father wrote, "Adolescence, as it is now understood, did not exist. A boy became a man when he could do a man's work." My father confessed to hot competition with his fellows when it came to rites of passage: "At what age had so-and-so been entrusted with a team of horses, a tractor, the family automobile, and how many cows did one milk." But, then again, by his own admission, it was his sister who was the athlete: "She could run faster than her brothers, do cartwheels, walk on her hands, and wielded a mean bat at the softball plate." He was proud of his sister's physical prowess, and when two of his daughters, his oldest not among them, turned into champion horsewomen, no one was more pleased with their trophies than my father. Despite his beginnings on the farm, my father became an intellectual and worked as a professor. Reading too much took him elsewhere.

But, like all of us, he was shaped by his early experiences. He watched his parents' farm fail during the Depression and suffered the indignities and humiliations of extreme poverty. His boyhood helplessness in the face of these terrible events became the catalyst for a life lived to repair what had been broken. The winds of chance and devastation were not going to blow down *his* family if he could help it. He would work himself to death if he had to. This is the old story of the good boy who becomes the duty-bound father. What he could never say was that his parents' marriage was one of conflict and alienation. He, too, idealized and identified with his father, a tenderhearted and rather meek man, who by the time I met him seemed resigned to his fate. My grandmother, on the other hand, was indomitable and outspoken, admirable traits that sometimes veered toward the screeching and irrational. For a temperamentally sensitive boy like my father, his mother's invective must have cut to the quick. But these were wounds he hid.

About three years after my father's death, I had a conversation with my mother that made such an impression on me I can reproduce it almost word for word.

"He wanted his girls to marry farmers."

"He wanted us to marry farmers?" I said. "You can't mean that seriously."

"Well, farmboys like him, who went on to other things."

"Farmboys who became professors?" I said incredulously.

My mother nodded.

"But, Mamma," I said, "how many farmboys turned college professors are there? It's tantamount to saying that we shouldn't marry or that we should have married *him*!"

My mother and I laughed, but this strange notion of my father's reinforced the fact that it was difficult for him to let go of his daughters, to tolerate our growing up. He wanted to continue to find himself reflected in our childish eyes and see the ideal father shining back at him. It took me a long time to understand this, in part because I never stopped hungering for his love and approval, and he remained a measure for me, if not of all things, of many. But I suspect now that there was a part of him that thought he had lost me to my husband, to my work, and because real dialogue was often difficult for us and unequal to some degree—I remained a respectful daughter—there were unspoken misunderstandings between us.

I don't remember when I began to realize that I wanted to be *like* my father, but it wasn't in my earliest days. I think I became ambitious around eleven, which was just about the time I was suddenly able to read "small print" books, when I first read William Blake and Emily Dickinson. Poems and stories became an avenue for my psychic cross-dressing, or rather, discovering my masculinity. I was twelve when I first heard the story of Joan of Arc, that legitimate intruder branded as a witch. The man who told it to me was my seventh-grade history teacher at a Rudolf

Steiner School in Bergen, Norway, Arne Krohn Nilsen, a tall rangy man with long whiskery eyebrows that made him look as if he were permanently surprised. He was an intense teacher, and he told Jeanne d'Arc's tale of glory and woe with a fervor I have never forgotten. He told it to the whole class, but listening to it, I felt like the recipient of a secret gift. I could not have said that the girl warrior appealed to me because, for a while anyway, she was allowed to play a role normally prohibited to women, but I am certain that I felt it. As my teacher spoke, as his voice rose and fell, and his sweeping gestures emphasized the drama, I was Joan of Arc. In a blank book, he drew me a picture of the historical heroine in armor with a sword on a white steed. I still have it. I relate this because not only did Joan collapse the hard lines of sexual difference, but she came to me through a man who genuinely believed in my abilities, a father figure.

Portrait of the Artist as a Young Woman. "Identity and memory are crucial for anyone writing poetry," says Susan Howe in her book *My Emily Dickinson*. "For women the field is still dauntingly empty. How do I, choosing messages from the code of others in order to participate in the universal theme of Language, pull SHE from all the myriad symbols and sightings of HE."[16] Emily Dickinson constantly asked this question in her poems:

> *In lands I never saw—they say*
> *Immortal Alps look down—*
> *Whose Bonnets touch the firmament—*
> *Whose Sandals touch the town—*
>
> *Meek at whose everlasting feet*
> *A Myriad daisy play—*
> *Which, Sir, are you and which am I*
> *Upon an August Day?*[17]

Dickinson stayed at home to read and write. There she inhabited the immensity of her own inner life. Her mentors lived on the page. Hundreds of fathers. But Howe takes her title from a letter Dickinson wrote to her cousin after reading in the newspaper that George Eliot had died. "The look of the words as they lay in the print I shall never forget. Not their face in the casket could have had the eternity to me. Now, *my* George Eliot."[18] And *mine*. Translator, scholar, intellectual, brilliant novelist, Mary Ann hid behind the mask of George. How well I understand that pseudonym—the need to evade the fixity that comes with the brand "woman writer." If reading was for me the route to legitimate power under the sign of my professor father, it was nevertheless my mother who fed me books, one after another, to stave off a mounting hunger, which at times veered toward the compulsive. She had read widely, and so the *idea* of literature belonged to both my father and my mother, and *my* literature, the English-language books I read at eleven, twelve, and thirteen, were my mother's choices for me. I read under the auspices of two polestars, one paternal and more remote, the other maternal and closer.

What did I want? *More*. Reading is internal action. It is the intimate ground where, as my husband says, "two consciousnesses touch." I would add two unconsciousnesses as well. Reading in our culture has become so attenuated that all reading is now considered "good." Children are admonished to read in general, as if all books are equal, but a brain bloated with truisms and clichés, with formulaic stories and simple answers to badly asked questions is hardly what we should aspire to. For the strange thing is that even books we can no longer actively recall are part of us, and like a lost melody, they may return suddenly. I have discovered my own borrowings from texts through rereading books. These liftings, never exact, were always done unconsciously. As a young person, I read the canon, as I perceived it. Great books signified achievement and mastery, but also apprenticeship. I wanted to know everything, to enlarge myself, to get a fat mind, and that mind, as it has turned out, is mostly made of men. "The process of literary influence," Harold Bloom wrote in *The Anxiety of Influence,* "is a battle between strong equals, father and son as mighty opposites . . ."[19] Freud's *Civilization and Its Discontents,* with its rapacious sons murdering the tyrannical father, isn't far away from Bloom's blanket declaration that literature is the domain of men duking it out—*strong equals.* There are no daughters in this narrative. And there's the rub. It is too easy to say that the canon is patriarchal, that casting out John Milton for George Sand is a solution to the problem, but that is to ignore quality in the name of parity.

What of women who write? We, too, have literary fathers and mothers. For most of my life, I have felt that reading and writing are precisely the two places in life where I am liberated from the constraints of my sex, where the dance of being the other takes place unhindered, and the free play of identifications allows entrance into a multitude of human experiences. When I am working I feel this extraordinary freedom, my plurality. But I have discovered that out there in the world, "woman writer" is still a brand on a writer's forehead, not easily erased, that being George remains preferable to being Mary Ann.

I am not arguing that Bloom is entirely wrong. I think he is right that many male writers struggle to overcome influence. I have seen it up close in some men I know who have had to tangle with a beloved author before they can write themselves. A classic example is Beckett's overwhelming admiration for Joyce, an influence he had to purge before becoming the writer he became. The question is not whether women writers are influenced; every writer takes from the past. It is how it happens. I was a sponge for books, but I have never had a bellicose relation to writers I love, men or women, even those who have influenced me the most strongly. My love for Henry James doesn't make me want to fight it out and get *over* him. Is this because, as a woman, I have a different relation to the paternal and the maternal? Are writers like Emily Dickinson, Jane Austen, Emily and Charlotte Brontë, George Eliot, Gertrude Stein, and Virginia Woolf not part of the pantheon of English letters? I don't believe that their sex is what one thinks of first when one thinks of their books, is it? But didn't they make themselves in a different way from men who write? Didn't they have to? Notably, not one of the writers in the list above was a mother. Is the question of equality with men so fraught for women that their battle is a different one? Are we part of a crooked line outside the patrimony? "Which, Sir, are you, and which am I?" Immortal Alps or daisy? Note that Dickinson's alps wear bonnets. Howe quotes Dickinson's second letter to the mysterious "Master," in which she writes,

If you saw a bullet hit a bird—and he told you he wasn't shot— You might weep at his courtesy, but you would certainly doubt his word.

One more drop from the gash that stains your Daisy's bosom—then would you believe?[20]

Is she not both alps and daisy? Wounded here. Whole elsewhere. Is she not *myriad*? Howe directs her reader to *David Copperfield,* to David, Master Davy, but also to Daisy, Steerforth's affectionate and feminizing name for his younger friend.[21] Literary mingling. Sexual mingling. Language isn't owned by anyone. It is inside and outside; it belongs to men and to women. Does it matter that women are mostly latecomers to the table of literature? Perhaps. Perhaps not.

There have been moments in my life when I felt like the legitimate intruder—at the defense of my doctoral dissertation in English literature, for example. I sat at a table with six men, my judges. They were not unsympathetic. Most of them were admiring. The single exception was an aging pedant who had painstakingly checked my footnotes for accuracy and, finding no errors, resorted to the comment "I did find some of the editions you used egregious, however." As I waited in the hall for their verdict, I didn't expect them to suggest any changes. I knew what I had written was good, but for me that seven-year adventure of getting a degree was an ongoing encounter with paternity, not because nearly all my professors were men, which they were, but because the institution itself offered a fatherly stamp of approval, as Dickens would say, "three dry letters": Ph.D. The fact that my father had also undergone those rigors no doubt haunted the entire enterprise. I have since discovered that it is much harder for young women to give up the lure of a higher degree than it is for young men. A poet who had been languishing in a Ph.D. program for years confessed to me that although she had no intention of becoming a professor, giving up the hope for a degree felt like a painful loss of stature. I understand. For women, letters after their names can be a form of armor. This is probably even more true in the sciences, where there are fewer women than in the humanities. It is in these worlds that one feels the problem of femininity most deeply, because it is here that it shouldn't *show*. The awareness of sex acts as a disturbance to the collegial pursuits of the mind—those unnameable openings in the structure begin to emanate dangerous powers, and the maternal witch is back.

A physicist friend of mine told me that women in his field generally disguise their bodies in manly attire to fit in with the powers that be, but he had also noticed a trend: when a woman has reached a position of respect and acclaim, when she has secured her reputation as brilliant, her sartorial discipline begins to unravel. Colors formerly unseen, high heels, makeup, and jewelry appear in rapid succession on her body, as if these accoutrements of womanliness were the tokens of a long-restrained sexual energy, as if the poor thing has suddenly been allowed to burst into bloom. For all its strides in the right direction, the Enlightenment elevated Reason to an impossible stature, and because women were lumped with its opposite, with the irrational forces in human life, no longer inexplicable or mystical, just situated on the wrong side of the fence, women languished there until they could claim Reason and the Rights of Man as their own. But climbing into the patriarchy entails some distortion. I learned to lower my voice when I spoke at seminars in graduate school, to try to sound dispassionate, even when I was quaking with feeling. I called on masculine forms to ensure I was taken seriously, to hide the girl. Over time, those forms became me, too. We are not static beings. We age and change.

In my novels, I have written as a woman and as a man. I have written as a father. I have written as a son. A young woman dresses as a man. She puts on her armor and wanders the streets. A man paints his self-portrait as a woman. A man dresses as a woman and comes into his own. We are myriad, all of us. Daisies. Witches. Alps. Masters. And skeletal little children looking up at the enormity of Dad. Contrary to Montaigne's statement about fathers and children, late in his life, not so long before he died, my father and I became friends. Although he was proud of me and carefully pasted my good reviews into a scrapbook, he had never said much to me about my work. I had become accustomed to brief, cryptic comments that could be construed in many different ways. My father was very ill when I finished my third novel and sent my parents the manuscript, but he was still living at home. That book was the first I wrote in the voice of a man. One afternoon, the phone rang, and to my surprise it was my father. He rarely called. I usually spoke to my mother, and she would then put my father on for a chat. Without warning, he launched into a disquisition on the book, heaping praise on my literary efforts. And I began to sob. He talked, and I sobbed. He talked more, and I sobbed more. Years of tears. I would never have predicted so violent a reaction. But then, you see, he *knew*. He knew how much I wanted his sanction, his approval, his admiration, and his knowing what I had mistakenly assumed he had always taken for granted became the road to each other. We were changed then, my father and I. At least some of the distance between us fell away, and when we sat together in the months before his death, we talked as friends, as strong equals, as two real people, not ideal people, who had found each other again.

2008

FLOWERS

WHEN THERE ARE FLOWERS IN a room my eyes are drawn to them. I feel their presence in a way that I do not feel chairs, sofas, coffee tables, curtains. Their fascination for me must be connected to the fact that they are alive, not dead. The attraction is prereflective—it rises up in my body before any articulated thought. Before I can name the flowers (if I can), before I can tell myself that I am attracted to the blooms, the pleasurable sensation has arrived. The color red is especially exciting. It is hard to turn away from red flowers—to not look at amaryllis at full stretch, their broad pale-green stalks erect or leaning slightly behind the glass of a vase. When snow is falling outside, my happiness is augmented—red against the white seen through a window. And in summer, I cannot resist gazing for two, three, four minutes at peonies that have spread open into fat, heavy clusters of petals with their stamens of yellow dust.

Dying flowers don't have this power over me. In my garden, I pick off wasted blossoms, snip rosehips, pluck withered, browning leaves. I neaten up the dead, but I hover over the living blooms. I watch a bee sit on the beaded orange heart of an open daisy.

Sometimes I adjust a flower's head toward the light, careful not to bruise its petals. And I find my encounters with these quickening but senseless plants so absorbing that I do not narrate them. This is odd because I am continually putting words to living, always forming sentences that accompany me as I greet a person, sit at a dinner party, stroll on the street, but there is no inner voice that follows me in the garden. My head goes silent.

When I was a child, I lived in a house outside a small town in Minnesota. Behind the house was a steep bank that led down to a creek. In spring, after the snows, the water rose and flooded the flat bottom ground. It was on the slope above the creek that I found the first bloodroot growing in the soil. I remember the cold moisture seeping through my pants as I sat down to examine the flowers. When there were plenty of them, I gave myself permission to pick a bouquet for my mother. Their tiny white heads drooped as if in sorrow, but their true enchantment was located at their roots, in the rhizomes that contained a reddish sap that bled onto my hands. As I plucked them, I thought of wounds and of grief, and was overtaken by a satisfying melancholy. My infantile animism had a long life, but in my conscious memory, these personifications were never complete. I lived in a state of only partial belief, not true belief. Because it could bleed, the early bloodroot was more human than the bluebell that came later. I remember how much I liked to open my palms once I was home and examine the red stains the flowers had left on my skin and that I felt a kind of awe, an awe, I suppose, about the living and the dead and the injured.

2011

THINKING

THE REAL STORY

IN 1996, I CAME ACROSS an article in *The New York Times Magazine* about the explosion of personal memoirs in the publishing business and read the following: "If Proust were writing today about his penchant for observing handsome young men stick hatpins in live rats, he wouldn't hide behind the narrator of his novel. *A la Recherche du Temps Perdu* would be a memoir."[1] I found the comment highly irritating and have never forgotten it. The implication is that while fiction once served as a convenient screen for taboo personal material, it has now outlived its usefulness in a confessional culture that permits, even welcomes, every revelation, no matter how sordid. It is doubtful that the author, James Atlas, was serious about his claim; the sentences have the ironic, condescending tone we have come to expect from a good deal of cultural journalism, but it is interesting, nevertheless, to entertain how the memoir is different from the novel and see what comes of these musings. It is indisputable that Proust and many other novelists have borrowed events, feelings, thoughts, and people from life, and, in one way or another, transported them into their works. Scholars have diligently picked over Proust's biography for every morsel of his "real" experience, just as they have analyzed and reanalyzed the seven volumes of his master-work. But the two Marcels, the one in life and the one in fiction, are not identical. Even when there is a close familial resemblance between an author and his fictional character, the two remain distinct. What about an author and her persona in an autobio-graphical work? The question touches on the puzzling boundary between what we regard as the real and the imaginary.

Writing fiction takes place in a mental zone of free invention that memoir does not (or should not), for the simple reason that when a person picks up a book labeled "memoir," she expects that the writer of the volume has told the truth. The implied contract between writer and reader is simple: the author is not prevaricat-ing. The contract holds even though the explicit, conscious memo-ries we retain are only a fraction of what we remember implicitly, unconsciously, and the autobiographical memories we keep are not stable but subject to change, as Freud repeatedly observed. Memories are revised over time, and their meanings change as we age, something now recognized by neuroscience and referred to as the *reconsolidation* of memory. The act of remembering is not retrieving some original fact stored in the brain's "hard drive." What we recall is the last version of a given memory. The writer of a memoir is not asked to occupy a third-person perspective, but rather to inhabit his or her first-person position fully and write what he or she remembers. That said, my husband and I, who have now been living together for almost thirty years, often re-call the same event differently. He argues that the moment our daughter declared she wanted to be a performer the three of us were in the subway; I say it happened in a cab. Sophie, the object of the dispute, does not remember where it occurred or exactly what she said. Even more dramatically, a memory I am convinced belongs to me alone, is, according to my husband, his private men-tal property. He remembers it perfectly and is sure I must be mistaken. One of us is in error. What this anecdote clarifies about memory is that when we listen to a person tell a story, perhaps especially a person with whom we are intimate, that tale can spawn a mental image so vivid, it enters the mind as a subjective experience that originated outside the mind, not within it. The *I* adopts the recollection of the *you*. Memory, like perception, is not passive retrieval but an active and creative process that involves the imagination. We are all always reinventing our pasts, but we are not doing it on purpose. Delusion, however great, is not the same as mendacity. *We know when we are lying.* Lying is a form of double consciousness. There are two utterances: the one spoken or written and the unsaid, unrecorded one. The public outrage over memoirs that are actually fictions suggests that the contract implied by a work of nonfiction is still in effect, despite the fact that many memoirists seem to be equipped with supernatural abilities for recalling the past.

Several times over the years, I have heard one novelist or another refer to him or herself as "a professional liar." The words signal the fact that fiction writers can make up anything, that they, unlike their comrades writing nonfiction, are not tied to describing what *actually* happened. This is indubitably true, and yet I have always balked at the idea of the novel as a form of falsehood, which is to say, I believe that some novels do lie, but the good ones do not. How can a novel be fallacious? It cannot be held to any absolute standard. If I want my novel's narrator to have been born underwater from the eye of a giant octopus, who is going to stand in my way? If I begin my autobiography in this manner, however, there are those who will object. A birth certificate is on record that states otherwise. I might begin a memoir with an eight-legged aquatic mother had she been an early fantasy of mine, however. When my niece Ava was three, she repeatedly told her parents she had been born from a Chinese egg. Neither her mother nor her father is able to trace the origin of this personal myth. And no ambitious journalist can document the veracity of my inner imaginative life. The lies that have gotten memoirists into trouble are inevitably whoppers that can easily be identified by searching public records. The controversy over James Frey's *A Million Little Pieces* centered on the fact that the author had exaggerated or fabricated his crimes and arrests, had made them *worse* than they actually were. Like a novelist, he created a storytelling persona, one he apparently preferred to his own more benign and possibly more bathetic self. Frey hid behind the narrator of his memoir, who served as a novelistic vehicle of disguise, but the deeper issues of masks and revelations in nonfiction and fiction are multiple and go far beyond an addict rewriting his own pathology for more dramatic reading.

Many successful memoirs *read like novels*. They borrow the established conventions, indeed clichés, of the form to use for autobiographical writing. I have read elaborate descriptions of people's physiognomies, their clothing, of rooms and landscapes, and page after page of continuous dialogue in "memoirs." Frankly, I regard most of these passages as improbable, if not impossible. Although I remember the rooms, for example, in the house where I grew up in some detail, the particularity of the interiors I occupied only briefly—a hostel in London, say, when I was seventeen—have nearly vanished from my mind or have been supplanted by some vague but workable fictionalized space. I remember a single sentence or two uttered by people important to me over the years and the gist of significant conversations, but I could never reproduce them verbatim, nor would I attempt to. Even the face of my mother as she was in my childhood cannot be reproduced in my mind's eye, and that is why I sometimes take out photographs to remind myself of her youthful image. And I have a fairly good visual memory. The popular memoir has little to do with the peculiar realities of human memory. It has become a successful literary form, often fashioned on the journeyman novel, and, as with every hardened genre, it arrives with a set of expectations. A number of the memoirs exposed as frauds (to greater and lesser degrees) in recent years share a single quality: they are all stories of inspired survival: Frey's book, Herman Rosenblat's death camp love story, *Angel at the Fence*, and Margaret P. Jones's story of growing up among violent gangs, *Love and Consequences*, follow the same essential narrative line. Against all odds, the hero or heroine of the tale triumphs in the end. In each there is an obstacle—drug addiction, Nazi horror, and the Bloods. Although these three can hardly be called parallel afflictions, the broader narrative in which they find themselves is the same, and it exploits a deep human wish: to conquer (whatever it is) and stay alive, not as a broken, traumatized, weak bit of human wreckage, but as a strong, reborn noble figure.

The narrative machinery of such tales is as old as literature itself. The trickster who outwits death is a figure in many tribal and folk cultures. Odysseus finally comes home. The seven voyages of that inimitable sailor, Sinbad, are survival tales par excellence. Over and over again he is saved by chance or by his own wiles, often literally from the jaws of death—snakes, sea monsters, gigantic birds, cannibals. The fairy-tale child of multiple traditions suffers adversity but overcomes evil in the end. Moll Flanders, Defoe's resilient heroine, endures multiple assaults and the startling twists and turns of fortune to die of old age, and a penitent at that. These are characters of irresistible Darwinian appeal. Like Wile E. Coyote from the Looney Tunes of my girlhood, they have the wonderful gift of popping back into shape. There are true stories, as well, of people who defy the odds, people who despite grotesque experiences do not end up in hospitals, who, with far more than Beckettian resignation, go on.

In his book *Abnormalities of Personality*, Michael H. Stone, a professor of clinical psychiatry, presents the reader with two briefly summarized cases of men who had what appear to be

equally horrible childhoods. Both men were extremely intro-
verted when they were young. Both had parents who mistreated
them, and both were the victims of violence and sexual molestation. One man was Stone's patient, "a person of a decidedly paranoid caste" who after years of inertia and therapy was able to
resume his graduate studies. The other was Jeffrey Dahmer, the
notorious mass murderer. "The point of these stories," writes Dr.
Stone, "is that if either one had been identified in advance as the
serial killer of young men, most people would have said, 'Well,
with a background like *that*!'"[2] But true stories cannot be told "in
advance," only on hindsight. Whether Stone's patient or others like
him have a particularly robust genetic temperament or whether
there is some person in his story, a teacher or aunt, a grandmother
or sibling, who helped to keep him from disintegration, I do not
know. But Stone's comment is relevant to memoir: *there is no formula
for predicting the evolution of a particular human story.* And yet, we cling
to our standard narratives, although they change over time. Think
of all the stories of seduced and fallen women in eighteenth- and
nineteenth-century novels. Child sexual abuse and subsequent ru-
ination is a more contemporary narrative, but even this explosive
category, which includes everything from a grope in the locker
room to brutal rape, cannot stand in as an explanation for an entire
life. While it is certainly true that years of research on attachment
phenomena—the psychobiological dynamics of emotional bonds
between infant and caretaker—have shown how vital early interactions are to a person's development and that many people who
suffer neglect and/or violence as children grow up to have psychiatric problems, we must be careful about making simple equations.
Fraudulent or otherwise, many memoir narratives partake of the
broader culture's need for crude reductions of complex human realities into a salable package of victimology. In this, they are no
different from many popular novels that employ precisely the same
formula but lack the stamp of *reality*.

Fake or partly faked autobiographical works would not exist if they were not valued more highly than fiction in the contemporary American marketplace. When Frey's book was first submitted as a novel, it met with rejection. Were publishers equally attracted to fiction, we might be flooded with countless versions of the roman à clef. True crime, true sex, true abjection, reality TV, movie stars who debase themselves in private or public are daily media fare. Our many technologies give us access to high doses of Schadenfreude or inspiration, depending on one's point of view. But this, too, is nothing new. Since the expansion of literacy, people have greedily consumed stories, both fictional and nonfictional, that titillate and shock them. As the reading public grew in England in the late seventeenth and through the eighteenth century, so did the materials to satisfy their needs. Accounts of the lives of criminals were especially popular and were often published as inexpensive chapbooks or broadsides. A typical title: *News from Newgate: or an exact and true account of the most remarkable tryals of several notorious malefactors.* The words *true* and *authentic* recur continually in this literature. There was also a hankering for "Last Dying Speeches" and verbatim reports from the trials at Old Bailey, all written with an eye to entertainment. Newspapers competed as well with their accounts of crimes, arrests, and trials:

17 September 1734. Yesterday Mary Freeman, alias Frisky Nan, but commonly called by the Name of Diving Moll, was committed to the Gatehouse, Westminster, by Justice Cotton, for picking a gentleman's pocket of 15 guineas, a silver snuff box, and two gold rings of considerable value. (*Daily Journal*)

The same "notorious Moll," with another alias, Talboy, gets much fuller treatment in the *Grub Street Journal* the same day. The reader is told that this "creature," declared an "idle and disorderly person" by the justices, was supported by "several noted gamesters and sharpers about Covent Garden" and was wont to "draw in young cullies in order to make a prey of them." The writer of the account indulges in a bit of pathos as well: ". . . and poor Moll, to her great mortification, was remanded back again to perform her task of beating hemp till the next Quarter session." The fledgling novel soon got into the act, and fictional accounts of crime, debauchery, and seduction competed with "true" stories for the attention of readers.

> The world is so taken up of late with novels and romances that it will be hard for a private history to be taken for genuine where the names and other circumstances of the person are concealed; and on this account we must be content to leave the reader to pass his own opinion upon the ensuing sheets and take it just as he pleases.[3]

So reads the ambiguous first sentence of the preface to another Moll story, Daniel Defoe's *Moll Flanders*. The fictitious editor informs the reader that an original manuscript exists, but he has rewritten it to cleanse it of what might be morally contaminating. What the reader has in his hands is a "new dressing up of the story." Moll, whose first-person saga relates her adventures of extreme poverty; thievery; prostitution; five marriages, including bigamy; multiple children, all, except one, dead or cast off; imprisonment; deportation; and eventual reformation, is a creature born of the popular genre of criminal biography mingled with another form ascendant in the seventeenth century: the Protestant spiritual autobiography in which the sinner finds his way to God and redemption. Many recent memoirs partake of this very same movement from a state of damnation—abuse, addiction, handicap, or potentially fatal illness—which is then overcome by an act of will or some form of personal enlightenment. The conventional forms for relating true-life stories—memoirs, letters, trial reports, rogue and whore biographies—infected eighteenth-century fictions because they were deeply concerned with the idea that they depicted ordinary human beings *as they really were.*

The ideas of authenticity and realism were essential to the raison d'être of early novels, even when they didn't include prefaces by editors claiming to have cleaned up a genuine confession for polite consumption. In *Tom Jones,* Fielding's narrator regularly justifies his story as truthful to nature, albeit with heavy doses of irony: ". . . it is our business to relate the facts as they are; which when we have done it, it is the part of the learned sagacious reader to consult that original book of nature; whence every passage in our work is transcribed, though we quote not always the particular page for its authority."[4] In John Cleland's famous and infamous *Memoirs of a Woman of Pleasure* or *Fanny Hill,* the narrator tells her correspondent on the very first page that hers will be a true story: "Truth! stark naked truth, is the word, and I will not so much as take pains to bestow the strip of a gauze-wrapper on it, but paint situations as they actually rose to me in nature . . ."[5] Part of the author's seduction of the reader is the promise of unvarnished realism, in this case, undressing rather than "dressing up" the story.

Novels were regularly decried as a cause of mental pollution during the eighteenth century. In his 1778 essay "On Novel Reading," Vicessimus Knox articulated a commonly held view that resonates nicely with more recent anxieties about, for example, the dangers of violent computer games: "If it be true, that the present age is more corrupt than the preceding, the great multiplication of Novels has probably contributed to its degeneracy." Reading novels weakened the mind and made it vulnerable to "the slightest impulse of libidinous passion." Knox preferred romances because "their pictures of human nature were not exact."[6] Of course, what an exact picture of human nature might look like is a bewildering question. For Knox, novelistic exactitude seems to have meant the exposure of the seamier side of human beings—their appetites and frailties—an image of life that was more "real" than in earlier literary forms.

Jean-Jacques Rousseau promises to "tell all" or rather "tell everything" in his *Confessions*. He begins with this declaration to the reader: "I have begun on a work which is without precedent, whose accomplishment will have no imitator. I propose to set before my fellow-mortals a man in all the truth of nature and this man shall be myself."[7] Of course there were many memoirs before Rousseau's, and there were many memoir novels. Among other fictional autobiographies, the philosopher from Geneva especially loved Defoe's *Robinson Crusoe*, and this invented narrative influenced the telling of his own life. Both St. Augustine and Michel de Montaigne famously preceded Rousseau as writers who unveiled their personal lives. The difference was that for both of them self-revelation came in service of ideas beyond themselves. Rousseau believed in the validity of telling for the sake of telling. He believed in a transparency that would allow the reader to peer into his very soul. In this, he was modern. He is not confessing to God. He is unburdening himself in the sight of all humanity, warts and all.

I have to admit that when I first read Rousseau's life history at twenty, I felt variously amazed, delighted, appalled, and embarrassed. I had not expected him to reveal the sexual pleasure he had taken in being spanked as a boy, one he claims shaped his lifelong "affection for acts of submission."[8] I was horrified by the fact that he had abandoned his children, something which he attempts to justify, and amazed by his candor about any number of other shameful acts—both petty and more serious—of disloyalty, self-deception, and meanness. Writing about his own life, Rousseau is intent on not prettifying himself. The appetites and frailties depicted in the novels that so worried Knox are on full display in Rousseau's autobiography. At the same time, the narrator of *The Confessions* echoes the English critic across the channel. The philosopher admits that his imagination has a quixotic side and claims that reading novels as a child has addled him permanently. These fictions are responsible for "bizarre and romantic notions of human life, which experience and reflection have never really been able to cure me."[9] Or, to put it another way: the novels he read became part of who he was.

Was Rousseau truthful? A number of details and dates he cites have been proven wrong. Moreover, he has been accused of fabricating or softening some scenes in the book. The busy scholar, like the journalist sniffing out memoir fraud, can cite inaccuracies and obfuscations in Rousseau's account of himself, a narrative that also periodically falls into the trap I mentioned earlier of including dialogue and speeches too long for any normal human being to remember, which undermine the urgent, autobiographical tone of the book. At the same time, when I read him I never feel that Rousseau is an out-and-out liar. He is at junctures brilliant, wise, tender, hyperbolic, paranoid, totally convincing, and less so because I feel he is working so hard to justify himself that he moves into the terrain of self-deception. Then again, he openly declares that while he may stumble over facts, what he cannot be mistaken about are *his own feelings*. His appeal is to the truth of sentiment, to *emotional truth*. Although it is doubtful that any one of us can fully recover feelings and sensations from the past any more than we can perfectly reproduce events, it is clear that memory is consolidated by emotion, that the fragments of the past we recall best are those colored by feeling, whether it is joy or grief or guilt. Also, it is fair to allow that the writing self looking back on a former self can at least be acutely aware of feelings in the present about that earlier incarnation.

The art of autobiography, as much as the art of fiction, calls on the writer to shape himself as a character in a story, and that shaping requires a form mediated by language. What scientists call episodic or autobiographical memory is essential for creating

a coherent narrative sense of a self over time. It is part of our consciousness, but that consciousness is also shaped by unconsciousness. What it means to be a thinking subject is an enormously
complex philosophical and neurobiological issue, which remains
unsolved. But if you ask yourself how you would tell the story of
your life or tell a particularly dramatic part of your life, you will
soon discover the quandaries involved. My own memories can
only be called hodgepodge. The images and words retained in
my brain-mind are not sequential; they come and go in my reveries. They are triggered by the words of others, by my own associative thoughts, by smells and sounds and sights. As William
James stated in *The Principles of Psychology* (1890): "There is no such
thing as mental retention, the persistence of an idea from month
to month or year to year in some mental pigeon-hole from which
it can be drawn when wanted. What persists is a tendency to connection."[10] Memory is flux.

Moreover, the first two years of my life are lost to amnesia. In
order to report on them, I would have to rely on the stories my
mother and father told me, not my own memory. I know half a
dozen people who grew up deceived about their parentage. We
are not truly present at our own births and, although learning and
development are rapid and crucial during those initial months of
our lives, the self-reflective recollections of the autobiographical
"I" have not yet begun. In human beings, that "I" has tremendous
flexibility. It is dependent on the fact that we recognize ourselves
in a mirror, and so begin to imagine ourselves through the eyes of
another person. A human being can become a character to herself,
if you will, a being seen from the outside, a personage we can
place in the past and imagine in the future.

After about the age of six, I begin to have what some have
called a continuous autobiographical memory, but what does this
mean? It does not mean that I can recall every day of my life and
its incidents. As David Hume writes in *A Treatise of Human*

Nature: "For how few of our past actions are there, of which we have any memory? Who can tell me, for instance, what were his thoughts and actions on the first of January 1715, the eleventh of March 1719, and the third of August 1733?"[11] A continuous memory means only that I can locate the memories I do have in *places* I have known: my family house; Longfellow School; Way Park; an apartment in Bergen, Norway; Butler Library at Columbia University. By summoning these mentally familiar spaces, I put my young self within them and construct a rhythmic formula of a routine reality, punctuated by events significant to me. Between those important events are fogs and lapses. I forget. I forget. I forget. And I sometimes displace, condense, project, and generally get things wrong about my life as well. I have stolen "memories" from photographs, unwittingly, it is true, but when confronted with snapshots of my early childhood, I have been forced to accept that what I imagined was a mental picture of my own is, in fact, an image borrowed from an album. My errors are hardly unique. No doubt there are innumerable others I will never discover, but I accept the imaginative dimension of my remembering. The writing of memoir, then, is not about my "real" life in some documentary sense. Rousseau's optimism about recovering the past, even its feelings, is unwarranted. Writing a memoir is a question of organizing remembrances *I believe to be true and not invented* into a verbal narrative. And that belief is a matter of inner conviction; what feels true now.

When I'm writing a novel, it is very much like dredging up a memory, trying hard to find the "real" story that is buried somewhere in my being, and when I find it, it feels true. But I have also written passages that are wrong, that *feel like lies,* and then I must get rid of them and start again. I am measuring the truth of my fictional story against some inner emotional reality that is connected to my memories. That is why I rebel against the idea of novelists as "professional liars."[12] It demeans an enterprise that for me is exactly the opposite. The link between recollection and creativity has long been acknowledged in philosophy, as well as disavowed. In *The New Science* (1725), Giambattista Vico equated the two. "Hence memory is the same as imagination . . . Memory has three aspects: memory when it remembers things, memory when it alters or imitates them, and invention when it gives them a new turn and puts them in a proper arrangement and relationship."[13] Wilhelm Wundt, the German researcher who is credited with establishing psychology as a distinct field of study, blurs the two entirely in his *Outlines of Psychology* (1897). "It is obvious that practically no clear demarcation can be drawn between images of imagination and those of memory . . . All our memories are therefore made up of 'fancy and truth' (*Wahrheit und Dichtung*). Memory changes under the influence of our feelings and volition to images of imagination and we generally deceive ourselves with their resemblance to real experiences."[14] Invention is part of human experience, whether voluntary or involuntary, and everyone has fantasies and daydreams made possible by the projected "I." We can move ourselves mentally into real and unreal spaces:

> I can see myself as a famous singer performing in Yankee Stadium.
> What if my beloved died, and I were left alone?
> I have sprouted wings and am soaring happily over New York City.

Young people are particularly prone to spending hours inside their private fantasies. In "Imagination and Creativity of the Adolescent" (1931), the Russian psychologist Lev Vygotsky beautifully articul.tes the double experience of fiction:

> When with the help of fantasy, we construct some sorts of unreal images, the latter are not real, but the feeling which

they evoke is experienced as being real. When a poet says: "I will dissolve in tears over this fiction," he realizes that this figment is something unreal, but his tears belong to the realm of reality. In this way an adolescent finds a means of expressing his rich inner emotional life and his impulses in fantasy.[15]

There is mounting neurobiological evidence that the same regions or systems of the brain are at work in both episodic memory and the imaginative act of projecting oneself into the future. The neuroscientists Randy Buckner and Daniel Carroll put it this way in their paper "Self-Projection and the Brain," published in *Trends in Cognitive Sciences*:

> Accumulating data suggest that envisioning the future (prospection), remembering the past, conceiving the viewpoint of others (theory of mind), and possibly some forms of navigation reflect the workings of the same brain network. These abilities emerge at a similar age and share a common functional anatomy that includes frontal and medial temporal systems that are traditionally associated with planning, episodic memory, and default (passive) cognitive abilities.[16]

The "default system" is the rather ugly name scientists have given to what happens in our brains when we are not busy with some specific task, when we are at rest and not concentrating on stimuli outside ourselves—reverie mode, fantasy mode. It turns out that the brain is very active when we are doing nothing but hanging out inside ourselves. Note the scientists' list of connected activities. Envisioning the future is an out-and-out fictional act, a projection of the present self elsewhere into a time that has not yet arrived, but then so is autobiographical memory to an important degree. We must reimagine a former self and move it backward in time. All animals remember. Eric Kandel's groundbreaking work on the snail, aplysia, has shown that even that simple animal learns and remembers what it has learned. Living creatures all have motor-sensory memories that are implicit, and these mostly unconscious learned abilities underscore much of our habitual movement in the world. But a sea snail does not have episodic autobiographical memories, nor does it fantasize or imagine itself as another aplysia. Without the ability to conceive the viewpoint of others—to imagine being that other person—we would not be self-conscious, and without self-consciousness we could not construct the labile self we all have, the one that can be cut off from the present and *navigate* in other realms, both real and unreal. The authors of the paper do not mention philosophy or psychology, nor do they note that the increasing mobility of this projected self is connected to mirror recognition and our later acquisition of language and abstract thought. They do not extend their argument to fantasy, creativity, or the imagination in general. In their very cautious way, however, they step into the memory versus fiction question.

> . . . this explanation helps us to understand why memory is constructive and why it is prone to errors and alterations. Perhaps a feature of this core network that is involved in self-projection is its flexibility in simulating multiple alternatives that only approximate real situations. The flexibility of the core network might be its adaptive function, rather than the accuracy of the network to represent specific and exact configurations of past events.[17]

It seems to me that we have come to a cultural moment in the United States that is inherently suspicious of fiction and attached to an idea of "real memory" or "the true story" that is in itself a fantasy. Why write a novel when you can tell the real story? Isn't this what James Atlas was proposing in his reference to Proust?

Not long ago, I received a novel in the mail with a letter asking me for a quote. In the form letter, the editor explained that the book is about a rape and that the author herself had been raped. Moreover, the author was willing to talk about her experience of the real rape while doing publicity for the novel about a fictional rape. I have not read the book; it might be good. It might be subtle. What interests me is the inference that the fiction I was being asked to read was more genuine because life and fiction had crossed, as it were. What are we to make of this? The book in question is not a memoir but a novel, and yet it is being marketed as a form of hybrid. The factual rape is used to give credence to the fictional rape. There is nothing new about novelists using their own experiences to make a fiction. What seemed new was the need for the publisher to declare what those experiences were.

Let us return to Proust. Proust's biographers have written extensively about his sadomasochism. Apparently, he did enjoy torturing rats. His housekeeper Celeste Albaret relates that after one of his visits to a male brothel, he returns and tells her that he had peered through a small window and witnessed a man being whipped "till the blood spurts all over everything. And it is only then that the unfortunate creature experiences the heights of pleasure."[18] Proust then talks to the shocked Celeste for hours about the flagellation he has seen. In her book on Proust, *Time and Sense,* Julia Kristeva argues that "Proust uses the good woman's participation-indignation to help him reconstruct the scene from a distance. In this way, he can create a quasi-comedy that will allow him to detach himself from his sensations . . ."[19] In *Time Regained,* Proust's narrator also sees a flagellation, but before he sees it, he hears groans of pain, then two voices, one begging for pity, the other menacing, "and if you yell and drag yourself about on your knees like that, you'll be tied to the bed, no mercy for you," then the noise of a cracking whip. Moments later the narrator discovers "a small oval window" and peers through it.

And there in the room, chained to a bed like Prometheus to his rock, receiving the blows that Maurice rained upon him with a whip which was in fact studded with nails, I saw, with blood already flowing from him and covered with bruises, which proved that the chastisement was not taking place for the first time—I saw before me M. de Charlus.[20]

There is nothing "quasi-comic" about this passage in isolation, but in the context of the novel, it is, in fact, kind of funny. After his bout in the theater of cruelty, the baron, weak and tottering to be sure, but, remarkably, up on his pins, jokes with the hotel's "boys." We discover that Maurice plays the torturer for a few francs and that his heart is decidedly not in it. But this comes later, after I, as a reader, have participated in the fascinated horror of that other "I" who creeps "stealthily in the darkness" toward the peephole and then sees that the abject person on the bed is *someone I know*. This is not the nameless "unfortunate creature" Proust described to Celeste Albaret; it is the Baron de Charlus, the depraved but also generous dandy, the gallant, absurd survivor of his own perversion for pain, the same man, who, recovering from a stroke in his dotage, delights in reeling off the names of dead friends as World War I rages not far away and men howl and die in the trenches. Does it matter that Proust stole some of the baron's other character traits from Count Robert de Montesquiou-Fezensac, who was privately mortified by the novel because he recognized parts of himself? The transpositions from real experience to art are like the strange mingling that happens in dreams. I dream of a friend, who does not look like my friend, but like someone else. The name seems to be attached to the wrong person. One person, one thing, blends into another, or two stories from my waking life collapse into one. A minor character in my novel *What I Loved* (2003), Lazlo Finkelman, gained his first name and his hairdo from a friend's baby boy; his last name from my daughter's pediatrician; his hip, laconic patter from yet another friend; and his penchant for stealing food at parties and stuffing it into his raincoat from a story I once heard about the young, impoverished Henry Miller.

Would we prefer that Proust had catalogued his voyeuristic experiences as his very own, that he had stuck to the facts and not taken the horrific spectacle of an unknown man being whipped and turned it into an image of the baron? Would Proust's autobiographical memory of real events, in his vast book about memory and time, have served him better than his memories and fantasies, that Janus face of a single human capacity? There is a distance in writing fiction, in writing as another person, in allowing the slippage of remembering and imagining, always in the service of emotional truths, but from another perspective than one's own, even when the narrator is a kind of self-double, as Proust's narrator is. Comedy and irony both rest on this step backward. I often see more clearly from somewhere else, as someone else. And in that imagined other, I sometimes find what I may have been hiding from myself. In the free play of the imagination, in the words that rise from unconscious sources, as well as in the bodily rhythms that accompany the act of writing a novel, I am able to discover more than I can when I simply try to remember. This is not a method for disguising reality but for revealing the truth of experience in language.

In my first novel, *The Blindfold* (1992), I took my own first name and reversed it for my narrator: Iris. She was given my mother's maiden name as her last name: Vegan. I placed her in the apartment where I once lived: 309 West 109th Street. I robbed some close friends of mine of their various characteristics and mixed them together with fictional ones, and I used parts of my own experience as a patient in the neurology ward of Mount

Sinai Medical Center. But Iris's adventures are not mine. I invented them. They came to me as necessary, as true, but they are fictions. And yet, there were those, including a close friend of my parents, who were certain that everything had happened exactly as it was related in the book. I have been told that inhabitants of the town where I grew up have amused themselves by identifying every single character in my second novel, *The Enchantment of Lily Dahl* (1996), with real people in the town. Although the book's Webster is a fictional version of Northfield, Minnesota, and there are several minor characters based on actual persons, many, including all the main characters, were born of my imagination. Throughout my fiction I have borrowed bits and pieces from my life and the lives of others and reimagined, combined, condensed, and reconstituted them, but this is a far cry from telling my life story. In the autobiographical essays I have written and in the single memoir (which is less about me than about medicine, diagnosis, and what illnesses of the mind-body might mean), I have honored the pact of nonfiction with the reader—which is simply not to lie knowingly.

And, however unreliable our memories may be, we can tell the difference between our present given reality—the chair on which I am sitting now before my computer in my study as I write this essay—and the world of my fantasies, which I inhabit when I write a novel and am sitting in the very same chair. As Maurice Merleau-Ponty argues in *The Phenomenology of Perception,* "the normal subject" does not confuse the phenomenal present with the potential space of the imagination.[21] I would say it like this: unless we are mad, we can recognize the difference between the here and now and the mental there and elsewhere of remembering and fantasizing.

But robbing one's own memory for fiction can have a peculiar effect on the recollection itself. In his memoir, *Speak Memory,* Vladimir Nabokov addresses this change.

I have often noticed that after I had bestowed on the characters of my novels some treasured item of my past, it would pine away in the artificial world where I had so abruptly placed it. Although it lingered on in my mind, its personal warmth, its retrospective appeal had gone, and presently, it became more closely identified with my novel than with my former self, where it had seemed to be so safe from the intrusion of the artist.[22]

I have imagined this myself. Once a person or place or even just parts of those persons and places from the past have been transplanted into a novel, the fictional transformation can at times subsume the memory, but it happens only when the person or place is no longer a part of your daily experiences. Once, years after I had written my first novel, I met the original model for one of my characters in a restaurant. We chatted amiably and, when we parted, and I was about to say good-bye to him, the name of the character appeared in my mind before his real name, and I had to suppress the former. I almost said good-bye to a figment. This slip of the tongue, which I fortunately censored in time, revealed not only that the book had, to one degree or another, supplanted my memory of him, but that my emotional connection to the novel, to the writing of it, and to the character I had made, had become in some way more real to me than the man himself. As Kristeva puts it when she is writing about Proust, the beaten man, and the flagellant's reappearance with another face in fiction: "*what is experienced* gradually becomes *what is represented.*"[23] And word representations are different from both mental images and sensory experiences. Don't we all have memories that have hardened into stories? We remember how to tell the story, even though the sensations and pictures that accompanied it have begun to fade. The words master a dimming past.

Proust's dream was to bring back the past, not to cheat time so much as reincarnate it and its vicissitudes as it surged back into the real present, and he wrote and wrote and wrote, and the writing was an active, aching search for bringing then into now. Johannes the Seducer, a character in Søren Kierkegaard's *Either/Or*, has a similar wish:

> It would be of real interest to me if it were possible to repro-duce very accurately the conversations I have had with Corde-lia. But I easily perceive that it is an impossibility, for even if I managed to recollect every single word exchanged between us, it is nevertheless out of the question to reproduce the ele-ment of contemporaneity, which actually is the nerve in con-versation, the surprise in the outburst, the passionateness, which is the life principle in conversation.[24]

To long for the immediacy and presence of what we have lost is human. What we retain from that former time in words, images, and feelings is not stable. Only rarely can we measure our memo-ries against documentary evidence and, even then, our phenome-nological perspective is missing—the "I" who is experiencing the family gathering, the sailboat, the dinner party. For memory itself exists only in the present. I remember Arne Krohn Nilsen. He was my history teacher during the year I spent in Norway when I was twelve and turned thirteen. I am calling him forth now. He had remarkably long eyebrows that reminded me of sprouting plants, and he moved in a jerky, awkward way, and he could be very irri-table with the children, who poked fun at him in his absence. But I loved him. I cannot summon him whole, not in an inviolable pres-ent, not as he was in 1967. And yet, what if he returns as a character in a work of fiction? Then he might find a new reality, an imme-diacy and presence born of a recollection that moves forward rather than backward. That is the magic of fiction. Great memoirs also partake of a vivid re-experiencing, a re-seeing of the past that is also a fantasy, but it is nevertheless true to the present self, the one who recalls hoarfrost on a window long ago and, with that image, experiences an intense feeling of melancholy.

Just as memoirs may lie by borrowing hackneyed forms and spouting nothing but received knowledge, novels can do the same. And both genres can reveal small or large truths about what it means to be human. Perhaps my most gratifying moment as a novelist occurred after I had published *What I Loved*. I read from the book in Iowa City, and when the reading was over, a woman came up to me and said she had a verbal message for me from her father. She explained that like the novel's narrator, Leo Hertzberg, her father was a Jew who had been born in Berlin. He had fled the Nazis with his parents, first to London, but had eventually ended up in the United States. He was now living in Florida. The message was: 'Tell her I am Leo.'"

Of course, this cannot be true in any literal way, despite the similarities between the fictional and the true story. Leo recounts his early life only briefly, and it takes up very little of the book. The woman's father was speaking to some other reality, one of feeling, perhaps a feeling of exile and grief. I don't know. What I do know is that in my own life as a reader, I, too, have felt *I was* the narrator of a novel. I also know that, like Rousseau, I have taken those people and their stories into myself, and they have changed who I am. Fictions are remembered, too, and they are not stored any differently in the mind from other experiences. They *are* experience.

                                                              2010

EXCURSIONS TO THE ISLANDS
OF THE HAPPY FEW

Both the semiotic model of the index and the linguistic model of performativity (and often their combination) become central to the aesthetic of Conceptual art and they also define the specific visuality and textuality of Lamelas's filmic and photographic work of the late sixties. If, in the former, depiction and figuration are displaced by the mere trace and pure record that the photograph or the film or video recording supply when reduced to *pure information,* then we encounter in the latter a model of texuality where rhetoric, narrative plot and fiction, agency and psychobiography, are all dismissed as integrally participating in the conditions of the ideological and of myth (in Barthes's definition).

Benjamin H. D. Buchloh[1]

More fundamentally, however, an examination by pharmacological means, of the mechanism by which the granularity of activation is engendered (results not shown) indicates that the areas of silence between patches of activity at 40 Hz are generated by active inhibition. Thus, in the presence of GABA

A blockers, the spatial filtering of cortical activity described above disappears. These results are clearly in accordance with the findings that cortical inhibitory neurons are capable of high-frequency oscillation (Llinás et al. 1991) and with the view that, if such neurons are synaptically coupled and fire in synchrony, they might be formative in generating cortical gamma-band activity.

R. Llinás, U. Ribary, D. Contreras and C. Pedroarena[2]

Primary narcissism, however, is not in the focus of the ensuing developmental considerations. Although there remains throughout life an important direct residue of the original position—a basic narcissistic tonus which suffuses all aspects of the personality—I shall turn our attention to two other forms into which it becomes differentiated: the *narcissistic self* and the *idealized parent imago*.

Hans Kohut[3]

I DIDN'T GO FAR TO find the passages quoted above. Buchloh's book, the scientific paper on consciousness, and Kohut's essay on narcissism are all in my study, on bookshelves only steps away from my desk. I have read all of them because in one way or another they have been part of my research. Countless other books I've read could have served my purpose just as well, which was simple: I wanted to show that without considerable reading in the fields represented above—theoretical art history, neuroscience, and psychoanalysis—it would be difficult to understand what these people are talking about. What they share is more important to me than what distinguishes them. They are rarefied texts that rely on words known to "the happy few" who are reading them. They all require a reader who is steeped in the subject at hand. He or she already knows what Roland Barthes thought about myth and ideology, can readily identify GABA as gamma-aminobutyric acid, an important inhibitory neurotransmitter in the central nervous system, can distinguish GABA A from GABA B, and has some idea what a "basic narcissistic tonus" might be.

We live in a culture of hyperfocus and expertise. "Experts" on this or that particular subject are continually consulted and cited in newspapers and magazines, on television and the radio. Just think how many times we've heard the term "Middle East expert" in recent years, perhaps with some further qualification: "Dr. F. is the leading expert on Syrian and Iranian relations at Carbuncle University." Each field carves out a domain and pursues it relentlessly, accumulating vast amounts of highly specific knowledge. Except when brought in to make declarations to the culture at large, these people inhabit disciplinary islands of the like-educated and the like-minded. As a roaming novelist and essayist with an academic background in literature, I've found myself swimming toward various islands for some time. I've reached the shores of a few of them and even stayed on for a while to check out the natives. What I've discovered is both exciting and dismaying. Despite the hardships I've had penetrating abstruse texts and learning foreign vocabularies (not to speak of innumerable acronyms and abbreviations), I've been forever altered by my excursions. My thoughts about what it means to be a human being have been changed, expanded, and reconfigured by my adventures in art theory, neuroscience, and psychoanalysis. At the same time, I've been saddened by the lack of shared knowledge. It can be very hard to *talk* to people, have them understand you, and for you to understand them. Dialogue itself is often at risk.

Some years ago, I did extensive research on psychopathy, also called sociopathy and antisocial personality disorder, for a novel I was writing. I read everything I could get my hands on without discrimination. I read psychoanalytic and psychiatric books. I read statistical analyses of psychopaths in inmate populations. I read science papers that measured seratonin levels in criminal sociopaths, and I read neurological cases of people with frontal lobe damage who shared traits with classic psychopaths. It turned out that bibliographies tell all. You see those the authors quote or refer to and you know where they live intellectually. Even people researching the same subject are often wholly isolated from one another. For example, a statisician doesn't give a jot about what Winnicott had to say about sociopathy in his book *Deprivation and Delinquency*,[4] and neurologists don't bother to investigate what John Bowlby wrote about the effects of early separation on both children and primates in his masterwork, *Attachment and Loss*.[5] Ours is a world of intellectual fragmentation, in which exchanges between and among fields have become increasingly difficult.

Thomas Kuhn, in his book *The Structure of Scientific Revolutions*, identified these circles in science as "disciplinary matrixes."[6] These groups share a set of methods, standards, and basic assumptions— a *paradigm* of values. In other words, the people in these groups all speak the same language. In a lecture, the German philosopher Jürgen Habermas addressed these isolates, which are by no means limited to science: "The formation of expert cultures, within which carefully articulated spheres of validity help the claims to propositional truth, normative rightness, and authenticity, attain *their own logic* (as well, of course, as their own life, esoteric in character and endangered in being split off from ordinary communicative practice) . . ."[7] The parenthetical comment is crucial. It has become increasingly difficult to decipher the logic of these expert cultures because their articulations are so highly refined, so remote from ordinary language that the layperson is left thoroughly confused. Indeed, when reading some of these specialized texts, I can't help but think of Lucky's tirade in *Waiting for Godot*, during which his creator, the erudite Samuel Beckett, made inspired poetic nonsense from the overwrought articulations of academe: "Given the existence as uttered forth in the public works of Puncher and Wattman of a personal God quaquaquaqua with white beard quaquaquaqua outside time without extension who from the heights of divine apathia divine athymbia divine aphasia loves us dearly with some exceptions for reasons unknown but time will tell . . . that as a result of the labors left unfinished crowned by the Acacacacademy of Anthropopopometry of Essy-in-Possy of Testew and Cunard it is established beyond all doubt all other doubt than that which clings to the labors of men . . ."[8]

About a year ago, I was on a flight from Lisbon to New York and beside me was a man reading a neurology paper. Although I usually refrain from speaking to people on airplanes, my abiding curiosity about neurology was too great, and I asked him about his work. He was, as I had expected, a neurologist, an expert on Alzheimer's disease, it turned out, who ran a large research center in the United States and worked indefatigably with both patients and their families. He was bright, open, affable, and obviously knew as much about Alzheimer's disease as any human being in the world, an esoteric knowledge I could never hope to penetrate. After we had talked for a while, he looked down at the book I had with me and asked what it was. I told him I was re-reading Kierkegaard's *Either/Or*. He gave me a blank look. I then explained that Kierkegaard was a Danish philosopher and refrained from using the word *famous* because I was no longer sure what fame was. I don't think everyone in the world should have read Kierkegaard. I don't even believe that everyone should know who Kierkegaard is. My point is that I, too, often find myself in a closed world, one in which I make assumptions about common knowledge only to discover it isn't common at all. Somewhat later in the conversation I asked him what he thought about "mirror neurons." Mirror neurons, first discovered by Giacomo Rizzolatti, Vittorio Gallese, and their colleagues in 1995, made a splash in neuroscience and beyond. The researchers discovered that there were neurons in the premotor cortex of macaque monkeys that fired in animals who were performing a task, such as grasp-

ing, and also fired in those who were merely *watching* others perform that same task. A similar neural system has been found in
human beings. The implications of the discovery seemed enormous and a great deal of speculation on their meaning began. My
Alzheimer's companion didn't know about mirror neurons. No
doubt they had never been crucial to his research, and I had made
another presumptuous gaffe.

The truth is that being an expert in any field, whether it's
Alzheimer's or seventeenth-century English poetry, takes up most
of your time, and even with heroic efforts, it's impossible to read
everything on a given topic. There was an era before the Second
World War when philosophy, literature, and science were all considered crucial for the truly educated person. The Holocaust in
Europe, the expansion of education beyond elites, the postwar
explosion of information, and the death of the Western canon (no
more necessity for Greek and Latin) killed the idea that any human
being could master a common body of knowledge that traversed
many disciplines. That world is gone forever, and mourning it may
well be misplaced for all kinds of reasons, but its loss is felt, and a
change is in the air, at least in some circles. In his introduction to
Autopoiesis and Cognition, a book written by Humberto Maturana
and Francisco Varela, Sir Stafford Beer praises the authors for
their ability to create "a higher synthesis of disciplines" and assails
the character of modern scholarship. "A man who can lay claim to
knowledge about some categorized bit of the world, however tiny,
which is greater than anyone else's knowledge of that bit, is safe for
life: reputation grows, paranoia deepens. The number of papers increase exponentially, knowledge grows by infinitesimals, but understanding of the world actually recedes, because the world really
is an interacting system."[9] Anyone who has even a passing acquain-
tance with academic life must recognize that Beer has a point.

I remember a conversation I had with a young woman at Columbia University when I was a student there. She told me she

was writing her dissertation on horse heads in Spenser. Of course it's entirely possible that examining those heads led to staggering insights about Spenser's work, but I recall that I nodded politely and felt a little sad when she mentioned her topic. Years of work on that particular subject did seem incommensurate with my fantasies of an impassioned intellectual labor that uncovered something essential about a work of literature. When I did research for my own dissertation on language and identity in Charles Dickens's novels, I plodded dutifully through the endless volumes written about his work and realized in the end that only a handful of books had meant anything to me. Linguists, philosophers, psychoanalysts were far more helpful and, had I known then what I know now, I would have turned to neurobiology as well to explicate the endlessly fascinating world of Dickens. The theories I drew from then often came from the same pool as my fellow students in arms. In the late seventies and early eighties, French theory was the intellectual rage in the humanities, and we eagerly digested Derrida, Foucault, Barthes, Deleuze, Kristeva, Guattari, Lacan, and various others who were called upon to explicate not just literature but the textual world at large. Hegel, Marx, Freud, Husserl, and Heidegger also lurked in the wings of every discussion, but science was never part of a single conversation I had during those years. Wasn't science part of the ideological superstructure that determined our dubious cultural truths?

While I was doing research for an essay I was writing on the artist Louise Bourgeois, I read a book called *Fantastic Reality* by Mignon Nixon.[10] The author uses psychoanalytic concepts, Melanie Klein's idea of *part objects,* in particular, to elucidate Bourgeois's work. Nixon's analysis is intelligent and often persuasive. Along the way she mentions Klein's famous patient, Little Dick, whose behavior, she says, resembles Bruno Bettelheim's description of autism in *The Empty Fortress.* After discussing Bettelheim's machinelike patient, the autistic Joey, she moves on to Deleuze and Guattari's description of him in *Anti-Oedipus: Capitalism and Schizophrenia.* They also use Joey to further their particular argument. My purpose is not to critique Nixon's analysis of Bourgeois or *Anti-Oedipus,* a book I read years ago with interest, but rather to suggest that at every turn Nixon's sources are predictable. They indicate a theoretical education rather like the one I acquired during my years as a graduate student. She follows a preestablished line of thinkers worth mentioning, moving from one to another, but never steps beyond a particular geography of shared references. An investigation of contemporary ideas about Theory of Mind or the current science on autism, which is entirely different from and at odds with Bettelheim's ideas, doesn't enter her discussion. She is not alone. Islands are everywhere, even within a single discipline. I've noticed, for example, that continental and Anglo-American analytical philosophers often don't acknowledge that the other exists, much less do they deign to read each other.

The realization that the strict borders drawn between one field and another, or between one wing and another within a field, are at best figments may well be behind a new desire for communication among people with varying specialties. Philosophers have turned to neuroscientists and cognitive researchers to help ground their theories of consciousness. Their various musings are printed regularly in the *Journal of Consciousness Studies,* which has even published a literature professor or two. The philosopher Daniel Dennett draws from both neuroscience and artificial intelligence to propose a working metaphor for the mind—multiple drafts—in his book *Consciousness Explained.*[11] The neurologists Antonio Damasio[12] and V. S. Ramachandran[13] evoke both philosophy and art in their investigations about the neural foundations of what we call "the self." The art historian David Freedberg, author of The *Power of Images,* has leapt into neuroscience research to explore the effects of images on the mind-brain.[14] He was among the organizers of a conference I attended at Columbia University that hoped to establish a dialogue between neuroscientists and working visual artists. And yet, it isn't easy to make forays out of one's own discipline. The experts lie in wait and often attack the interlopers who dare move onto their sacred ground. This defensiveness is also understandable. Specialists in one field can make reductive hash of another they know less well. To my mind, conversations among people working in different areas can only benefit everyone involved, but the intellectual windows that belong to one discipline do not necessarily belong to another. The result is a scrambling of terms and beliefs, and often a mess is made. The optimistic view is that out of the chaos come interesting questions, if not answers.

In the last couple of years, I've attended the monthly neuroscience lectures at the New York Psychoanalytic Institute, and through Mark Solms, a psychoanalyst and brain researcher who has spearheaded a dialogue between neuroscience and psychoanalysis, I became a member of a study group that took place after those lectures led by the late psychoanalyst Mortimer Ostow and the neuroscientist Jaak Panksepp. The group has since been reconfigured, but during the year I regularly attended meetings of the first group, I found myself in a unique position. I was the lone artist among analysts, psychiatrists, and neuroscience researchers and was able to witness the dissonant vocabularies of the various disciplines, which nevertheless addressed the same mystery from different perspectives: how does the mind-brain actually work? Although the language of psychoanalysis had long been familiar to me, I knew next to nothing about the physiology of the brain. During the first meeting, I worked so hard to understand what was being said and felt so mentally exhausted afterward that I fell asleep at a dinner party that same evening. I ordered a rubber brain to try to learn its many parts, and began to read. It took innumerable books and many more papers before

I was able to penetrate, even superficially, the neuroscientific aspects of the discussion, but as the fog lifted somewhat, I felt I was in a position to make a few observations. Unsurprisingly, our conversations were riddled by language problems. For example, was what Freud meant by *primary process* equivalent to a similar idea in neuroscience used by Jaak Panksepp? Both sides agreed that most of what the brain-mind does is unconscious, but is the unconscious of neuroscience harmonious with Freud's idea of the same thing? Or, for example, when scientists use the word neural *representations* when they talk about brain function, what do they mean? Exactly how do neurons represent things, and what are those things they're representing? Is this a form of mental translation—the internal reconfigurations of perception? The words *neural correlates* are also interesting. I have a better sense of this. I'm feeling angry, and when I'm feeling angry, there are neuronal networks in parts of my brain that are actively firing. In order to avoid saying that those excited neurons *are anger,* scientists speak of correlates. Language counts. Not always, but often, I listened as people talked right past each other, each one speaking his own language.

Words quickly become thing-like. It has often fascinated me how a psychoanalytic concept such as *internal object,* for example, can be treated as if it weren't a metaphor for our own inner plurality that necessarily includes the psychic presence of others, but as if it were something concrete that could be manipulated—like a shovel. I've also listened in amazement to analysts talk about the *ego* almost as if it were an internal organ—a liver, say, or a spleen. (I can't help feeling that Freud's *Ich,* our English *I,* with its pronominal association, might have been a better translation choice than *ego.*) A pharmacologist I met in the group referred to this phenomenon as a "hardening of the categories," a phrase that struck me as both funny and wise. Names divide, and those divisions can easily come to look inevitable. Neurons, of course, aren't like internal objects, egos, or ids. They are material in a way that psychic categories aren't, but making sense of them calls for interpretation, nevertheless. As Jaak Panksepp likes to say, scientific research doesn't make *reality* pop up like magic. He is not a victim of a naïve realism that reaches out for "the thing in itself" and grabs it. Hard science is a plodding business of findings and refindings and findings again. It is incremental, often contradictory, and dependent on the creativity of the mind doing the research, a mind that can grasp what the research *means* at the time, a meaning that may well change. At the end of many science papers there is a section called *Discussion,* where the researchers tell the reader how their study might be understood or how it could be followed up. Results rarely speak for themselves.

In the group, the problem of the *self* came up several times. What constitutes a *self*? True to my education, I had often located the self in self-consciousness, a dialogical mirroring relation between an *I* and a *you,* and I believed that we create ourselves through others in narratives that are made over time. From this point of view, the self is a convenient if necessary fiction we construct and reconstruct as we go about the business of life. It was always clear to me that most of what we are is unconscious, but that unconscious reality has never seemed singular to me, but plural—a murmuring multitude. I have since modified my views. Language is important to forms of symbolic self-consciousness, an ability to see oneself as another, to hurl oneself forward into the future and remember oneself in the past, but not to consciousness or a feeling of selfhood. Surely animals, even snails, have some form of a self and are awake, alive, and aware. Does that awakeness, with its desires and survival instincts, its aggressions and attachments, constitute a core or primordial self, as some would have it, or is a *self* simply the sum of all our conflicted and fragmented parts, conscious and unconscious? People with damage to left language areas of their brains often hold on to a strong sense of themselves and can be profoundly aware of what they

have lost. Some people with devastating lesions nevertheless retain an inner sense of who they are. Luria recorded a famous case
of just such a person, Zazetsky, in *The Man with a Shattered
World*.[15] After suffering terrible head injuries in the Second World
War, he spent his days trying to recover the bits and pieces of his
ruined memory in a journal he kept until his death. Other forms
of neurological injury, in the right hemisphere especially, can
cause far greater disruption to a person's sense of being, which
suggests that while language is important, it doesn't *determine* our
identities. But for this discussion what interests me is not my
own evolving view of what a self might be, but that for neurobiologists and analysts alike this global question of *what we are* is
tortuous and necessarily calls upon a philosophical orientation,
an ability to loosen the categories, juggle the frames, and be free
enough to question even those ideas one has held most dear. Human inquiry requires making borders and categories, and dis-
secting them, and yet these divisions belong to a shared, articulated
vision of *how things are* that is not arbitrary, but neither is it absolute. Unless one believes in an ultimate view, a supreme, disembodied scientific observer, we cannot find a perfect objective image
of things as they are. We are neither angels nor brains in vats, but
active embodied inhabitants of a world we internalize in ways
we don't fully understand. Merleau-Ponty makes a distinction between philosophy and science that is valuable: "Philosophy is not
science, because science believes it can soar over its object and
holds the correlation of knowledge with being as established,
whereas philosophy is the set of questions wherein he who questions himself is himself implicated by the question."[16] Whether
one agrees with Merleau-Ponty's phenomenology or not, it seems
clear that in science, as well as in philosophy, the observer's relation to the object must be considered.

Every discipline needs its philosophy, or at least its ground
rules. Another one of my island excursions has been to a hospital.

I have a volunteer job as a writing teacher for psychiatric inpatients at the Payne Whitney Clinic. For its inmates, the clinic on the eleventh floor of New York Hospital is a world unto itself. The patients live in locked wards, are under continual supervision, and many of them don't know when they will be able to leave. Some are eager to get out. Others are afraid to return to their lives. Some of those who are released come back before too long, and I wonder how warmly I should greet them when they walk through the door of the classroom, even when I've missed them. Each person has been diagnosed with one or several of the many disorders that are found in the *Diagnostic and Statistical Manual of Mental Disorders,* now in its fourth edition. The authors of the manual state in their introduction: "In the DSM IV, there is no assumption that each category of mental disorder is a completely discrete entity with absolute boundaries dividing it from other mental disorders or from no mental disorder."[17] Despite this caveat, I've discovered that at least for patients these diagnoses can become surprisingly rigid. The diagnosis and the patient are identified to such a degree that there is no escape, no blur, nothing left over for the person to hold on to once he's been designated as bipolar, say, or schizophrenic. In many ways, this is not strange. A mental disorder isn't a virus or a bacteria that attacks the body from the outside. If I am continually hearing voices from another dimension or am so depressed that I lie in my bed without moving day after day or am churning out fifty pages of poetry during a period of a few hours in a flight of manic joy or am reliving an assault in horrifying uncontrollable flashbacks, who is to say these experiences are not *of* me?

One afternoon, several students in my class began to talk about their diagnoses. A young woman turned to me and said in a pained voice, "To call someone a borderline is the same as saying 'I hate you.'" It wasn't a stupid comment. She had understood that the characteristics that define borderline personality disorder in the DSM, "inappropriate, intense anger" among them, could well be construed as unflattering traits, and ironically and perhaps true to her diagnosis, she had interpreted the clinical name as a blow. Another patient then helpfully volunteered: "My doctor says she treats symptoms, not diagnoses." This more flexible position is also complicated. I have noticed that patients are often dealt with as a jumble of symptoms—sleeplessness, anxiety, thought disorder, auditory hallucinations—almost as if these traits were disembodied and easily distinguishable problems, each of which calls for a pharmacological solution. I am not an antidrug person. I have seen people who over a period of a couple of weeks improve remarkably when they change their medicines. I also witnessed a wild, incoherent, out-of-control patient, who after ECT, once called electroshock, the nightmare treatment of popular imagination, seemed so much better, so *normal,* that it took my breath away. I know the effects don't always last. I know there are risks. A psychiatrist I met who works with inpatients said she was continually aware, not only of the potential dangers of treatment, but that fixing one thing may mean the loss of another. "How are you?" I asked a talented writer who had been in my class for over a month. She seemed quieter than I had ever seen her and far less delusional. "Not so good," she answered, tapping her temple. "Lithium head. I've gone dead in there." Is the dead self the well self? Would a little less lithium help to create a more *normal* self? As a person who has what psychiatrists would call *hypomanic* phases, which manifest themselves in excessive or perhaps obsessive reading and writing, often followed by crashes into migraine, I was full of sympathy for the patient. The difference between us is one of degree. Somehow I manage, and she doesn't.

No one would argue that a person *is* his diagnosis, and yet no one would argue that the characteristics that define an illness aren't part of the person. Even I, layperson that I am, have found myself silently diagnosing students in my classes, especially those with florid symptoms. Once you are immersed in the jargon and have read enough, it seems to come naturally. And yet, I know that in another era, or even a few years ago, the names and boundaries for the various illnesses were different and, to my mind, not necessarily *worse* than the ones that exist now. With each new edition, the DSM shifts its descriptive categories. New illnesses are announced. Old ones drop out. What interests me is that my perception of patients' *disorders*, colored by doubt as it is, has been shaped by the givens of current psychiatric expert culture. I have begun to *see* what I'm looking for. The discursive frames orient my vision. My familiarity with them certainly makes it possible for me to talk to people in that world, to ask informed questions, to find out more, to continue my life as a curious adventurer. But one may well ask: just because I like hanging out on islands and chatting up the inhabitants, is there anything really wrong with specialization, with knowing as much as one can about Alzheimer's or borderline personality or horse heads in Spenser? Would reading philosophy, history, art theory, linguistics, neuroscience, literature, or even psychoanalysis (now that it's marginal to the profession) be beneficial, for example, to the doctors on the wards where I go to teach every week? Do we really want psychiatrists deep in Immanuel Kant, Hippolyte Taine, Erwin Panofsky, Roman Jakobson, D. O. Hebb, Fyodor Dostoyevsky, and the inimitable but still controversial Sigmund Freud? What's the point? Nobody can know everything. Not even in the lost world of the thinkers who shared a vision of the educated man (it was *a man,* I'm sorry to say) did people know all. Even then there were too many books, too many fields, too many ideas to keep track of.

In *The Man Without Qualities,* Robert Musil's character, General Stumm, hopes to search out "the finest idea in the world." Chapter 100 of Musil's huge, unfinished novel is Stumm's account of his visit to the library. He is too embarrassed to use the phrase "the finest idea in the world" when he asks for a book, confessing that the phrase sounds like a "fairy tale,"[18] but he hopes that the librarian, familiar with the millions of books to be found in that palace of knowledge, will guide him toward it. He can't specify what he wants—the book in his mind isn't about a single subject.

> My eyes must have been blazing with such a thirst for knowledge that the man suddenly took fright, as if I were about to suck him dry altogether. I went on a little longer about needing a kind of timetable that would enable me to make connections among all sorts of ideas in every direction—at which he turns so polite it's absolutely unholy, and offers to take me into the catalog room and let me do my own searching, even though it's against the rules, because it's only for the use of the librarians. So I actually found myself inside the holy of holies. It felt like being inside an enormous brain.[19]

The endless volumes, the bibliographies, the lists, categories, compartments for this subject and the other have a traumatizing effect on poor Stumm, who becomes only more disoriented when the librarian confesses that he never actually reads the books in the collection, only their titles and tables of contents. "Anyone who lets himself go and starts reading a book is lost as a librarian," he tells Stumm. "He's bound to lose perspective."[20]

Musil's comedy summons a truth. Losing perspective is an intellectual virtue because it requires mourning, confusion, reorientation, and new thoughts. Without it, knowledge slogs along in its various narrow grooves, but there will be no leaps, because the thinner my perspective, the more likely it is for me to accept the preordained codes of a discipline as inviolable truths. Doubt is the engine of ideas. A willingness to lose perspective means an openness to *others* who are guided by a set of unfamiliar propositions. It means entertaining a confounding, even frightening and radical form of intersubjectivity. It also means that however happy you are among the few residents of your particular island, that little island is not the whole world.

2007

ON READING

READING IS PERCEPTION AS TRANSLATION. The inert signs of an alphabet become living meanings in the mind. It is all very strange when you think about it, and perhaps not surprising that written language came late in our evolutionary history, long after speech. Literacy, like all learned activities, appears to alter our brain organization. Studies have shown that literate people process phonemes differently from illiterate people. Their knowledge of an alphabet seems to strengthen their ability to understand speech as a series of discrete segments. Before my daughter learned to read, she once asked me a question I found hard to answer. She pointed at a blank space between two words on the page of a book we were reading and said, "Mommy, what does the nothing mean?" Articulating the significance of that emptiness did not come easily. My illiterate three-year-old did not understand the sequencing and divisions that are inherent to language, ones that are more apparent on the page than in speech.

There are any number of theories about how reading works, none of which is complete because not enough is known about the neurophysiology of interpreting signs, but it is safe to say that reading is a particular human experience of collaboration with the words of another person, the writer, and that books are literally animated by the people who read them because reading is an embodied act. The text of *Madame Bovary* may be fixed forever in French, but the text is dead and meaningless until it is absorbed by a living, breathing human being.

The act of reading takes place in human time; in the time of the body, and it partakes of the body's rhythms, of heartbeat and breath, of the movement of our eyes, and of our fingers that turn the pages, but we do not pay particular attention to any of this. When I read, I engage my capacity for inner speech. I assume the written words of the writer who, for the time being, becomes my own internal narrator, the voice in my head. This new voice has its own rhythms and pauses that I sense and adopt as I read. The text is both outside me and inside me. If I am reading critically, my own words will intervene. I will ask, doubt, and wonder, but I cannot occupy both positions at once. I am either reading the book or pausing to reflect on it. Reading is intersubjective—the writer is absent, but his words become part of my inner dialogue.

It happens that I find myself half-reading. My eyes follow the sentences on the page and I take in the words, but my thoughts are elsewhere, and I realize that I have read two pages but haven't understood them. Sometimes I speed-read abstracts of science papers, zooming through the text to glean whether I want to read the whole article. I read poems slowly, allowing the music of the words to reverberate inside me. Sometimes I read a sentence by a philosopher again and again because I do not grasp its meaning. I recognize each word in the sentence, but how they all fit together requires all of my concentration and repeated reading. Various texts call for different strategies, all of which have become automatic.

I have vivid memories of some books that last in my consciousness. Novels often take pictorial form in my recollection; I see Emma Bovary running down a grassy hill on her way to the chemist's shop, her cheeks flushed, her hair loosened by the wind. The grass, the cheeks, the hair, the wind *are not in the text*. I provided them. Philosophy usually does not stay with me in pictures, but in words, although I have formed images for Kierkegaard, for example, because he is a philosopher-novelist, a thinker-storyteller. I see Victor Eremita, the pseudonymous editor of *Either/Or,* with his hatchet as he smashes the piece of furniture in which two manuscripts have been hidden. Other books have vanished almost entirely from my conscious mind. I recall reading Danilo Kis's *A Tomb for Boris Davidovich* and liking it very much, but I cannot bring back a single aspect of the story.[1] Where did it go? Could an association prompt it back to mind? I clearly recall the title, the author, and my feeling—admiration for the book— but that is all that has remained.

And yet, explicit memories, however dim, are only part of memory. There are implicit memories, too, which can't be retrieved on demand but are nevertheless part of our ongoing knowledge of the world. A simple example is reading itself—a learned skill I do, but I can't remember *how* I do it. The rigors of long ago, puzzling over letters and sounding out words, have disappeared as conscious processes. Another example of subliminal recollection is looking for a particular passage in a book. I take the volume off the shelf, often without any sense of where the passage is among the many hundreds of pages. I certainly have no number in my mind, but once I have the object in hand, I am able to go directly to the paragraph I want. My fingers seem to remember. This is a proprioceptive ability. Proprioception is our motor-sensory capacity to orient ourselves in space—our ability to negotiate our way into chairs, dodge obstacles, pick up cups, and remember unconsciously where the crucial passage is to be found.

Cognitive scientists often talk about encoding, storage, and retrieval in relation to memory. These are computer metaphors that only approximate the actual experience of remembering and, I would argue, distort it as well. There are no warehouses in our brains where material is stored and waits to be retrieved in original form. Memories aren't photographs or documentary films. They shift over time, are creatively and actively perceived, and this applies to the books we remember as well. They dim in time and may mutate. Others seem to imprint themselves deeply. Books, of course, are made only of words, but they may be recalled in images, feelings, or in other words. And sometimes we remember without knowing we remember. This insight is hardly new. In *The Passions of the Soul* (1649), Descartes claimed that a terrible episode in childhood could live on in a person despite his amnesia for the event.[2] In his *Monadology* (1714), Leibniz developed an idea of unconscious or insensible perceptions that we aren't aware of but which can nevertheless influence us.[3] In the nineteenth and into the early twentieth century, William Carpenter, Pierre Janet, William James, and Sigmund Freud all investigated unconscious memories, although memories of reading did not figure in their contemplations.

I recently reread George Eliot's *Middlemarch*. I had read it three times before, but many years had passed since my last encounter with the book. I had not forgotten the broad sweep of the novel or its characters, but I could not have reproduced each one of the multiple plots in detail. And yet, the act of reading the book again triggered specific memories of what would come later in the same text. Rereading became a form of anticipatory memory, of remembering what I had forgotten before I reached the next passage. This suggests, of course, that reacquaintance unearths what has been buried. The implicit becomes explicit. Cognitive scientists have a term called "repetition priming." They don't give their subjects eight-hundred-page novels but various verbal tasks, and then much later quiz them on a list of words, for example, and others not previously seen. It is clear that even without any conscious awareness of their earlier exposure to the words, participants in the studies have unconscious recall and perform better than if they had not been primed.

But no reading experience, even of an identical text, is the same. I discovered ironies in *Middlemarch* I had not fully appreciated before, no doubt the product of my advancing age, which has been paralleled by the internal accumulation of more and more books that have altered my thoughts and created a broader context for my reading. The text is the same, but I am not. And this is crucial. Books are either unleashed or occluded by the reader. We bring our life stories, our prejudices, our grudges, our expectations, and our limitations with us to books. I did not understand Kafka's humor when I first read him as a teenager. I had to get older to laugh at "The Metamorphosis." Anxiety can also block access to books. The first time I tried to read Joyce's *Ulysses* at eighteen, I worried so much about my ignorance that I couldn't get through it. A couple of years later, I told myself to relax, to take in what I could, and the novel has become a vivid jumble of visual, sensory, and emotional memories that are dear to me.

Some readers read a book and wish it had been another, one closer to their own lives and concerns. Writers have the fortune (and sometimes misfortune) to encounter their readers, either in person or through reviews and academic articles. A reviewer of one of my books, *The Shaking Woman or A History of My Nerves* (which is about the ambiguities of diagnosis and how illnesses are framed in various disciplines) was annoyed because I did not address the sufferings of those who care for sick people. This particular subject was so entirely outside the book's argument, I couldn't help wondering if there wasn't some personal reason for the reviewer's irritation: she wanted a book about caretakers, not about the people stricken by an illness. Sometimes books get scrambled in memory. Not long ago, a friend of mine told me she had reread

Catch-22, expectantly waiting for her favorite scene. It never came. Her guess was that two books had mingled in her mind. And the beloved passage? To what novel did that belong? She couldn't remember.

Openness to a book is vital, and openness is simply a willingness to be changed by what we read. This is not as easy as it sounds. Many people read to solidify their own views. They read only in their own fields. They believe they know what a book is before they have opened it or they have rules they imagine should be followed and react with dismay if their predictions are dashed. To some degree, this is the nature of perception itself. Repetitive experience creates expectation, which shapes how we perceive the world, books included. In recent years a lot of work has been done on something called "change blindness."[4] Most of these experiments involve visual scenes in which large numbers of people fail to notice significant changes. For example, in a film: after a cut, two cowboys switch heads. Buñuel's *That Obscure Object of Desire* makes use of this form of ingrained expectation: two very different-looking actresses play the same role, but many viewers failed to notice for quite some time that one woman was not the other.

Reading has its own forms of change blindness. We necessarily come to books of a particular literary genre—detective fiction, romance novels, memoirs, and autobiography—with prejudgments about what the work will be. And if we don't pay attention, we may miss essential departures from the form and fail to recognize what is there. Similarly, ideas of greatness or badges of honor, such as prizes attached to a book, predispose readers to think well of what they are reading. As a high school student I remember reading and disliking Archibald MacLeish's poetry. I remember thinking that something was wrong with me because the man had won every literary prize it was possible to win in America. I now believe my early opinion was right. I also no longer feel alone. MacLeish's star has plummeted.

It also happens, however, that I recognize a writer's intelligence or her fluid and elegant style, but I am left feeling very little else. Such books seem to evaporate almost immediately after I have read them. Experiences of powerful emotions linger in the mind; experiences of tepid ones don't. Great books, it seems to me, are distinguished by an urgency in the telling, a need that one can feel viscerally. Reading is not a purely cognitive act of deciphering signs; it is taking in a dance of meanings that has resonance far beyond the merely intellectual. Dostoyevsky is important to me, and I can place him in Russian intellectual history. I can talk about his biography, his ideas, his epilepsy, but that is not why I feel so close to his works. My intimacy is a product of my reading experiences. Every time I remember *Crime and Punishment,* I relive my feelings of pity, horror, despair, and redemption. The novel is alive in me.

But books may also return from thought's underground into the daylight without our knowing where they have come from. I know that when I write the books I have read are implicated in what I am composing. Even novels I have forgotten may come to play a role in the unconscious generation of my own texts. Exactly how books are carried inside us after we have read them is not well understood and varies from person to person. Most of us are not savants. Except for poems or passages we have actively memorized, the books we read are not fixed in recollection as complete texts that we can turn to as we would a volume on the shelf. Books are made between the words and spaces left by the writer on the page and the reader who reinvents them through her own embodied reality, for better and for worse. The more I read, the more I change. The more varied my reading, the more able I am to perceive the world from myriad perspectives. I am inhabited by the voices of others, many of them long dead. The dead speak, and they speak in shouts and whispers and in the music of their poetry and prose. Reading is creative listening that alters the reader. Books are remembered consciously in pictures and words, but they are also present in the strange, shifting rooms of our unconsciousness. Others, which for some reason have no power to rearrange our lives, are often forgotten entirely. The ones that stay with us, however, become us, part of the mysterious workings of the human mind that translates little symbols on a page into a lived reality.

2011

STIG DAGERMAN

The snakes are loose.
Robert Mitchum in *Crossfire* (1947), directed by Edward
Dmytryk

*T*HE SNAKE IS A NOVEL of hallucinatory urgency written by a
person barely out of his adolescence.[1] Stig Dagerman was
twenty-two years old when the book was published in 1945, and
this fact alone makes it a rare work in the history of the novel.
Poets, musicians, mathematicians, and visual artists often bloom
young, but great novels have usually been produced by somewhat
older people. Like F. Scott Fitzgerald, who published *This Side of
Paradise* when he was twenty-four, Dagerman hit it big fast, and
his early genius has become part of his identity as a writer.*

---

*Dagerman was born in 1923 to working-class parents outside the village of
Älvksrleby. Dagerman's mother abandoned him when he was still a baby, and
he was raised by his grandparents. At twelve, he moved to Stockholm to live
with his father and became active in the youth organization of the Syndicalist
Union. When he was sixteen, a lunatic murdered his beloved grandfather,
and his grandmother died not long after. Between the ages of twenty and

But this is received knowledge. What is the power of *The Snake*? When I opened the book for the first time and began reading, I confess I felt hammered by the metaphors and similes that came down on me hard and fast, one after the other. I asked myself if I had run into a hopped-up European version of Raymond Chandler and his tough-guy prose, but as I read on, it became clear that something altogether different was happening. This is a text in which the metaphorical and the literal mingle to such a degree that by its end, the two have merged entirely. The process begins in the introductory paragraph of the novel. Dagerman's narrator views the train station of a "sleepy hamlet" on a burning-hot day, a town which is personified when it gets a "dig in its flank," a dig that presumably wakes it up. The theme of sleep, dreams, and stupors is under way from this sentence on and will return again and again before the novel ends.

In the paragraphs that immediately follow, the reader is introduced to further tropes that will dominate the book and from time to time metamorphose into actual creatures and objects: the old woman at the station "with her quick rat-like eyes" who becomes "Rat-Eyes"; her grotesque companion (later identified as Irene's mother), has a tongue that sways in her mouth "like the head of a snake"; and the train that cuts the silence "like a razor blade." Rodents, snakes, and cutting instruments will reappear relentlessly in multiple guises and incarnations, as will images of mouths and throats, of suffocation and strangulation, of biting and

---

twenty-six, Dagerman wrote four novels, four plays, a collection of stories, articles, essays, and poems. In 1946, he traveled in Germany and wrote *German Autumn,* a strikingly human portrait of the country after the war. His prolific abilities, however, began to wane, and he suffered from writer's block. In 1954, at age thirty-one, suffering from depression and perhaps schizophrenia, he committed suicide. Although his work has been translated into English and is admired by many writers in England and America, Dagerman's fame has been mostly confined to Europe. This is sad because he is a writer of uncommon urgency and power.

the fear of being bitten, of suppressed or actual screams, of silence and speech.

The novel is structured as a concatenation of stories told from varying perspectives. It begins with its longest section, "Irene," a third-person account, closely identified with the heroine but which also enters the mind of the sadistic soldier Bill and, briefly, Sergeant Bowman, who is terrified of the snake Bill shows him. The following section, "We Can't Sleep," about half the length of the first, is a collective narrative, told in the first person plural, but which incorporates the stories of individual men, as the soldiers lie awake on their bunks in a state of shared insomnia and dread, after which come five additional third-person tales, all titled, and none of which is more than half the length of the novel's second section. The five stories revisit individual conscripts whom we have met earlier and do not follow a chronological timetable. In this way, the structure of the novel's second half can reasonably be called snakelike; it moves, not straight ahead, but slithers in and out and around the characters' narratives.

The two halves of the novel are bound by place and by a literal snake that appears and disappears in the camp, terrifying the men who feel it is lurking somewhere near, ready to strike. And even after it is found dead, one of the soldiers, Gideon, is startled to realize that his fear is not extinguished; it lives on. The snake's metaphorical aptness for Sweden's precarious neutrality during the Second World War is clear, but what interests me is Dagerman's evocation of embodied dread, a human state that is notoriously difficult to pin down because, as Gideon notices, it needn't have an object. Anxiety's object can be nameless.

In *Inhibitions, Symptoms, and Anxiety* (*Hemmung, Symptom, und Angst*) (1926), Sigmund Freud writes about the ambiguity of angst: "What we clearly want is something to tell us what anxiety really is, some criterion that will enable us to distinguish true statements from false. Anxiety is not so simple a matter."[2] Freud changed his theory of angst in this book, but the central thought that applies here is that the person suffering from anxiety has been blocked from releasing a necessary discharge of energy, without which he can't find satisfaction. The feeling of anxiety is a signal of danger, a danger, Freud argues, we save ourselves from through repression.

The characters in *The Snake* are bellyful of seething anxiety. Both their emotions and their words are smothered by all manner of restraints. Eventually, however, the internal pressure mounts, becomes unbearable, and the characters give in to volcanic outbursts. Besieged by jealous thoughts that Bill is with her rival Vera, Irene "holds a [figurative] knife to her throat to prevent her from saying anything . . ." Later, after she had pushed her mother off the train, she fears "being suffocated, of not getting enough air to her voice . . ." After being raped or nearly raped by the butcher boy, she breaks out in hysterical laughter. The fear and guilt she suppresses are compared to a little rodent inside her, gnawing away at her insides, but finally it must be let out. "Her terror is the little animal that nothing can keep shut in any longer. All of a sudden, she screams, in fact it's the little animal that screams." Bill presses down on his opponent during a fight "in order to loosen the scream" that will clinch his victory, but instead he sees the man's strangled tongue, one that resembles the earlier snake-like tongue of Irene's mother and is unmistakably phallic: "He could see his tongue being sort of pressed out of his mouth, stretching out like a neck." The soft-spoken, well-mannered girl in "The Mirror" reaches her limit and howls at the dense Lucky, "Don't you see, you idiot, I'm blind! Blind! Blind!" In "The Rag Doll," the boy Sorensen could have saved from sexual molestation by a predator returns home and, in a scene of genuine horror, vomits his guts out on the man who should have acted to help him. Gideon, the outsider, tormented by his fellow conscripts, suppresses the scream of his mounting anxiety. After he is brutally attacked by them, he lies paralyzed on the floor long after his cohorts have done with him. "Then he screams."

The sexual danger that runs through the stories turns on a need for and terror of orgasmic release. Irene's vacillations between inhibition and freedom, between soporific boredom and arousal, between her dread of and masochistic attraction to Bill are subtly evoked in a kind of Dagermanian phenomenology of embodied emotion and sensation that tracks her shifting internal realities in an ongoing present. These fluctuations in the characters between lassitude and longing, silence and speech, are continually explored through the lens of their immediate experience. And for many of them this dialectical tug of feeling crescendos in an act of sudden violence. When the reader first encounters Irene, she is lying naked in bed in a state of sensual torpor and moral ambivalence, which continues as she talks to Bill through the window. Her lax mood ends abruptly when Bill hurls his bayonet into the wall that separates them, bites her mouth when they kiss, and then she cuts her wrist on the bayonet's blade. He also nips his other conquest, "quickly as a razor blade, he bites Vera's ear." The sexual violence of "The Rag Doll" is never seen, but it is ominously portended when the pederast bribes his victim with a knife in a sheath. The myriad associations prompted by the knives in the novel, both metaphorical and real, of cutting, butchery, wounds, sexual sadism, and running blood, permeate the text. At one moment the earth itself appears to have been gored: "Then he comes into the dense, suffocating spruce forest, where clusters of berries have been ripped out of the ground, which seems to be bleeding with deep black wounds."

The novel's insistent tropes move seamlessly from the subjectivity of a single character to personifications of a town or a landscape as asleep or bleeding. Accompanying this metaphorical motion is a contagion of feeling that moves from one character into another and blurs the boundaries between them. The fear is individual and collective: it bleeds. Without Dagerman's psychological acumen, however, I don't think the roiling metaphors and linked stories would have the power they do. He is a master of the momentary, of the fleeting emotional and ethical muddles we all find ourselves in, and then wonder what on earth has happened. He is also sensitive to the ongoing delusions between self and other and how often we confound the two. In "The Mirror," Lucky's attraction to the girl is a projection and so, ironically, a form of blindness:

> Lucky suddenly felt sorry for her, because she was so alone. It was his own self-pity that spread to her. He'd worked himself into one of those moods now—everyone around him seemed to have a companion they could exchange ideas with; he was the only one who was so wretchedly lonely.

Lucky's painful isolation infects his perception, and his identification with the pitiable position of the blind girl culminates in a vicious blast of self-hatred, and he smashes a mirror in the apartment, after which he is summarily beaten by his cohorts.

In *The Snake* the furious repression of confused and confusing sexual desire and its sadistic aspects epitomized in the narrative of Irene, Bill, and Vera merges with the more overt political messages delivered in the book's second half and the collective failure to speak out and act, perhaps best articulated by Edmund through another image of restraint: "I feel pressurized . . . I feel there's an iron band pressing into my skull when I find there are laws nobody's asked me to accept that make me practically defenseless." This message is further complicated by an additional statement. "You're not wearing it because you deserve it, but because of so many people's cowardice and your own inadequacy." In the "Iron Band" chapter, it is words that go "to sleep in their

sleeping bags" and must be shaken and woken up. Edmund finds
his voice and his words; he speaks loudly, too loudly, addressing
the angst he feels directly, claiming that no one's is greater than
his. As Joker listens to his comrade, he feels a sudden desire to
speak, to achieve "clarity," but the words are "strangled" and instead of coherent sentences, he emits gibberish, which is followed
by a hallucinatory dream of two adjacent rooms, which are contained in Joker himself—a hiccoughing, chortling, jiggling living
room and a second threatening angst-room with chairs that speak
and fear that hovers near the ceiling. The double rooms clearly
address the political present, one is full of drunks, furniture, a
radio; the other is an impoverished place rife with paralyzing
dread, but the fantasy is too bizarre to be agitprop or to be read
only in terms of the war.

In *The Concept of Anxiety*, that paradoxical, ironic, parodic,
difficult text by Søren Kierkegaard, the pseudonymous Vigilius
Haufniensis famously yokes anxiety and dizziness.

> He whose eye happens to look down into the yawning abyss
> becomes dizzy. But what is the reason for this? It is just as much
> his own eye as in the abyss, for suppose he had not looked
> down. Hence anxiety is the dizziness of freedom, which emerges
> when the spirit wants to posit the synthesis and freedom looks
> down into its own possibility, laying hold of finiteness to sup-
> port itself. Freedom succumbs in this dizziness. Further than
> this psychology cannot and will not go. In that very moment
> everything is changed, and freedom when it again rises sees
> that it is guilty. Between these two moments lies the leap,
> which no science has explained and which no science can ex-
> plain.[3]

The Concept of Anxiety is a maddeningly complex examination of original sin and effect of the fall: the alienation from

nature fundamental to human beings—guilt, innocence, and freedom. The spirit is that which is linked with God and the infinite, the body and the psyche are tied to the finite. As for Freud, for Kierkegaard anxiety serves as an inward subjective signal and needs no object. There is something ambiguous about dread itself, something that can't be pinned down. Science has no access to this reality because it posits only a third-person objective view, and the "leap" made is not rationally explicable.

Dagerman's snake necessarily evokes the story of the fall with its serpent, Eve, Adam, the original loss of innocence, and the insistent question of free will. In fact, the book may be read as a meditation on what it means to act freely. Joker's hallucination of anxiety is the dizziness of freedom. The two rooms do not remain separate but merge in a terrifying image of collapsing walls, wild laughter, and blurring borders, in the monstrous confusion of unbearable dread. When Joker wakes from his horror dream, in which he feels he will burst apart, he again longs to speak his mind but doesn't. He does not embrace his freedom or address his guilt. He does not act but remains silent in the world of his fantasy, only imagining that he has spoken, and his comrades have answered him by assuaging his sense of culpability with the words "You don't need to have a guilty conscience." The ethical dilemma, the parsing of innocence and guilt, is not simple and, as a reader, I have immense sympathy for Joker and his confused wish to be aided by his companions, somehow to articulate the complexity of his feelings, and for his inability to get the words out. Guilt spreads, too. It seeps into the whole culture and stains everyone.

It does not matter whether Dagerman read Kierkegaard or not, because in the early forties when he wrote *The Snake,* Kierkegaard was in the air, reread through the lens of Existentialism, a name mostly rejected by those who were labeled with it, but which nevertheless serves a useful purpose here because I am talking about ideas that seem to circulate like winds and blow into people's ears as if no reading were necessary. When I was at Columbia University in the late seventies and early eighties, I sometimes felt that French theory had so permeated the humanities departments that one could simply stand on campus and inhale it. Such was existentialism in the early forties.

Although Sartre remained in denial about his debt to Kierkegaard, the Dane is all over *Being and Nothingness* (1943) in Sartre's references to "vertigo" and "anguish" and in his insistence on freedom as an unavoidable human fate.[4] But it is not only existentialism that infected the author of *The Snake*. Eras have moods, too, and in light of the monstrosities of Nazism, it is hardly strange that a fateful pessimism hung over the ideas and the art of the day and in the years that followed in American film noir, for example, which borrowed from European cinema to create its own dark stories of human brutality. Dagerman's interest in American prose writers is well known, but their influence is reinvention in *The Snake*. Hard-boiled metaphors become a philosophical device, one that emphasizes, rather than limits, ambiguity.

Dagerman's novel is a cry for individual responsibility and freedom, as well as a spirited work of resistance to the conventions of bourgeois life, which restrain and stupefy people. And it is a call for free thought and speech to clarify what should be done. It is acutely aware of the unspeakable horrors of the war, the sadism, the blood, and destruction, but none of these explains the book's power. The allegory, the symbolism, the bleeding metaphors work because they are embodied in characters and scenes of genuine psychological force and nuance, because the visual world of the novel is astutely observed and refuses banal conventions, and because the narration has an intensity and drive that is irresistible. Also, the book is shot through with ironies and humor.

The author even makes fun of his own metaphorical indulgences through his alter ego in the novel, Scriber, the scribe, the author character. In the second chapter, we are told that Edmund has poked fun of Scriber as a guy who compares a fire extinguisher to a bottle of India ink and a bottle of India ink to a fire extinguisher. "But just think if he needs both the India ink bottle and the fire extinguisher in the same sentence. How's he going to manage it without mixing them up, without the firemen starting to spray ink on a fire and the artist drawing his sketches with carbon dioxide?" A welcome moment of self-referential levity.

In the last chapter of *The Snake,* "The Flight That Didn't Come Off," Scriber falls. After an unknown quantity of beer and an extended argument with two interlocutors, a cultural critic and a poet, during which Scriber has insisted that "the tragedy of modern man is that he no longer dares to be afraid," he acts on an impulse to prove a point. He wants to "carry his reasoning to its logical conclusion." Scriber climbs out the window and moves along the parapet. When the poet calls for him to come back because he might fall, Scriber says, "No bloody fear." Surely this is a moment of hubris, not the dizziness of freedom for the one who looks into the abyss. There is something wrong with his fearlessness. Has he not been arguing for the merits of fear and dread? He loses his footing, and the last thing he hears is not his own scream but the cry of the prostitute who is standing in the doorway below.

The snake in the garden does not cause the Fall. He is only the tempter. But I don't believe that Scriber's fall can be read in any single way, nor do I think that the end evokes despair. It is, above all, ambiguous. Scriber's fall is also a stupid accident. An energetic, argumentative, tipsy young man finds himself out on a ledge and falls to his death for no good reason. That is life, too—the sudden slip into the abyss. And there is irony in Scriber's fickle fearlessness at the end of a novel that treats anxiety as its theme. Only a few pages before, Scriber has insisted that his own fear "is the greatest in the world." We are not rational creatures. In the best art something always escapes us and bewilders us. If it didn't, we would never return to it.

2010

THE ANALYST IN FICTION
Reflections on a More or Less Hidden Boing

THE FOLLOWING PASSAGE IS FROM an early draft of my most recently published novel, *The Sorrows of an American*. The narrator, Erik Davidsen, is a psychiatrist/psychoanalyst who lives in New York City. I have rescued the deleted passage from my closet, home to dozens of manuscript boxes stuffed with rejected material, because although it never found its way into the finished book, it speaks to the uneasy position the psychoanalyst occupies in contemporary American society.

The story of psychiatry has been bedeviled by the problem of naming from the beginning, a tortured puzzle of herding a diffuse cluster of symptoms under a single designation. The wounded psyche is not a broken leg. An X-ray won't reveal the fracture, and the brain images from PET scans and fMRIs cannot show us thoughts, only neuronal pathways. What invades or grows within a mind and causes people to suffer is not, as in a case of the measles, a single pathogen. Despite its earnestness and longing for precision, psychiatry's Bible, the *DSM*, now in its fourth edition, is a muddle. "Disorder" is the word of choice these days. Mental illness is a state of chaos and the job of mental health professionals is to restore order by all means at their disposal. New disorders are added with each edition of the *DSM*; others fall away; their presence or absence isn't necessarily founded on new science, but on consensus and, for lack of a better word, fashion. Half of Sonya's classmates have been diagnosed with ADHD. The *DSM* begins its description like this: "Attention Deficit/Hyperactivity Disorder is a frequent pattern of inattention and/or hyperactivity-impulsivity that is more frequently displayed and more severe, than is typically displayed in individuals at a comparable level of development." *Typically* is the word to notice. Exactly what is typical? I am not alone in thinking that thousands of American boys have been fed stimulants for no reason. I do believe that the disorder is real and that medicines can sometimes help, but its presence as an epidemic is a cultural phenomenon, the product of an evolving idea of what a normal child is supposed to be.

I have prescribed many drugs in my day and have seen their undeniable benefits. When screaming inner voices fall silent, a depression lifts or panics subside, the relief can be incalculable. I've also seen what the profession politely calls adverse effects: ataxia, blackouts, seizures, incontinence, renal crises, akathisia—the restless, wiggling sensations that make it impossible to sit still—and tardive dyskinesia—the tongue wagging, jaw rotating, hand and foot jerking caused by narcoleptics. The inability to achieve orgasm is such a common "side" effect of SSRIs, drug of choice for the masses, few doctors even bother to mention it to their patients. Insurance companies will pay for only short-term care, which means that after a brief interview or during a short hospital stay, a physician must assign a name to an array of often murky symptoms and prescribe a drug. Most American psychiatrists have become little more than prescription-writing machines, who leave

psychotherapy to social workers. What has been forgotten in all
this is how we draw the lines between one thing and another,
that the word is not the thing. The problem is not a lack of
good will among physicians. It is, as Erwin Schrödinger once
mourned, "the grotesque phenomenon of scientifically trained,
highly competent minds with an unbelievably childlike—
undeveloped and atrophied— philosophical outlook."

I am also a psychoanalyst, a member of that beleaguered
group of cultural outcasts who are only now regaining respect with the revelations of neuroscience. Psychoanalysis,
too, has suffered from "hardening of the categories," as a colleague of mine once put it, of treating metaphorical concepts
as if they were chairs or forks, and yet, it is at its best a discipline that values patience and tolerates ambiguity. What happens between two people in the analytic room cannot be easily
quantified or measured. Sometimes it cannot even be understood, but after years of practice I have become a man changed
by the stories of others, a human vault of words and silences,
of speechless sorrows and shrouded fears.

Erik's use of the word *outcast* may be strong, but his view that
for years psychoanalysis has been losing ground to drug-oriented
psychiatry is a fact, and our culture's representations of the analyst have suffered as a result. To see this clearly, one needs only to
ask the question: How many absurd or demeaning caricatures of
neuroscientists have you encountered in the media lately? Surely
it would be easy to poke fun at some of their widely reported
studies: a "God spot" discovered in the brain, for example, or
fMRI results of Republicans and Democrats in the throes of
"partisanship," as if religion and American politics can be found
in the temporal lobe or the amygdala, wholly isolated from language and culture. Neuroscientists often ridicule such research as
examples of "a new phrenology." But the doubts articulated by

people inside the field do not reach the hordes of journalists eager to record the explorations of "the last frontier" and embrace the newest brain discoveries as if they were absolute truths handed down from some divine source.

I am deeply interested in the neurobiology of mental processes, in brain plasticity and its role in the development of every human being over time. But I do not believe that the subtle character of human subjectivity and intersubjectivity can be reduced to neurons. As Freud wrote in *On Aphasia: A Critical Study*, "The psychic is therefore a process parallel to the physiological, a dependent concomitant."[1] The conundrum of the brain/mind relationship is as mysterious now as it was when Freud wrote those words in 1892. Erik's observation that the insights of neuroscience, some of which appear to confirm long-held psychoanalytic ideas about the unconscious, repression, identification, as well as the effectiveness of the talking cure, have helped redeem psychoanalysis is, I think, accurate. But it also reflects a truism: if you can locate an illness in some body part, it's more *real* than if you can't. Although this belief is philosophically naïve, it is nevertheless held by multitudes of people, including any number of doctors who have spent little time examining the taxonomies that shape their perceptions of illness and health.

Mass culture is often crude. The portraits of the analyst as a bearded, tight-lipped, aging character with a Viennese accent, a sly seducer hopping into bed with his clients, an egghead spouting jargon, a deranged monster, or merely an innocuous buffoon reflect various clichéd, and often hostile, views of psychoanalysis that have become familiar to many of us. But silly as these images are, they may also unearth a genuine suspicion of a discipline that, despite its enormous influence on popular thought, remains fundamentally misunderstood.

Priests, physicians, and psychoanalysts are repositories for, among other things, secrets, and the need for trust and the fear of betrayal are always present when a secret is told. Like the priest, the analyst inhabits a realm outside the ordinary social world. He or she is neither friend nor family member but nevertheless becomes the container of another person's intimate thoughts, fantasies, fears, and wishes—precious materials that must be handled carefully. There are forbidden behaviors in the psychoanalyst's office, but no subjects that cannot be spoken about.

The patient's rare freedom of speech in a sacrosanct space has provided a number of writers with the perfect frame for the fictional confession. The very first psychoanalytic novel, Italo Svevo's *Zeno's Conscience* (1923), opens with a preface written by our hero's analyst: "I am the doctor occasionally mentioned in this story, in unflattering terms. Anyone familiar with psychoanalysis knows how to assess the patient's obvious hostility toward me."[2] Holden Caulfield of Salinger's *Catcher in the Rye* (1951) unburdens himself to a hidden psychiatrist. In *Lolita* (1955), Nabokov, like Svevo, includes a "Foreword," written by one John Ray, Jr., Ph.D., who offers Humbert Humbert's story as a case study, and while acknowledging its author's literary gifts also excoriates him as "a shining example of moral leprosy."[3] Philip Roth's *Portnoy's Complaint* (1969) also includes a brief introduction in the form of a dictionary entry, which defines the term "Portnoy's complaint" and refers to the doctor who has coined the name for this particular "disorder," O. Spielvogel, author of an article, "The Puzzled Penis." After this little parody, the reader meets the garrulous narrator, who for 270 pages prattles, expounds, and fulminates at his analyst, who then famously utters a single line at the end of the book: "So (said the doctor) Now vee may perhaps to begin. Yes?"[4]

These books are essentially bracketed monologues. There is no back-and-forth, no dialogue, no world made between therapist and patient. They are not fictional versions of therapeutic practice but narratives that employ psychoanalysis as a literary device to unleash an uncensored first-person confession. The analyst or psychologist remains mostly *outside* the narrative. Svevo's doctor, as he himself points out, plays only a small role in the pages to come. He also proclaims that he is publishing the memoirs "in revenge" for his patient's untimely departure from treatment, and adds the vituperative quip "I hope he is displeased." Nabokov's condescension to American academics displays itself, not only in the text of his foreword, but in the addition of *Jr.* after his psychologist's name. In Salinger and Roth, the analyst is a remote, hidden being, not a *you* for the narrative *I*. Salinger's psychiatrist never speaks, and Roth's is never answered. They are objects, not interlocutors. The image of a distant, implacable doctor who nods, says "Ah" or "Vell," and only occasionally offers an abstruse comment, usually involving complexes or fixations, has become a stereotype, but it is one rooted in the history of psychoanalysis.

The analyst as a *neutral* figure has long struck me as a flawed idea, but then so does the notion of *objectivity* in the sciences. Is it possible to drain any person of subjectivity, whether she is an analyst or a researcher in a laboratory? Even in the lab, human beings must interpret results, and those interpretations cannot be expunged of the interpreter's thought, language, and culture. There is no third-person or bird's-eye view detached from a breathing bodily presence. Despite the fact that they are not free from human prejudice, the experiments of the hard sciences can be controlled and repeated over and over again. This is not true of the nuanced atmosphere of the analytic environment. From its early days, psychoanalysis has had to defend itself against the accusation that mutual suggestions passing between analyst and patient would contaminate the process and destroy its legitimacy. As George Makari points out in *Revolution in Mind,* "In the hopes of containing the analyst's subjectivity, Freud created the ideal of an analyst whose desires and biases were held back. But there was a hitch. The imagined analyst floating in evenly suspended attention must be without resistances, without blind spots."[5] In other words, the ideal demands that the analyst be superhuman, that his or her first-person reality be transformed into the disembodied third-person view heralded by science. It is not hard to see how this perfectly neutral floating personage might be employed for comic or satirical purposes, or how that same withdrawn and mostly silent figure might vanish from a story altogether.

Although some psychoanalytic theorists, such as Kernberg,[6] continue to champion an ideal neutrality, many have let it go for a more attainable posture, which recognizes that therapy is an intersubjective process, but not one between equals. The effective analyst holds back, maintains distance through her role, her professional attitude, her considered interventions. An analysis is necessarily hierarchical. The patient puts himself into the hands of an expert, but the substance of analysis is the patient and his inner life. The analyst's thoughts become apparent only in moments, and only in relation to the patient. The analyst's family, her joys, pains, and anxieties, remain hidden unless she chooses to share information for a particular purpose. If intimacy becomes truly two-sided, the treatment has failed. Alex Portnoy is free to rave, but his analyst isn't. In some fundamental way, the psychoanalyst must be a mystery, a mystery filled by the patient's loves and hates, emotions that can turn very quickly from one to the other. The most vulgar depictions of the psychoanalyst in our culture may be a form of splitting. The idol falls, and an evil demon takes his place. A truly human portrait of a working therapist, therefore, depends on a point of view that can accommodate ambivalence. It must also address the problem of the between, the charged space that is neither analyst nor analysand, but a mutual creation. This is not an easy territory to articulate. It is not subject and object, but two subjects who necessarily mingle. This is a human reality, which analysis magnifies, and which the history of the discipline has tried to find words for: transference and countertransference, Bion's container and contained, Winnicott's transitional object all touch on this bewildering area of the middle. Novels use many languages that slip and slide. Their diction moves from high to low and in and out of the voices of different characters. As a patient does in analysis, the writer searches for the words that will have a true meaning, not ultimately true, but emotionally true.

Works of fiction that depict the back and forth of psychoanalysis are quite rare. As Lisa Appignanesi pointed out in an article in *The Guardian*: "Shrinks in novels, if they appear at all, are largely devoid of that very inner life which is meant to be their trade; they often strut the fictional stage as grotesques."[7] She mentions the appearance of psychiatrists and analysts in a number of novelists' works and finds the portraits largely hostile until the appearance of a couple of recent novels: Hanif Kureishi's *Something to Tell You* and Salley Vickers's *The Other Side of You*. Although she mentions Virginia Woolf, Vladimir Nabokov, Doris Lessing, Iris Murdoch, Philip Roth, D. M. Thomas, Sylvia Plath, Simone de Beauvoir, and Erica Jong, she does not write about F. Scott Fitzgerald's *Tender Is the Night,* published in 1933. Fitzgerald's psychoanalyst, Dick Diver, is not a figure of ridicule, an empty sounding board, or an authority introducing a "case." Of all the novels I have read that treat analysis, Fitzgerald's is the one that most deeply enters the land of the between. The novelist's knowledge of psychiatry came mostly through the many physicians who treated his wife, Zelda, including Eugen Bleuler, who diagnosed her with schizophrenia. The novel's strengths do not come from a mastery of psychoanalytic theory, however, although the ideas of transference and countertransference clearly caught Fitzgerald's attention. Dr. Diver *marries* a rich patient, Nicole Warren, whose illness is central to the story, and the two are caught in an unsettling tug-of-war. Roles and personalities—doctor/husband/

Dick, patient/wife/Nicole——merge, dissolve, and disentangle themselves over the course of the book, and for a time, Dick and Nicole refer to themselves by a single name that suggests a borderless psychosis: *Dicole*.

For me, the most wrenching passage in the book, however, takes place between Diver and another patient in the Swiss clinic where he works. This nameless woman is described as "particularly his patient." She is an American painter who suffers from an agonizing skin affliction, which has been "unsatisfactorily catalogued as nervous eczema."

> Yet in the awful majesty of her pain he went out to her unreservedly, almost sexually. He wanted to gather her up in his arms, as he had so often done with Nicole, and cherish even her mistakes, so deeply were they part of her. The orange light through the drawn blind, the sarcophagus of her figure on the bed, the spot of face, the voice searching the vacuity of her illness and finding only remote abstractions.
>
> As he arose the tears fled lava-like into her bandages.
>
> "That is for something," she whispered. "Something must come out of it."
>
> He stooped and kissed her forehead.
>
> "We must all try to be good," he said.[8]

The goodness is all Fitzgerald. Throughout his work, there are repeated strains of longing for the moral verities of his Midwestern childhood, a paradise of lost goodness that bears little resemblance to the founding Oedipal myth of Sigmund Freud. But Fitzgerald's description of Diver's inner motion toward his patient that is "almost sexual," his aching compassion, and his understanding that a wide chasm lies between her speech and her suffering articulates truths about psychoanalytic work. Words are often circling the wordless, seeking an explanation for pain that will bring sense to what feels like nonsense. In art, as in psychoanalysis, what *feels right* must always have resonance, even when it is impossible to fully explain why a passage has taken on that strong emotional echo. It is no accident that the woman in Diver's care is a painter. Just before he feels the urge to take her into his arms, he meditates on her fate, one he feels can never include her work.

> The frontiers that artists must explore were not for her, ever. She was fine-spun, tubred — eventually she might find rest in some quiet mysticism. Exploration was for those with a measure of peasant blood, those with big thighs and thick ankles who take punishment as they took bread and salt, on every inch of flesh and spirit.[9]

While even a cursory survey of the lives of innumerable artists could easily serve as a disclaimer to this statement, its truth value is not what makes it compelling. Fitzgerald's creatures are generated from the dreamlike action that produces fiction out of lived experience. As is the case with many writers, he robbed his own life and transfigured it. Fitzgerald was adamantly opposed to his wife's ventures into the arts, to her writing, dancing, and painting, and one obvious way to read this passage is to turn it into a fictionalized explanation of his resistance: She wasn't strong enough. Fitzgerald may even have been thinking about Zelda when he wrote the paragraph. And yet, I believe that the scabrous, bandaged woman on the bed, whom Diver feels for so intensely, is also an image of himself, and by extension his creator. Dr. Diver's narrative wends its way toward alcoholism and failure. Fitzgerald's drinking was legendary. After *Tender Is the Night,* he never finished another novel. He wasn't strong either. And although he sometimes feared his femininity (he was homophobic), Fitzgerald, like Henry James, had an imagination as feminine as it was masculine. The miserable spectacle of artistic failure finds itself in the body of a woman too weak for work. Of course, if my little interpretation demonstrates anything, it is how quickly the reader of any literary text becomes like the analyst, and how much we writers of fiction are often unconscious of when we write.

In 1933, when Fitzgerald wrote his book with an analyst as hero, the image of the psychoanalyst had not hardened. The Second World War and its devastation lay ahead, and the field was still in the process of an often messy and fractured creativity. A serious, knowledgeable portrait of a postwar analyst can be found in Simone de Beauvoir's character Anne in *The Mandarins* (1956). She is given extended first-person narrations inside the novel, and her patients are all people who have been traumatized by the war in some way.

> The white-haired young woman was now sleeping without nightmares; she had joined the Communist Party, had taken lovers, too many lovers, and had been drinking immoderately. True, it wasn't a miracle of adjustment, but at least she was able to sleep. And I was happy that afternoon, because little Fernand had drawn a house with windows and doors; for the first time, no iron fence.[10]

De Beauvoir was well versed in psychoanalysis, and Anne's descriptions of her patients ring with authenticity. The passage above makes it clear that although she does not expect miracles, she takes pleasure in small successes. Her attitude is strictly professional. And yet, perhaps because the novel is a roman à clef, modeled closely on de Beauvoir's life with Sartre, their circle, and her love affair with the American writer Nelson Algren, Anne thinks about her patients too little and leaves them too easily. There is nothing in *The Mandarins* about the psychoanalytic encounter that comes close to the depth of feeling, the soaring moment of identification Diver feels when he stands beside his ailing patient.

When I began writing as Erik Davidsen, I was not thinking of literary precedents for his character. I thought of him as my imaginary brother, a man who worked at a job I can imagine having had in another life. What if I had grown up with a brother, I wondered, born to parents much like mine? What if, rather than four daughters, there had been one son and one daughter? And because I was writing the novel after my father's death or rather *out of* his death, a character like my father and grief like my grief, but also not like it, became part of the narrative. I transformed my experience, changed sex, wrote in a different voice, found a doctor self and several patient selves. Being Erik meant having a fictional practice. Writing the sessions between my narrator and the people he treats came from places in me both known and unknown.

I have been reading about psychoanalysis since I was in high school, but being Erik also meant immersing myself in psychiatric diagnoses, pharmacology, and innumerable neuroscience papers. I also read countless memoirs of mental illness, some good, some poor; interviewed several psychiatrists and analysts in New York City; joined a discussion group about neuropsychoanalysis led by a psychoanalyst; and began teaching weekly writing classes to psychiatric patients at Payne Whitney. That is the *known* part. Books, conversations, and perceptions enter us and become us.

The *unknown* part is far more diffuse and difficult to reach. I cut the passage I reproduced in this paper because it was a bit of contemporary sociology that did not advance the narrative, but also because I wanted the novel to take place mostly on the terrain of a man's inner life, a psychic landscape inhabited by both the living and the dead. Erik knows he is not neutral, knows that

psychotherapy happens in the land of Between, that wilderness
between you and me. Although the patient's narration must dominate, the analyst can steer, probe, wonder, and interpret, while
he or she maintains a thoughtful, sympathetic professional distance. A holding environment is not just a space for confession; it
is where truths can be discovered and narratives remade.

The sense of hearing was crucial to the novel. The analyst
listens, and as I wrote, I realized that Erik was extremely sensitive to sounds, not only to words spoken, but to the intonations
and cadences of the human voice, as well as to pauses and silences,
and that his auditory acumen extended to the myriad nonhuman
sounds of the city. His patients are part of his inner world, and he
thinks about them. They variously hurt, arouse, bore, move, and
gratify him. During sessions, he has sudden mental images, as-
sociates to words his patients use, and examines his own emotional response to what he hears and sees. His experience with
his patients is not exclusively intellectual. Unarticulated tensions
bristle in the air. Meanings are confused. Ghosts enter the room.
Erik loses his balance with a borderline patient, Ms. L., and seeks
advice from Magda, his training analyst. He breaks through with
another patient after a long period of stasis. I suspect that it is the
multifaceted reality of being a psychoanalyst that is so seldom
caught in fictional portraits. The analyst as purely cerebral or as
convenient deposit box leaves out the substance of psychoanalysis: the unconscious. Discussing the dynamics of transference in a
symposium talk called "Counter-Transference," D. W. Winnicott
comments on transference through a hypothetical statement, "You
remind me of my mother":

> In analysis the analyst will be given clues so that he can interpret
> not only the transference of feelings from mother to analyst but
> also the unconscious instinctual elements that underlie this, and
> the conflicts that are aroused, and the defenses that organize. In

this way the unconscious begins to have a conscious equivalent and to become a living process involving people, and to be a phenomenon that is acceptable to the patient.[11]

Obviously, writing fictional versions of psychoanalytic sessions is not the same as being in analysis. There is no *real other* in a novel, only imagined others. But writing novels is nevertheless a form of open listening to those imagined others, one that draws on memories, transmuted by both fantasies and fears. And it is an embodied act, not an intellectualization. Unconscious processes struggling toward articulation are at work in both psychoanalysis and art. It is impossible to fully understand how a book comes about, because the words are born elsewhere. In fact, when a work of fiction is going well, it seems to write itself. It is no longer a question of authorship, but midwifery—allowing a birth to take place.

Writing as Erik, I felt an underground music that determined the rhythms of the book's form. I knew I was writing a verbal fugue, point and counterpoint, themes chasing themes, and variations on them that kept returning: telling and not telling, listening and deafness, parents and children, the past in the present, one generation's sorrows living on in the generation that follows it. And so, I have come to understand that it wasn't only the parts of the novel that explicitly explored Erik's relations with his patients that were about psychoanalysis, but that the book as a whole was generated from the discipline's particular form of dialogue and search for a story that feels right and makes sense.

2010

CRITICAL NOTES ON THE VERBAL CLIMATE

EVERY POLITICAL MOMENT HAS A particular rhetorical climate. Language matters, not only because it expresses the dominant ideologies of a period, but because it creates, alters, and determines our perceptions of the world. We have been living for some time now in what I think of as bad linguistic weather, a verbal fog that is both contagious and damaging to political discourse in the United States. Manipulation of language for ideological purposes is nothing new. When it is effective, it inevitably creates an emotional response in the listener, a rush in the limbic system that calls on the deepest feelings we have as human beings. These appeals fall essentially into two categories: a call to empathy or a call to fear.

When I was a child, I remember listening to Martin Luther King and being moved to tears by his words. Although I didn't understand everything he was saying, I grasped what was essential. The minister was talking about human rights, arguing that freedom and justice for all were legal and moral imperatives. Racism and its shameful policies were a stain on the United States that had to be eradicated in order that all of its citizens might be free. As unsophisticated as I was as a nine- and ten-year-old, King's rhetoric was a door to my empathic imagination. What would it be like if I were not a white girl but a black girl subject to indignities and cruelty for no reason? I knew I would be furious. I would fight for my rights. My emotional identification created a primitive but genuine political position, one that has developed, but at the same time, not changed in any fundamental way.

The word *freedom,* as King used it, with its call for sympathy and imagination, has receded from public discourse. It has been replaced by its double, a word with connotations that inevitably evoke fear. George W. Bush has repeatedly used the word *freedom* in his speeches as a word to signal alarm. We are protecting our "freedom" from "the enemies of freedom," fighting the "evil-doers" who "hate freedom." It is well known by now that the rationale for the invasion of Iraq was bogus, that the administration continued to argue that Saddam Hussein was somehow mixed up with September 11 although this wasn't true. Applying the well-worn propaganda technique of repeating falsehoods over and over, the Bush administration succeeded in convincing significant numbers of people in the country that these prevarications were true. More interesting to me, however, is why this worked. It's much too easy to argue that Americans are just ignorant and will swallow anything. There are intellectuals, ideologues, and informed people on both sides.

When the president speaks to Americans about freedom, he is using a word that *sounds* good to just about everybody. The entry in *Webster's* under *freedom* is long, but the first definition reads: "state of being at liberty rather than in confinement or under physical restraint." Surely this is the most common sense of the word. I'm free, not in bondage, enslaved, or in jail. The word also resonates strongly with the founding principles of American government born of the Enlightenment, the freedom Immanuel Kant evoked in his 1784 essay, "What Is Enlightenment?"

"Enlightenment is the freedom to make public use of one's reason at every point." Before the philosopher arrives at this, however, he cautions that accepting such freedom is not a given.

Laziness and cowardice are the reasons why so great a portion of mankind, after nature has long since discharged them from external direction, nevertheless remains under lifelong tutelage, and why it is so easy for others to set themselves up as their guardians. It is so easy not to be of age. If I have a book which understands for me, a pastor who has a conscience for me, a physician who decides my diet, and so forth, I need not trouble myself. I need not think, if I can only pay—others will readily undertake this irksome work for me.[1]

This passage has lost none of its pertinence. Knee-jerk patriotism, calls to support the president simply because he is the president, literal interpretations of the Bible, are all versions of Kant's "tutelage," a state of mind that evokes feudalism, not democratic republics. And yet, we were all children once. Desires for parental protection, for letting someone else decide, for safety in a frightening world, aren't bizarre. They are familiar, and I believe that many Americans after September 11 sought comfort in the paternalism that George W. Bush seemed to represent.

But the word *freedom* also connotes a deep-rooted American myth—that Wild West, out-of-my-face, doin'-as-I-please, gun-toting, anarchic fantasy that has little in common with Kant's sober argument about maturity and the solitary work of an enlightened individual: independent thinking. The administration has been savvy enough to be unbothered by definitions of exactly what kind of freedom they're talking about or for whom, but they created an idea attractive to many: a swaggering Father Knows Best shod in a pair of cowboy boots wielding a smart weapon. Accompanied by simple slogans in which freedom was incessantly linked to protection from the monsters out there, this image packed a visceral punch. But beneath the administration's incantation for freedom lay wildly contradictory and irrational messages: we have brought freedom to Iraq, but Iraqis cannot walk in their own streets without fear, and it isn't only Islamic extremists and former Baathists they must look out for but strained and confused American soldiers who let bullets fly in fits of fatal, if understandable, paranoia. The United States trumpets freedom, but in the name of that freedom curtails civil liberties at home, defies the Geneva Conventions for prisoners of war, and through ugly legalisms, sets in motion a justification for torture already taking place. The freedom to worship or not worship as one pleases means bringing the precepts of one religion into every aspect of public life. Freedom means suppression: if the conclusions of scientific research on global warming are at odds with the reigning ideology in Washington, alter them. If evolution, a universally accepted scientific theory, offends biblical literalists, throw the weight of power and legitimacy behind its faux alternative: intelligent design. All of these outrages were reported in the newspapers, and yet the president won an election and remained reasonably popular until the floods came roaring into the Gulf.

Bush's endless repetition of the word *freedom* has swayed people who take comfort, not from an abstract political notion of protecting universal individual liberties under the law, but from a tribal mentality much older than the Enlightenment and the institutions in this country that came from it, one that reemerges when people sense danger from the Other, when the barbarians are howling at the gates. Fear is a powerful and mobilizing emotion, one that leaves little room for Kantian cogitations. No one in New York who saw the devastation wrought on September 11 would argue that those who planned and executed that horror aren't dangerous, but the Bush administration has manipulated the terror we all felt that day to ostracize many of the people it is supposed to represent. The Other in Republican rhetoric isn't limited to the radicals who murdered three thousand people in this city. Bush dehumanized them from the beginning. Over the years, the language of the Right has repeatedly exploited the real divisions in this country between Americans who live in a secular, urban world and those who live in a religious, often rural one. By casting liberals as effete and feminized (Schwarzenegger's "girlie men" as well as the absurd denigration of John Kerry's ability to speak French), unpatriotic (any criticism of administration policies), and godless (Republicans circulated a flyer during the last campaign claiming that liberals would ban the Bible), the *Other* has effectively become not only the rest of the world, but more than half the country.

We've been here many times before. A single example will suffice: the anti-immigrant movement of the 1840s and 50s. In April 1844, an election circular was printed in the *New York Daily Plebeian* which began like this: "Look at the hordes of Dutch and Irish thieves and vagabonds, roaming about our streets, picking up rags and bones, pilfering sugar and coffee along our wharves and slips, and whatever our native citizens happen to leave in their way." This little gem of fear-mongering goes on to mention "English and Scotch pickpockets and burglars," "Italian and French mountebanks," and last, but not least, "wandering Jews."[2] Although both comic and grotesque on hindsight, this text is a reminder of how, at every moment, arbitrary and entirely fictional thresholds are drawn among people for political gain. The Nativists or "Know-Nothings," as they were called, came from families who had all emigrated from *somewhere* at *some* point. The borders between *us* and *them* are continually sliding.

The need to divide is old, but the lines of those divisions keep changing. I'm not alone in feeling some amazement at the fact that a party that consistently supports giant corporations and tax relief for the very rich has been able to sell itself as populist. An entire book has been written on the subject: *What's the Matter with Kansas?*[3] Who are those people who voted against their own self-interest? Are they nuts or what? The Norwegian-American farming community where my father grew up and which I remember from my girlhood was decidedly left wing. Many of those second- and third-generation Norwegians suffered or were ruined entirely by the Depression. My grandparents lost much of their land to the bank when it foreclosed on their mortgage, and they had to stop farming altogether. The DFL, Democratic Farm Labor, was strong in Minnesota then, and my father, for whom the Depression remained a painful memory all his life and whose sympathies were inevitably with the downtrodden, was a wholehearted supporter of that coalition between rural and urban workers.

But there were prejudices in that world, too, a deep-seated anxiety about strangers, especially "city slickers," who were suspected of feeling superior to "ordinary folks." I remember conversations among some of the old farmers of my grandfather's generation that cast bankers, rich people, and most urbanites in a half-light of moral doubt. Their "fanciness" wasn't just foreign, it smacked of crookedness, of gambling, dancing, and all manner of corruption. But even when prejudice wasn't operating at full tilt, isolating difference was vital to that community's mode of being. The old people, all of Norwegian descent and all still Norwegian-speaking, habitually used qualifiers to signal that a person wasn't *of* them: "Sven, the Swede," they'd say, or "Fredrik, the Dane." It wasn't malicious, but it underscored the smallness of the world in which they lived. When my father was dying in a nursing home, he had frequent visitors, among them a Lutheran minister, who liked my father and was interested in his spiritual well-being. I was present at one of their conversations, during which the reverend mentioned a Bible study group he attended and brought up the name of one of its members. "A Methodist, you know," he declared as an aside, a hint of disapproval in his voice. I couldn't help smiling. Having spent twenty-seven of my fifty years in New York City with its inhabitants from all over the world, who speak dozens upon dozens of languages and subscribe to any number of religions, the distinction between Lutherans and Methodists struck me as rather fine.

The old people never lost their faith in the politics of the Left. They died believers, but many of their children and grandchildren, who inherited their prejudices, have moved to the Right. Playing on the age-old fear of malignant outsiders and foreigners, both those residing on American soil and elsewhere, has become the exclusive property of the Republican Party, and I understand how it happened. Egalitarian, anti-intellectual, paranoid feelings have long been tapped in this country; only the objects of those emotions change. "Evildoers," "enemies of freedom," and the exhortation that "If you're not with us, you're with the terrorists" are forms of political speech that make dialogue impossible. There is no legitimate response to such speech because anyone who counters with another thought has already been lumped with an inhuman enemy. In psychiatric patients, absolute polarities like those the president habitually makes are regarded as pathological, a form of dichotomous thinking often seen in patients with borderline personality disorder. The ill person is unable to tolerate ambiguity and insists on viewing the people in his life through an "all good" or an "all bad" lens. George W. Bush and his cohorts have been masters of angel/devil discourse, employing a language that gives no room for dialogue and necessarily distorts reality, which unfortunately is usually murky. This kind of speech that doesn't recognize an interlocutor, a real human other, is speech without empathy, and it is startlingly similar to the rhetoric of the Muslim radicals who spew venom at the West and "the enemies of Islam." Had the men who boarded those planes on September 11 been able to imagine their victims as people like themselves, they wouldn't have been able to complete their mission.

No doubt there is something all too human about this phenomenon of splitting. The need for simple juxtapositions of good and evil, heroes and villains, is ubiquitous. It is the stuff of most Hollywood movies and many popular books. Nuance is discarded for easy clarity. It is certainly possible that George W. Bush actually views the world in these black-and-white terms, that his mind is as blunt and unrefined as his impromptu sentences. His insistence on "loyalty" from those who work for him may be an indication of an "all for" or "all against" way of thinking. I don't know. I do know that a hurricane destroyed at least for a short time the seductiveness of the president's rhetorical polarities. Nature is amoral, after all, and its ravages are without guilt. In a vain attempt to keep the country's collective eyes on foreign devils, the president made a statement to the effect that were the terrorists to view the spectacular destruction, they would wish they had done it. I find this sad. I also find it sad that the images on television of drowned bodies and people stranded turned the media's attention to "poverty," as if it had suddenly been revealed overnight that huge numbers of people in this country, both white and black, are terribly poor, and that poor black people suffer the double burden of poverty and racism. It is never mentioned, of course, that race is yet another divisive category, another cultural fiction made real because it continually shapes our perception of the world around us. One need only ask where and how the arbitrary line between races is drawn to understand this clearly. Nevertheless, the public discourse shifted. It moved away from *us* and *them* to just *us*. The dead are our dead. The evacuees are ours, too. We had nobody to blame but ourselves and the indifferent government that supposedly represents us.

We will always feel more for those who belong to us, for our families, our neighbors, our fellow citizens. No one can completely escape tribal sentiments. As a resident of New York City, I was more affected by September 11 than by Hurricane Katrina. That said, I resist the idea of turning my private emotional attachments into public policy, because I don't want others to do the same. Any discourse that demonizes other people, near or far, is a betrayal of the idea of freedom. In a free society, political liberties belong to everyone, and when curbed are lost to everyone. In a free society, nobody *owns* the truth. It is strange to articulate the obvious, to feel that it's necessary to argue for principles long enshrined in our political system, but we have strayed from our Enlightenment heritage in these last years, not for the first time, it is true, but I am convinced that we must reexamine what we are saying, must begin to choose our public words judiciously and imaginatively. If we don't, we are in danger of going blind in the lowering fog of New Speak that has enveloped us.

2005

THREE EMOTIONAL STORIES

IN A 1995 ESSAY ON memory, "Yonder," I wrote the following sentence: "Writing fiction is like remembering what never happened."[1] It seemed to me fifteen years ago, and still seems to me today, that the mental activity we call memory and what we call the imagination partake of the same mental processes. They are both bound up with emotion and, when conscious, they often take the form of stories. Emotion, memory, imagination, story— all vital to our subjective mental landscapes, central to literature and psychoanalysis and, much more recently, hot topics in the neurosciences.

Ever since Plato banned poets from his Republic, philosophers have debated the role of imagination and its link to memory. Traditionally, imagination referred to the mental pictures we conjure in our minds, as opposed to direct perception. For thinkers as diverse as Aristotle, Descartes, Kant, and Hegel, the imagination occupied a middle zone between the bodily senses and intellect. Augustine connected imagination to both emotion and will. The will directs internal vision toward memories, but it also transforms and recombines them to create something new. "My memory," he writes in the *Confessions,* "also contains my feelings, not in the same way as they are present to the mind when it experiences them, but in a quite different way that is in keeping with the special powers of the memory." The emotions are all there, Augustine tells us—desire, joy, fear, and sorrow—and they can all be called to mind, but "if we had to experience sorrow or fear every time that we mentioned these emotions, no one would be willing to speak of them. Yet we could not speak of them at all unless we could find in our memory not only the sounds of their names, which we retain as images imprinted on the memory by the senses of the body, but also the idea of the emotions themselves."[2]

Surely, Augustine's thoughts remain cogent: remembering is not the same as perceiving. We remember what we have perceived, although we need ideas or concepts and names, *language,* to recognize and organize the material we have brought to mind. The seventeenth-century Italian philosopher and historian Giambattista Vico regarded memory and imagination as part of the same faculty rooted in sense perceptions. The imagination, he wrote, is "expanded or compounded memory," and memory, sensation, and imagination are skills of the body: "It is true," he insisted, "that these faculties appertain to the mind, but they have their roots in the body and draw their strength from it."[3]

Vico's comment is startlingly like the phenomenology of the twentieth-century French philosopher Maurice Merleau-Ponty (1908–1961), who understood imagination as an embodied reality, dependent on sensory perceptions, but which nevertheless allows us entrance into possible, even fictive spaces, *l'espace potentielle,* "potential space." D. W. Winnicott used the same term in relation to his thoughts on play and culture. Unlike other animals, human beings are able to inhabit fictional worlds, to turn away from the phenomenal present and imagine ourselves elsewhere. Rats, even sea snails, remember, but they don't actively recollect themselves as characters in the past or hurl themselves into imaginary futures.

How do we conceive of the imagination now? From Galen in the second century to Descartes and his pineal gland where he located *phantasie* or the imagination in the seventeenth, to phrenology in the nineteenth and Freud's abandoned *Project* near the dawn of the twentieth, thinkers have sought the anatomical sites of mental functions. We have not solved the mystery of the mind's eye, or what is now framed as a brain/mind problem. Terms such as *neural representations, correlates,* and *substrates for psychological phenomena* do not close the explanatory gap; they reveal it. There is a vast literature on this, and the debates are ferocious. A solution does not seem imminent. Suffice it to say that our inner subjective experience of mental images, thoughts, memories, and fantasies bears no resemblance to the objective realities of brain regions, synaptic connections, neurochemicals, and hormones, however closely they are connected.

I am not going to solve the psyche/soma problem here, but I can put some pressure on that old sentence of mine: *Writing fiction is like remembering what never happened,* or to rephrase it: *How are remembering and imagining the same and how are they different?*

The novelist, the psychoanalyst, and the neuroscientist inevitably regard memory and imagination from different perspectives. For the novelist, the story does all the work. When I am writing fiction, I am concerned with what *feels* right and *feels* wrong. I see images in my mind as I work, just as I do when I remember. Often I use landscapes, rooms, and streets that actually exist as backdrops for the actions of my fictional characters. I am directed by the story, by the creation of a narrative that resonates for me as *emotionally,* rather than literally, true. The novel develops an internal logic of its own, guided by my feelings.

For the analyst, a patient's personal memories are crucial, but so are fantasies and dreams. They exist within the dialogical atmosphere of the analytic room and the abstract conceptual framework the psychoanalyst brings to his work. When listening to a patient's memory, a psychoanalyst would keep in mind Freud's idea of *Nachträglichkeit,* what James Strachey translated as "deferred action." The adult patient may have memories from when he was five, but those memories have been reconfigured over time. The analyst would be alert to repetitive themes and defenses in his patient's speech, but also voice cadences, hesitations, and, if his patient is looking at him, the motions and gestures of a body. What is created between analyst and patient is not necessarily a story that represents historical fact, but one that reconstructs a past into a narrative that makes sense of troubling emotions and neuroses. For patient and doctor, as for the novelist, the narrative must also be felt; it must resonate bodily as emotionally true.

The neuroscientist is trained to conceive of subjective memory and creative acts through objective categories, which she hopes will unveil the neurobiological realities of a self that both remembers and imagines. Following Endel Tulving and others, she will probably divide memory into three categories: 1) episodic memories, conscious personal recollections that can be localized to a specific place and time; 2) semantic memories, impersonal recall of information—cats have fur, Kierkegaard wrote under pseudonyms—and 3) procedural memories, unconscious learned abilities—riding a bike, reaching for a glass, typing.[4] As a memory researcher, she would be aware of Joseph LeDoux's work on the enduring synaptic connections formed by emotion in memory, fear in particular,[5] and she would know that memories are not only consolidated in our brains, they are reconsolidated. Although it is unlikely that our neuroscientist has read Freud carefully, she would unwittingly agree with him that there is no original "true" memory; autobiographical memories are subject to change. Finally, theoretically, at least, her subjective feelings are irrelevant to her work.

In these three practices, we find the two modes of human

thought which William James in his essay "Brute and Human Intellect" called narrative thinking and reasoning.[6] Jerome Bruner, using a philosophical term, has called them two natural kinds, that is, essentially different.[7] Novelists think in stories. Analysts use both narrative thought and the categorical thinking of reasoning. Scientists may employ a case history as an illustration, but their work proceeds without story. Reasoning is sequential but not dependent on a representation of time. Narrative is embedded in the temporal. Unlike the flux that characterizes narrative, scientific categories are static. Memory and imagination have to be approached from a third-person perspective and placed in a broader taxonomy. In the reasoning mode, definitions become all-important, and therefore a frequent battleground. First-person experience is vital to narrative because there is always an agent whose subjectivity and intentionality are part of the story's movement, narrated from one perspective or another. In science the subject is nameless and normative.

What is the third-person point of view? Scientists cannot jump out of themselves and become God any more than the rest of us can. Through a largely unexamined agreement about what Thomas Kuhn in *The Structure of Scientific Revolutions* calls a paradigm—the bottom line of accepted theory, which changes over time, often in great convulsions—and an explicit consensus about methodology, scientists aim to avoid subjective bias.[8] Although Freud never used the word *neutral* himself, the idea of the neutral analyst is a direct importation from the natural sciences. The omniscient narrator in some novels plays this role as he looks down from on high at his characters and their follies, but we readers know that clever as he may be, Henry Fielding's narrator in *Tom Jones* is not God. Indeed, the cool "I-less" voice of nearly all academic writing adopts the pose of the third person. There is an author or authors, but they vanish as persons from the text. Still, as Kuhn argues in his book, there is no such thing as perceptual neutrality. The histories of science, psychoanalysis, and, of course, the novel, make this abundantly clear. This truth does not impede either discovery or innovation; it merely qualifies epistemology.

As Augustine points out, if we didn't have names and ideas for things, we couldn't speak of them at all. Both the reasoning and narrative modes of thought create linguistic representations. They exist on what the linguist Emile Benveniste refers to as a pronominal axis of discourse.[9] The *I* implies a *you,* even if that *I* is just listening to one's inner self. The language wars are as fierce as the brain/mind wars. Is there a universal grammar? as Noam Chomsky argued. Wasn't Wittgenstein right that there is no such thing as a private language? How is language acquired, and exactly what does it have to do with our memories and imaginations? There is no consensus. I am sympathetic to A. R. Luria's position that the advent of language *reorders* the mental landscape.[10] I do not subscribe to the postmodern notion that *it is* the mental landscape. Nevertheless, whatever innate abilities we may have to learn it, language, which is both outside and inside the subject, plays a crucial role in our reflective self-consciousness, in how we become creatures of not only "I remember," but "What if . . . ?"

We codify perceptual experiences in conscious memory through both placement—where and when it happened—and interpretation, what it means in the larger context of my life. In our autobiographical memories, as in a mirror, we become others to ourselves. Even if we don't see ourselves in the third person, we have projected the self elsewhere in time. As Merleau-Ponty notes in *The Phenomenology of Perception*: "Between the self which analyzes perception and the self which perceives, there is always a distance."[11] There is a difference, he argues, using Hegel's distinction, between the "in itself" and the "for itself" (*für sich*).[12] When I actively recall something from my past, what Augustine called "will" is involved. This is exactly how Aristotle distinguished human from animal memory. Only we people *will* ourselves backward in time.

And the episodic memories we recall have mostly been turned into stories. If narrative is, as Paul Ricoeur argues in *Time and Narrative,* a "grasping together" of various temporal actions or episodes[13] in both life and fiction into a whole that has meaning, I believe that meaning is crucially grounded in emotion. It makes sense that narrative, a ubiquitous form of human thought, would, mimicking memory itself, focus on the meaningful and leave out the meaningless. What I am indifferent to, I mostly forget. The stories of memory and fiction are also made by absences— all the material that is left out.

As early as 1895, the psychologists Alfred Binet and Victor Henri tested children's memories for lists of unrelated words as opposed to meaningful paragraphs.[14] The children remembered the meaningful passages far better, but they reported them back to their examiners in their own words. They retained, to borrow a term from the Russian formalists, the *fabula*. Cinderella can be told in many different ways, and the details may vary, but the *fabula,* the bones of the story, remain the same. The narrative mode contextualizes the meaning or valence inherent in every emotion. It pulls together and makes sense of disparate sensory and affective elements.

Augustine's insight that emotion dims in memory, however, is overwhelmingly true of our episodic memories. The cooling of the emotions that belongs to such recollections is built into the nature of this kind of memory, because it is quickly turned into narrative. The raw affective material of memories is restructured and then told as stories from a remove. Much, if not all, of this restructuring takes place unconsciously. When I remember, for example, that in 1982 I was hospitalized for eight days with an excruciating migraine that had lasted for many months, I do not reexperience either my pain or my emotional distress, although the pictures in my mind are colored gray for sadness.

I no longer remember what happened every day in the hospital, only a few highlights—a nurse who seemed to believe migraineurs were either neurotics or malingerers, the interns who asked me over and over who the president was, and my doctor who seemed exasperated that I didn't get well. (All of their facial features are now visually dim.) I remember lying in the hospital bed, but I no longer see the room clearly. Still, I have a mental image that probably combines several hospital rooms I've visited or seen in the movies. We deposit memorable emotional events into a visual setting that makes sense, but what we see in our minds may bear little resemblance to what actually was. What I've retained is the story and a few serviceable mental pictures, but much is missing from that verbal account.

The fact that I used that hospital stay in my first novel, *The Blindfold,* further complicates matters because I turned an episode from my life into fiction, an episode I had already, no doubt, fictionalized in memory. Both the memory story and the novel were created unconsciously. Furthermore, I don't truly recall my twenty-seven-year-old self. Too much time has intervened. I can easily shift the scene and see myself in the third person, a wan, blond young woman pumped full of Thorazine, staring at the ceiling. The hospital chapter of *The Blindfold* was turned into a movie, *La Chambre des Magiciennes,* by the French filmmaker Claude Miller. My experiences in Mount Sinai in 1982 generated three stories with the same *fabula*: my own narrative memory of an actual event, my character's story in the novel based on that event, and my character's story in the film, embodied by the actress Anne Brochet. Each one is different, and each one is constructed as a narrative, which partakes of the imaginary, the fictionalizing processes inherent to memories that are reflectively self-conscious.

Neuroscience research on the imagination is limited. However, a 2007 paper on patients with bilateral hippocampal lesions found they suffered from impaired imaginations as well as memory. A paper that same year by the same team, D. Hassabis et al., was published in *The Journal of Neuroscience*. This paper, "Using Imagination to Understand the Neural Basis of Episodic Memory," based on fMRI scans, concludes, ". . . we have demonstrated that a distributed brain network, including the hippocampus, is recruited during both episodic memory recall and the visualization of fictitious experiences."[15] The activated part of the brain is a large cortical network, which has been implicated in "high level" cognitive functions, not only episodic memory, but future thinking, spatial navigation, theory of mind, and the default network. The participants were given three tasks that fell under the rubrics recall, re-create, and imagine. Notably, they were asked to keep all of these scenarios emotionally neutral.

The authors divided episodic memory into what they call "conceptual components," among them a sense of subjective time, narrative structure, and self-processing. Although I enthusiastically endorse such research and believe episodic memory and imagination are fundamentally connected, I would like to focus on just one of their components: self-processing. The authors hypothesize that there will be less self-processing in imaginary other-oriented scenarios than in autobiographical ones, a reasonable thought until one asks oneself exactly what self-processing is. How exactly does an imaginary story I am generating about you, or her or him, not involve me? Aren't all of these narratives—recalled, re-created, or imagined—related to my self, a part of my subjective experience? Furthermore, aren't these narratives represented, at least in part, in language, and so necessarily located on the axis of discourse? There is no pronominal *I* without a *you*. When I think of you, are you not a part of me? What is being processed here? Shouldn't neuroscience look to other disciplines to refine this vague idea: self-processing? Isn't phenomenology's concept of an embodied self useful in this regard? And what about psychoanalytic theory, with its internal objects, transference, and countertransference? Even with a cooling effect, can episodic memory and imagination really be entirely divorced from emotion?

In a 2009 comprehensive review of neuroimaging studies on self-processing versus other-processing in the *Psychological Review*, Dorothée Legrand and Perrine Ruby state: "The authors of the aforementioned studies . . . hypothesized that a given cerebral substrate should be systematically more activated for the self than for the nonself. Our review demonstrates that the cerebral network they identified does not exhibit such a functional profile."[16] I politely suggest that many of the researchers reviewed by Legrand and Ruby have lost themselves in the philosophical wilderness of selfhood. At the explicit representational level of episodic and imaginative narration, a distinction between self- and other-processing strikes me as entirely artificial.

In a fascinating 2011 paper "Bodily Self: An Implicit Knowledge of What Is Explicitly Unknown," Frassinetti, Ferri, Maini, and Gallese conducted two experiments to untangle the following question: "We directly compared implicit and explicit knowledge of bodily self to test the hypothesis that bodily self-advantage, i.e., facilitation in discriminating self compared to other people's body effectors, is the expression of an implicit body-knowledge."[17] In the first experiment, subjects were confronted with three photographs, one on top of the other, of their own and other people's hands and feet, as well as objects belonging to them or others—mobile phones and shoes. They were asked to match the lower or upper image to the center "target" photograph. In this task a distinct self-advantage showed itself. In other words, people were considerably better at matching their own body parts than matching other people's. No such advantage was present with the objects. In the second experiment, there was no target image, just an empty white box in the center. This time, the subject was asked which of the two remaining images was his or her *own* hand, foot, mobile phone, or shoe. Not only was there no self-advantage in this case; there was a self-disadvantage in recognizing one's own body parts, one that was not seen in the recognition of one's own objects.

The hypothesis is that an unconscious motor representation of our bodies is at work in the first task, while what the authors call "body identity" must be summoned for the explicit task. Body identity (or what Shaun Gallagher in *How the Body Shapes the Mind* calls *body image*) is a conscious, not an unconscious idea.[18] It is the self perceived as an other. In the explicit task, the response is not automatic; the person has to think about it; and thinking often involves a linguistic construction as well as a visual one. Is that *my* foot? Is it someone else's? The authors' conclusion is worth quoting, "Taken together, our results show for the first time that the representation of our body-effectors is not only different from the way we represent inanimate objects, but—more importantly—it is accessible in a least two different ways: one way is implicit, while the other is detached, third-person like."[19] This unconscious/ conscious distinction is paramount to understanding what neuro-imagers call "self-processing."

William James said that all personal memories have a "warmth and intimacy," a quality of one's own.[20] To use the Latin word for selfhood or identity, my memories have *ipseity*. But so do my fantasies, the vicarious experiences I have while reading, my thoughts about others, my feelings about my fictional characters, and my dreams. James's "warmth and intimacy," that sense of ownership, is not emotionally neutral. And, as Freud stressed in *The Interpretation of Dreams,* however irrational or bizarre our dream plots may be, the emotions we feel are not fictional. He quotes the dream researcher Stricker: "If I am afraid of robbers in a dream, the robbers, it is true, are imaginary—but the fear is real."[21]

While Proust's tea-soaked bit of cake has become a facile reference for just about everybody, what is interesting is not that the petite madeleine opens the narrator to memories of his childhood, but rather that at first, the taste produces *only feeling.* "... this new sensation having had on me the effect which love has of filling me with a precious essence; or rather this precious essence was not in me, it was me." It is only after the swell of high feeling has passed that Proust's narrator asks himself this: "What did it mean?"[22] That meaning, explored in the seven-volume first-person narrative of *Remembrance of Things Past,* lies in the fluctuations of subjective experience—of an emotional self in space and time. First, the narrator perceives and feels. He is immersed in the prereflective consciousness of a sensual reality that is also somehow remembering. Only later does he reflect on it, and that reflection requires that he conceive of himself as an object to himself in the same way he conceives of others. Isn't it reasonable, then, that "self-processing" cannot be distinguished from "other-processing" at the explicit conscious level of storytelling?

The narrative self is the self in time. We are immersed in time, not clock time necessarily, although we adults refer to it, and certainly not the time of physics. We live in subjective time, the sequential time of our consciousness, and what happens before becomes the template for what we expect to happen later. Through repetition, past perceptions create future ones. In one of his 1925 lectures on phenomenological psychology, Edmund Husserl writes that "each . . . momentary perception is the nuclear phase of a continuity, a continuity of momentary gradated retentions on one side, and a horizon of what is coming on the other side: a horizon of protention, which is disclosed to be characterized as a constantly graded coming."[23] We are continually retaining and projecting, and the present always carries in it the thickness of before and after. Husserl, who was influenced by William James, argues that the experience of time, this perceptual stream is always pregiven in a first-person perspective. When he was five, my nephew Ty sat in the family car and made a startling discovery. Looking at the road behind him, he cried out, "That's the past!" Turning to the road ahead, he crowed, "That's the future!" The locus of that streaming reality of time and space, was of course, Ty himself.

We now know that a form of time, or rather, timing is also part of infancy. Psychoanalysis, attachment studies, and infant researchers, such as Daniel Stern, have been vital to our notation of what might be called the intersubjective music of early life, the preverbal melodies of the first human interactions. As John Bowlby postulated, these rhythms of attachment are crucial to affect regulation later in life. In an empirical study of adult-infant vocal interactions, *Rhythms of Dialogue in Infancy,* the authors proceed from a dyadic view of early communications. The nuanced analysis of the rhythmic dialectic between mother and child provides a foundation for a child's ongoing social and cognitive experiences by forming, as the authors put it, "temporal expectancies."[24] These bodily, emotional expectations form the ground for the axis of discourse and the narrative self. An infant's prereflective conscious perceptions are not yet *for herself* in an articulated story. Nevertheless, these deeply established corporeal metrics, the motor-sensory beats of self and other, merge with genetic temperament in the dynamic synaptic growth that accompanies early emotional learning. In his book *Affective Neuroscience,* Jaak Panksepp writes,

> From a psychological perspective, I would say that the main thing that develops [in a child's interactions with his world] in emotional development is the linking of internal affective

values to new life experiences. However, in addition to the epigenetic processes related to each individual's personal emotional experience leading to unique emotional habits and traits, there is also a spontaneous neurobiological unfolding of emotional and behavioral systems during childhood and adolescence.[25]

We are creatures of a subjective time founded in the wordless dialogues of infancy, which is further developed in language and its natural consequence, story. As important as the narrative self is, however, I am in complete concordance with Dan Zahavi, who writes in his book *Subjectivity and Selfhood,* "Is it legitimate to reduce our selfhood to that which can be narrated?" He goes on to add, "The storyteller will inevitably impose an order on the life events that they did not possess while they were lived."[26] Proust's "precious essence," which he claims is himself, resonates with Panksepp's revision of Descartes' famous *cogito ergo sum* to *I feel therefore I am.* In "The Neural Nature of the Core SELF," Panksepp locates his core SELF in the brain stem: ". . . the ability to experience raw affect," he argues, "may be an essential antecedent to foresight, planning, and thereby willful intentionality."[27] I add narrative to that list. Antonio Damasio, in his book *Self Comes to Mind,* discusses his protoself that produces "primordial feelings" reflecting the body's homeostatic reality, "along the scale that ranges from pleasure to pain, and they originate at the level of the brain stem rather than the cerebral cortex. All feelings of emotion," he continues, "are complex musical variations on primordial feelings."[28]

In *Instincts and Their Vicissitudes* (1915) Freud proposed his own homeostatic model of primitive selfness in an organism that can discriminate between outside and inside through "the efficacy of its muscular activity." For Freud, the regulation of internal drives and external stimuli are the origin of all feelings. "Even the most highly evolved mental apparatus," he writes, "is automatically regulated by feelings belonging to the pleasure pain series."[29] It is out of this core feeling self that a reflectively conscious, remembering, imagining narrative self develops.

Shaun Gallagher also posits a minimal self or a "primary embodied self" already present in the motor-sensory corporeal reality of an organism that is aware of its own boundaries.[30] Infant studies on imitation and deferred imitation give credence to the idea that a newborn has a greater awareness of his separateness from others and the environment than was thought earlier.[31] Exactly how memory develops in babies is controversial. What effects do an immature hippocampus and forebrain and incomplete myelination have on that development? What exactly do implicit and explicit memory mean in a preverbal infant? What roles do imitation, mirroring, and language play? How do we frame the reality of infant consciousness? How is it related to a minimal or core self? When does *in itself* become *for itself*? What is the neurophysiology of time perception and how does it develop? All of these questions remain unanswered.

Narratives from the Crib, edited by Katherine Nelson, focuses on the monologues of Emily Oster taped before she went to sleep between the ages of twenty-one and thirty-six months. These soliloquies are remarkable illustrations of what Vygotsky called private speech,[32] the stage before inner speech takes over. We witness the chattering play-by-play announcer who has not yet gone underground. Here is a monologue from when Emily was twenty-one months old. She is talking to her doll. I have truncated it slightly.

Baby no in night
Cause baby crying
Baby no eat supper in in in this
No eat broccoli no

So my baby have dinner
Then baby get sick
Baby eat no dinner . . .
Broccoli carrots cause rice
Emmy eat no dinner
Broccoli soup cause
No baby sleeping
Baby sleeping all night[35]

There are no fixed tenses here that situate past, present, and future, no pronominal "I." There is a third-person baby and a third-person Emmy, characters that mingle in what might be called a protonarrative. Emily verbally represents herself as an agent to herself, and describes a series of actions in order to make sense of her emotion: the memory of not feeling well, not eating, and not being able to sleep. The third-person "Emmy" precedes the first-person "I" because reflective self-consciousness, "for-itself" reality, emerges from seeing herself as others see her, those vital others who recognize Emmy as an agent and actor in the world. In a later monologue, at twenty-eight months, the little girl imagines herself in a fictional place, the future, to master her anxiety about what lies ahead. "We are gonna at at the ocean/ocean is a little far away . . . /I think it is a couple of blocks away."[34] After an associative stream that includes a fridge submerged in water and a river, the child imagines sharks biting her. The fantasy is driven by emotion, but her speech allows the flowering of creative speculation while she is still safely in her crib, away from the sharks in her mind. Emily's monologues are heavily analyzed in the book, but two points go unmentioned, perhaps because they are too obvious: having a narrator, external and voiced or internal and silent, is a way of keeping company with one's self. In language, the self is always touched by otherness, if only because it is represented.

Some memories have no narrator and no time except the present. In 1961, when my cousin Nette was one year old, she traveled to Africa with her parents and sister. Her father, my uncle, was a doctor who practiced in Bambuli in what was then Tanganyika. Nette learned Swahili, a language she later forgot. When she was three, she returned home to Norway with her family. Nette retained no conscious memories of Africa, but in 2007, she and her husband Mads visited Tanzania. As soon as she set foot in Bambuli, she was overwhelmed by sensations of familiarity. The smells, the colors, the sounds all contributed to a heady feeling that she had come home. One afternoon, Nette and Mads met some schoolgirls on the road, and although the two groups shared no common language, they communicated with smiles, laughter, and gestures. Mads suggested Nette hum a melody she remembered from childhood, a song the family had once sung together, the words to which had disappeared. When the girls heard the tune, they began to sing and, to her own amazement, Nette joined them. One after another, the lost Swahili lyrics returned to her, verse after verse, and Nette sang loudly and joyfully. In that moment of exuberant recall, forty-one years seemed to collapse. The forty-four-year-old woman and the small child met.

This memory is not episodic and, although I have told it as a story, the recovery of the lyrics and the flood of joy my cousin experienced is not a narrative, but a form of involuntary memory. The nineteenth-century neurologist John Hughlings Jackson called this kind of repetitive, learned knowledge *automatisms*. The automatism is proprioceptive, related to my bodily orientation in space, what Merleau-Ponty called a *body schema,* and it engages my motor-sensory capacities. The perceptual context—visual, auditory, and olfactory—acted as cues, and the once-learned but lost Swahili words came back automatically. Nette's eruption of memory accompanied by a flood of joy has meaning *in itself.* Affect marks experience with *valence,* positive or negative, part of the pleasure-pain series. It is purely phenomenal and prereflective until we ask ourselves: What did it mean?

By far the most dramatic form of bodily prereflective, involuntary memory is the flashback. After a car accident, I had flashbacks four nights in a row that shocked me out of my sleep. Rigid, repetitious, horrifying, this memory was a visuo-motor-sensory reexperiencing of the crash. As the psychoanalysts Françoise Davoine and Jean-Max Gaudillière argue in their book *History Beyond Trauma,* this form of traumatic memory is outside time and language.[35] It is not in the past. It is the kind of memory Augustine said nobody would *want* to have. In a 1993 paper, the neurobiologists van der Kolk and Saporta make the same argument. "These experiences may then be encoded on a sensorimotor level without proper localization in space and time. They therefore cannot be easily translated into symbolic language necessary for linguistic retrieval."[36] Translation into words means location in space and time; it also means distancing and, perhaps ironically, greater mutability in memory. This very mutability, however, serves the cooling and creative aspects of narration, whether in memory or in fiction.

In *Beyond the Pleasure Principle,* Freud cites Kant, for whom "time and space are 'necessary forms of thought,'" and then goes on to say, "We have learnt that unconscious mental processes are in themselves 'timeless.' This means in the first place that they are not ordered temporally, that time does not change them in any way and that the idea of time cannot be applied to them."[37] Unlike secondary process, what Freud called primary process does not distinguish past, present, and future. We glimpse this form of archaic thought in dreams, which are more concrete, emotional, and associative than waking thought, and in Emily's early monologues in which subjective time is not yet fully codified in language.

That creativity is mostly unconscious is hardly surprising. Psychoanalysis has long known that we are strangers to ourselves, and the idea of unconscious perception has been with us at least since Leibniz in the seventeenth century. All creativity in both modes of thought—reasoning and narrative—can be traced to this timeless dimension of human experience or, I would say, a dimension with motor-sensory timing, but not self-reflective time. In a letter to Jacques Hadamard, Albert Einstein wrote that neither language nor "any other kinds of signs which can be communicated to others" were important features of his thought. His work, he said, was the result of "associative play," was "visual and motor" in character, and had an "emotional basis."[38] In 1915, Henri Poincaré, the great mathematician, pointed to the unconscious origins of his own work:

> The subliminal self plays an important role in mathematical creation . . . we have seen that mathematical work is not simply mechanical, that it could not be done by a machine, however perfect. It is not merely a question of applying rules, of making the most combinations possible according to fixed laws. The combinations so obtained would be exceedingly numerous, useless and cumbersome.[39]

Every once in a while a formula, a poem, an essay, a novel bursts forth as in a waking dream. The poet Czeslaw Milosz once said: "Frankly all my life I have been in the power of a daimonion, and how the poems dictated by him came into being, I do not quite understand."[40] William Blake said his poem "Milton" "was written from immediate dictation . . . without premeditation and sometimes against my will."[41] Nietzsche described thoughts that came to him like bolts of lightning. "I never had any choice about it."[42] The last pages of my novel *The Sorrows of an American* were written in a trance. They seemed to write themselves. Such revelations may well be based on years of laborious living, reading, learning, and cogitating, but they come as revelations nevertheless.

A retreat to nineteenth-century science is needed to frame this creative phenomenon. F. W. H. Myers was a renowned psychical researcher and a friend of William James, who is now mostly forgotten. His magnum opus was called *Human Personality and Its Survival of Bodily Death*,[43] a title which no doubt hastened his oblivion. Still, he was a sophisticated thinker who applied the idea of automatisms to creativity. Unlike Jackson's habitual automatisms or the pathological dissociations of hysteria studied by Pierre Janet or Freud's idea of sublimation, Myers argued that subliminally generated material could suddenly find its way into consciousness, and that this eruption was not necessarily the product of hysteria, neurosis, or any other mental illness.

The definition of creativity in neuroscience research I have stumbled over again and again is: "the production of something novel and useful within a given social context."[44] Useful? Was Emily Dickinson's work considered useful? Within her given social context, her radical, blazingly innovative poems had no place. Are they useful now? This research definition must be creativity understood in the corporate terms of late capitalism. Another component of creativity featured in these studies is divergent thinking, or DT. In one study, subjects' brains were scanned as they "produced multiple solutions to target problems." The more solutions, the more creativity, but this is obtuse, as Poincaré pointed out so succinctly. We are not machines or computers but embodied beings guided by a vast unconscious and felt emotions.

I have often asked myself, Why tell one fictional story and not another? Theoretically, a novelist can write about anything, but she doesn't. It is as if the *fabula* is already there waiting and must be laboriously unearthed or suddenly unleashed from memory.

That process is not exclusively the result of so-called higher cognition; it not purely cognitive or linguistic. When I write, I see images in my mind, and I feel the rhythms of my sentences, embodied temporal expectancies, and I am guided by gut feelings of rightness and wrongness, feelings not unlike what has happened to me in psychotherapy as a patient. After my analyst's interpretation, I have felt a jolt of recognition, which is never merely an intellectualization but always has a felt meaning: *Oh my God, that's true, and if it's true, I have to rewrite my story.*

Fictions are born of the same faculty that transmutes experience into the narratives we remember explicitly but which are formed unconsciously. Like episodic memories and dreams, fiction reinvents deeply emotional material into meaningful stories, even though in the novel, characters and plots aren't necessarily anchored in actual events. And we do not have to be Cartesian dualists to think of imagination as a bridge between a timeless core sensorimotor affective self and the fully self-conscious, reasoning and/or narrating linguistic cultural self, rooted in the subjective-intersubjective realities of time and space. Writing fiction, creating an imaginary world, is, it seems, rather like remembering what never happened.

2010

FREUD'S PLAYGROUND

WHEN I WAS IN MY adolescence, I used to think that in every relation between two people, there was also a third entity—an imaginary creature the players made between them—and that this invisible thing was so important, it deserved to be given a proper name, as if it were a new baby. The insight arrived, I believe, because I had begun to notice that two people were able to create both fairies and monsters between them, especially if love was involved. As I got older and read more, I realized that this zone between people had not gone unnoticed. It had been given different names and conceived of through various metaphors, but forms of one plus one make three or, better, one plus one make one out of two, were important aspects of the philosophical thinking I found most compelling. Questions about self and other have been central to psychoanalysis, but they also rage beyond its borders in analytical and continental philosophy, other disciplines in the humanities, in psychiatry, and, more recently, in the neurosciences. *Subjectivity, intersubjectivity, mirroring, dialogue,* and *theory of mind* are all terms directed at the problem of the between.

A couple of years ago, I reread one of Freud's papers on technique, *Remembering, Repeating, and Working Through* (1914), and found myself fascinated by the following famous passage:

> The main instrument, however, for curbing the patient's compulsion to repeat and for turning it into a motive for remembering lies in the handling of the transference. We render the compulsion harmless, and indeed useful, by giving it the right to assert itself in a definite field. We admit it into the transference as a playground in which it is allowed to expand in almost complete freedom and in which it is expected to display to us everything in the way of pathogenic instincts that is hidden in the patient's mind.

This "creates an intermediate region between illness and real life,"[1] a geographical metaphor—*the between* is a road to wellness and realism.

James Strachey translated *Tummelplatz* as "playground." It's a sound choice as it evokes children romping at play, but the German carries additional connotations of hurry and commotion among adults, not just children, as well as a figurative possibility—a hotbed of action. Elsewhere, Freud characterized the transference as a field of "struggle" or, more dramatically, as "a battlefield" between doctor and patient. Whether a site of play or bloodshed, whether inhabited by benign characters or frightening ones, this intermediate region is where analysis happens. Just as dreams speak in archaic but overdetermined ways that must be interpreted, the expressive and resistant character of the transference is a language of repetitive actions, driven by primal bodily needs and affects that have become relational patterns, reenactments of early loves and hates that the patient does not consciously remember or understand.

The analyst sees in the patient what Anna Freud called defensive styles, individual modes of being with others in the world.[2]

Our need for other people is an essential drive, and that need is of us—body and soul. In his *New Introductory Lectures on Psychoanalysis* (1932–33), Freud introduces drive, *Trieb* (instinct), theory by saying openly that it is "our mythology," and that drives are "magnificent in their indefiniteness." Nevertheless, he continues, human beings are in the grip of "the two great needs—hunger and love."[3] We know from *Civilization and Its Discontents* that he is quoting Schiller: "hunger and love are what moves the world."[4] Freud makes it plain that he is articulating a "biological psychology"— "the psychical accompaniments of biological processes."[5] Our own age of neurobiology, which has mythologies of its own, returns us to the question of these "psychical accompaniments." What are they? Freud was most interested in love, as am I. In *Affective Neuroscience* (1998), Jaak Panksepp writes, "It is now widely accepted that all mammals inherit psychobehavioral systems to mediate social bonding as well as various other social emotions, ranging from intense attraction to separation-induced despair."[6] Mammals do not stay alive by just satisfying their hunger for food. Like rats we have social and sexual drives—a pleasure principle—that animates us and makes us feel good or bad.

Although the emotional systems of our brains have much in common with rats, we are born into a world in which people speak to one another. We represent ourselves to ourselves in language, and this complicates matters considerably. It influences *how* and *whom* we love. Freud writes, "The relations of an instinct to its aim and object are also open to alterations; both can be exchanged for other ones . . . A certain kind of modification of the aim and change of the object, in which our social valuation is taken into account, is described by us as sublimation."[7] Rats don't sublimate. Freud's admittedly murky idea of sublimation is one of transformation—primal erotic instincts or drives are redirected into creative work, both intellectual and artistic. Speechless affective forces find symbolic realization in the ornaments of culture. Love can be reconfigured.

The repetitive style of the patient's relation to the analyst is not articulated, but it has an object, and the analyst may well find herself playing somebody else—mother, father, sister, brother—which is why from the very beginning transference love was riddled with problems of illusion and reality. In *Studies on Hysteria,* Freud attributes his patient's desire to kiss him to "a false connection," a case of mistaken identity. The woman's memories of the true object have vanished. But in his postscript to the Dora debacle (1905), Freud argues that along with simple substitutions, transference may also create a *sublimated* version of the old love object, which borrows some "real" quality from the analyst.[9] In *Remembering, Repeating and Working Through,* the ghost of Charcot rises when we are told that transference "represents an artificial illness," that is nevertheless "a piece of *real* experience" with the character of 'genuine love.' "[10] In a 1906 letter to Jung, however, Freud had stated the issue far more simply: psychoanalysis, he wrote, "is a cure effected by love."[11] But is it one-sided or two-sided?

Sándor Ferenczi first addressed the complexities of countertransference. His acknowledgement that psychoanalysis is "an intimate human practice," his experiments in mutual analysis, and his rebellion against the unnatural, indeed *artificial* pose of the analyst, have taken on greater and greater significance in contemporary psychoanalysis.[12] Fond as Freud was of some of his patients, he believed countertransference was something the analyst should rise above. The truth is that transference is human, and it moves in both directions.

People fall in love on the playground, and falling in love there or anywhere else is often riddled with the imaginary, steered by phantom powers from the past we can't consciously remember.

I think Freud's ambivalence about what is real and unreal in transference is resolved with an insight he provided in *The Interpretation of Dreams,* "Our feeling tells us that an affect experienced in a dream is in no way inferior to one of equal intensity experienced in waking life; and dreams insist with greater energy upon their right to be included among our real mental experiences in respect to their affective than in respect to their ideational content."[13] *Emotions are not fictive* either in dreams or in transference. Transference love is real, even if it comes about under "special" circumstances.

Freud's *Tummelplatz,* Strachey's playground, became the catalyst for D. W. Winnicott's "potential or transitional space"—his arena of play, playing, creativity, and culture, surely one of his most important contributions to psychoanalytic theory. It was only through play that people could, as he put it, begin to "feel real." I have been unable to find in Winnicott a single mention of *Remembering, Repeating, and Working Through.* If it's there, I have missed it, but the inspiration, acknowledged or not, is obvious. Freud's language, via Strachey, suffuses Winnicott's prose. For Winnicott, not just neurotics in therapy, but normal infants require an "*intermediate* state between [their] inability and growing ability to recognize and accept reality."[14] Strachey's translation is *intermediate region between illness and real life.* Like Freud's, Winnicott's intermediate area is crowded with illusions generated by play, but it cannot be situated only inside the person. Winnicott's "potential space" is "not inner psychic reality. It is outside the individual, but it is not the external world."[15] The transitional object—that bear or bit of blanket—is a real object in the world, but also a "symbol" radiant with the infant's fantasies of union with his mother that helps ease his separation from her. It is at once "a piece of real experience" and a fiction.

For Freud, the word *illusion,* the Latin meaning of which is "to be in play"—*illudere*—had pathological implications. For

Winnicott, we never entirely give up our fictions for the so-called real world: "There is a direct development from transitional phenomena to playing, from playing to shared playing, and from this to cultural experiences."[16] Music, painting, dance, and the alternative worlds of novels are all generated by play. The connection between play and culture was hardly new. Thirteen years before Winnicott's paper "Transitional Objects and Transitional Phenomena," Johan Huizinga published *Homo Ludens* (1938), in which he argued that all culture is a form of play.[17] For Lev Vygotsky, play was also a developmental phenomenon, but he dated its advent later in a child's life than Winnicott did. For him, it began with the imaginary situation. When the child pretends, he "operates with alienated meaning in a real situation."[18] The symbol or word for a thing has shifted. The refrigerator box becomes a house or a cave deep in the woods or a monster that eats children, but in real life, the box is still a box.

It is easy to see how theoretically complex this intermediate region can be. How does one frame the subjects involved? Are they monads each in a private and often delusional psychic space sending messages to each other? Where is the border between them? Can they form a single unit of free-flowing mutuality? Can the interaction be seen as a third entity between them? How much of it is conscious and how much unconscious? What is real about it and what is imaginary? I have been borrowing Martin Buber's term "the Between." For the philosopher, "the Between," was an ontological reality that could not be reduced to either person involved and was more than both. The ideal relation between human beings resulted in "a change from communication to communion, that is, in the *embodiment* of the word dialogue" (my italics). It was not a relation of immersion or loss in the other person, not a schizophrenic confusion of I and you. It was a third reality. Buber writes, "Neither needs give up his point of view . . . they enter a realm where the point of view no longer holds."[19] The key word in Buber's communion is *embodied,* an embodied dialogue—this is not an engagement of two intellects but of two whole beings. For Buber, who was interested in psychotherapy, psychic illness happened in this between. Buber's I-Thou dialectic made deep inroads into psychoanalysis—in the work of Ludwig Binswanger and Carl Rogers, among others.

Buber and Freud were well aware of each other, but the odor of religious mysticism wafting through Buber must have been repellent to Freud, whose philosophical orientation was eminently rational. He regarded religion as illusion number one. Kant's idea that play is the antithesis of reason, that reason must triumph over imagination, and philosophy and science over art, is a continual ghostly presence in Freud. The Kantian hierarchy fit well with Freud's scientific temperament.

Science is ideally a discipline of remove. In fact, the scientist is supposed to vanish in the third-person objectivity of the observation or experiment. The I-You dialectic may be an object of study, but it is not part of the epistemological drama. When the cure in question is one enacted through a form of dialogue (two people alone together in a room), the remove, what came to be called *neutrality,* is an insistence that dispassionate reason guide the analyst, no matter how messy and wild the doings on the *Tummelplatz* become. "We admit it into the transference as a playground where it is allowed to expand in almost complete freedom . . ." And yet, there are echoes of Schiller here, too, and his play-drive, *Spieltrieb.* For Schiller, *Spieltrieb* generates the imagination and the arts that serve as *intermediaries* between *Stofftrieb,* sense drive (sensual, bodily reality), and *Formtrieb* (the rational vehicle of conceptual and moral order), between feeling and willing, between philosophical-scientific discourse and unknowable external reality, *das Ding an sich* of Kant. Schiller's location of the imagination is classical. Imagination, *phantasie,* or mental images as a meeting ground between body and intellect goes back to the Greeks. But for Schiller, the integration of passive feeling and active will-ing, the senses and reason, results in human freedom.[20] Of course, Freud was neither an Idealist nor a Romantic. Even the repetitions of transference expanding on his playground are not entirely free—his words are *almost complete freedom*. Freud was a scientist, a doctor, and a Jew. The phrase *complete freedom* was not in his vocabulary.

Freud's drive theory also seeks integration, a way to account for the inherited givens of the animal body and the labile charac-ter of the human psyche. He described a drive as "lying on the frontier between the mental and the physical."[21] Through yet another intermediate zone, Freud attempts to solve a problem that still baffles scientists and philosophers. How do *ideas* relate to neural networks? What are the psychical accompaniments to bi-ological processes? Freud answers by arguing that during a per-son's life, his essential need for love begins with a bodily excitement or tension, which attaches itself to a psychic representative, an idea or *Vorstellung,* which, when all goes well, finds its satisfac-tion in the love object. A drive pushes outward into the world, and its journey is always accompanied by a quota of affect, which results in our conscious subjective feelings—in the best cases, ones of relief. Our first experiences with others lay down unconscious memory traces—traces which become a link between affects and ideas. In *Inhibitions, Symptoms, and Anxiety,* Freud states that af-fects are "reproductions of very early, perhaps even pre-individual experiences of vital importance."[22] If this is true, we feel again what we have felt before.

Freud's "biologism," long derided in many circles, is enjoy-ing a resurrection. Intellectual climates change, and the winds are blowing in a new direction. For people in the humanities, the disembodied, culturally constructed, linguistic subject of late twentieth-century theory began to look both tired and in-complete. And in the hard sciences, the sweeping influence of behaviorism, with its contempt for inner life and subjective experience, grew equally dull. These are broad generalizations. Everywhere, always, there have been individuals pursuing their intellectual concerns, despite the atmospheric pressure, but we find ourselves at a moment of change, a change that has reinvigorated Freud's thinking about psychobiological processes and sheds light on the anatomical as well as the psychic reality of the playground.

But how do we read other people? Perhaps no discovery in neuroscience has created as much uproar, both in the field and outside it, as the finding by Gallese, Fadiga, Fogassi, and Rizzolatti published in 1996 that in the macaque monkey there are neurons in the premotor cortex of its brain that fire when an animal performs an action, such as grasping, but also fire when another animal simply observes the same action.[23] These aptly named mirror neurons have become part of a physiological explanation for human intersubjectivity, although it is vital to state that nobody knows whether this reflective action is innate or developed. What has become clear is that the neurons are involved not only in mimicry but in the comprehension of intentionality—the *why* of an action.

Research into biological mimesis of various kinds and into what is now called primary intersubjectivity, which begins from the first day of life, has exploded. However, if the idea of mirror neurons wasn't intuitively attractive and didn't resonate powerfully with thought outside of neuroscience, in psychoanalysis, phenomenology, linguistics, attachment studies, and infant research, the fate of the discovery might have been different. As it was, the prestigious journal *Science* rejected the paper by Gallese et al. at the time, because it was deemed lacking in general interest.

Both as literal experience and as metaphor, the mirror has a long history in Western thought. The tragic triangular love story of Echo and Narcissus continues to move us. In that myth, the third person in the drama is nobody—an illusory presence in the water. One of the first to research a child's relation to the mirror was William Preyer (1841–1897), who in *The Mind of the Child* meticulously charted his own son's reaction to his reflection over many months. His experiments led to the conclusion that mirror recognition marks the emergence of the ego (*Ich*), which allows the child to distinguish both himself and others from his and their images in the looking glass.[24] Jacques Lacan codified the mirror stage, influenced by his teacher Alexandre Kojève's reading of Hegel, the master-slave chapter of the *Phenomenology* in particular. Lacan also borrowed Charlotte Bühler's concept *transitivism*[25] (a term originally coined by Carl Wernicke) for the confusion of self and other in early childhood, a phenomenon that has been demonstrated over and over on real playgrounds: one small child takes a tumble and starts to cry. Another, who is only watching the fall, begins to cry as well. Winnicott, after reading Lacan, rethinks mirroring as a relation between mother and child. A contemporary example of this line of thought can be found in the psychoanalyst Jessica Benjamin. Through her critical reading of Hegel and Freud from a feminist, dialogical perspective, as well as her use of both Winnicott's transitional theory and the burgeoning infant research on reciprocity and attunement, she repositions the human and psychoanalytic playground. In *The Bonds of Love* (1988), she writes, ". . . intersubjective theory sees the relationship between self and the other, with its tension between sameness and difference as a continual exchange of influence." [26]

In one of his papers on analytic technique, Freud used, among other metaphors, the image of a mirror for the analyst: "The doctor should be opaque to his patients and, like a mirror, show them nothing but what is shown to him."[27] From the patient's perspective we might put it this way: *In you, I am able to see myself,* or *through you I become able to see myself.* One research study has shown that in successful psychotherapy sessions, therapist and patient engage in bodily mirroring.[28] Freud had nothing quite so literal in mind, but he did understand psychoanalysis as a conversation between two unconsciousnesses that communicated in ways well beyond purely cognitive operations. I suspect that it was Freud's clinical experience that pricked his interest in the idea of thought transference, despite the fact that it was laden with occult connotations.

The mirror metaphor for the other confirms a phenomenal reality: when I look at you, the symmetrical likeness of our two bodies is felt by me, although I am invisible to myself. Most of this mirroring is unconscious, but in some fundamental way, when I look at you, your face supplants mine. The now classic studies by Meltzoff and Moore and Kugiumutzakis that documented infants (some less than an hour old) imitating the facial expressions of adults amazed many in the scientific community,[29] but I must add here that the finding merely confirmed what every attentive parent has always known. In the first weeks of my daughter's life, she imitated my facial expressions, and she also engaged in what is now called protoconversation. I would talk, wait a little, and she answered me. There were scientists, too, who truly looked at infants, among them, Preyer, who documented the fact that when he stuck out his tongue, his seventeen-week-old son did the same. But their observations didn't stick. They drowned under a wave of opposing consensual theories.

The newborn as egocentric, asocial, solipsistic, autistic, has been replaced with an innately convivial being. In other words, as infant researchers point out regularly, the newborn that has come to light in the last thirty years is neither Freud's nor Piaget's nor Skinner's nor Mahler's. Colwyn Trevarthen writes, "The idea of infant intersubjectivity is no less than a theory of how human minds, in human bodies, can recognize one another's impulses intuitively with or without cognitive or symbolic elaboration."[30] The word *intuitively* is a slap in the face, not only to earlier child research, but to the cognitive theorists and analytical philosophers, who have addressed the problem of other minds by postulating convoluted, fully conscious, intellectual gymnastics based on a paradigm of the human mind as a locked room and the other as robotic alien.

Trevarthen, Daniel Stern, Stein Bråten, Gallese, and others articulate a theoretical position, which is remarkably similar to the embodied intersubjectivity of Maurice Merleau-Ponty. In *Phenomenology of Perception* (1945), the philosopher argues forcefully against the understanding of others by analogy. He writes:

> A baby of fifteen months opens its mouth if I playfully take one of its fingers between my teeth and pretend to bite it. And yet it has scarcely looked at its face in a glass, and its teeth are not in any case like mine. The fact is that its own mouth and teeth, as it feels them from the inside, are immediately, for it, the apparatus to bite with, and my jaw, as the baby sees it from the outside, is immediately capable of the same intentions. Biting has immediately, for it, an intersubjective significance. It perceives its intentions in its own body, and my body with its own, and thereby my intentions in its own body.[31]

None of the later researchers has said it better. The infant's grasp of the other is not reflectively self-conscious; it is an embodied, subliminal relation. Mother and infant make a dyad, the two-in-one unit proposed by John Bowlby. They engage in a Buberian "we space." Their mutual rhythms of gazing, vocal intonations, touch, and gesture are "attuned" to each other in a Winnicottian dialectic. They make music. They dance. They play. In this dynamic, the classical subject/object distinction begins to blur.

And through these repetitions, this shared bodily music, this emotional signaling back and forth, the immature brain of the infant develops enormously. By the end of the first year, there is a conspicuous enlargement of the brain's frontal region. In those first twelve months, it is particularly the right orbitofrontal cortex that develops, an area of the brain crucial to affect regulation—how we manage our emotional responses. Allan Schore has written extensively on right hemisphere interactions between child and caretaker and their importance for psychopathology, and there is growing evidence that attachment and failures in attachment between mother and child affect autonomic, neural-chemical, and hormonal functions in a growing brain.[32] In a 2006 paper in *Nature Neuroscience,* Mirella Dapretto et al. articulate the mutual reflections this way: "Typically developing children can rely on a right hemisphere mirroring neural mechanism—interfacing with the limbic system via the insula—whereby the meaning of the imitated (or observed) emotion is directly felt and hence understood."[33] Without dwelling excessively on the neurobiology, which is still in a state of flux, it is fair to say that what has emerged is a psychophysiology of the Between, which involves neither nature nor nurture, but both at once, merging without demarcation— genetic temperament and a specific human story become *personality* over time, a personality shaped by its affective story: the "reproductions of very early . . . experiences of vital importance."

Genetic research, the decoding of the genome, in particular, which some scientists hoped would serve as a fixed map for all human traits, has proved disappointing and given way to epigenetics. There is little evidence for simple, consistent effects of mutations in specific genes. The human story is far more complex. What does seem clear is that emotional styles or patterns of response, the repetitious forms of our relations to others and their primal meanings, are cocreated and probably begin even before birth. Brain plasticity implies dynamism, but also neural repetitions. There is no meaning without repetition, as Kierkegaard pointed out, and all recollection—implicit and explicit—is a form of repetition.

The early templates of our social relations are encoded prelinguistically in motor-sensory, emotional systems of our bodies, without symbolic representation, but they lie at the bottom of all higher meaning—as part of Freud's primal pleasure-pain series. They create temporal bodily expectations that become part of unconscious memory and are essential to our relations with others. They become a dialogical code of behavior that appears on the playground. As Rhawn Joseph puts it, ". . . early emotional learning" may occur "in the right hemisphere completely unbeknownst to the left; learning and associated emotional responding may later be completely inaccessible to the language centers of the brain. . . ."[34] Whether he knows it or not, he is echoing Freud. This is how what is not consciously remembered becomes repetition, an automatic affective response. We may intuitively perceive the actions of others through biological mechanisms, but those perceptions are also determined by past experiences. And so, illusions and delusions enter the playground. The person who was neglected as a child will read the wandering eyes of the other differently from the one who was not. Simply seeing his interlocutor or analyst look away from him may generate fear, sadness, or a feeling of persecution in the man who has felt unloved, and he then may create countless verbal explanations to explain why it is perfectly rational for him to feel that way, none of which touch on the actual wound.

What we don't explicitly remember, we repeat, and these reenactments of learned emotional responses, mechanical in their appearance, are like a musical phrase repeated, sometimes ad nauseam, between patient and analyst in an echoing drama that often goes back to our earliest, unsymbolized relations. And it is not easy to bring these dissonant phrases to consciousness, and when we do they are translations only. Relational pathologies appear as an adaptation, after all, a defense against a cacophonous Between. Buber was right, psychological illnesses do grow up between people. And it seems that as much as milk, the neonate craves recognition, the eyes of the other on her, through which she finds her own eyes and mouth and tongue, arms and legs and torso, long before she can identify those various body parts in the mirror as herself.

The melodies of interaction become unconscious memories or, in Freud's terminology, *mnestic traces,* the proprioceptive and emotional underground of each one of us, and this music must be distinguished from what Endel Tulving called episodic memories, that can be rooted to a time and place in a narrated personal autobiography.[35] As Freud said in *The Ego and the Id* (1923), things become available to consciousness through corresponding "word presentations."[36] I am convinced that Freud was right about words: self-conscious narrative memories gain their flexibility—motion in time—and their mutability—they are not reliable but continually reconstructed over a lifetime—in language. They depend on our ability to see ourselves as others see us—that's me in the mirror—a character in my family, a player in the social world, and this otherness becomes most highly articulated in words, which allow us to gather up ourselves in the past, project ourselves into the future, and create fictional worlds that are always in essence dialogical.

Reflective self-consciousness is a form of alienation that brings with it Vygotsky's imaginary situation, "Let's pretend the box is a dragon," but what he did not say is that this form of imagining is predicated on the affective mirroring relations that came before it. Words are the ultimate emissaries because they travel from inside the body to the outside, and they are shared, not privately owned. My mental images, my dream pictures can reach you because I tell you about them. And when you respond, we have a dialogue in the real world or in the special circumstances of the analytic space. And, as M. M. Bakhtin, the Russian theorist, argues, the word is dialogic in itself, charged with per-

sonal intentionality in relation to the other and to whole histories of use and context by others, and it cannot be reified, given
some fixed, final meaning.[37] Even when I am alone, the rhythmi-
cal realities of the back and forth between self and other are embodied in me, and their meanings are both implicit and explicit.

This brings us to Freud's *Beyond the Pleasure Principle,* and to
his grandson, the "good" little one-and-a-half-year-old boy, who
does not cry when his mother leaves him or disturb his parents at
night, but plays his fort-da game instead, reenacting and master-
ing his mother's absence by throwing her away and bringing her
back again.[38] The "symbolic" significance of this game, the role of
the words *fort* and *da* as vehicles to cover absence, has, of course,
been heavily glossed by Lacan,[39] but the game is also rhythmic
and physical. The spool attached to a string is thrown and retrieved; a corporeal enactment of a relation in its back-and-forth
motion. Freud's grandson plays the Between game. He is too
young to turn his spool and string into a true imaginary situation, which means, according to Vygotsky, "separating the field
of meaning from the visual field."[40] The boy cannot say, "Let's
pretend the spool is Mommy, and I have the power." But there is
potent emotional meaning in the fort-da game, as Freud noticed,
a meaning which is not yet fully articulated or alienated in Vygotsky's terms. It is an illusion of mastery seen in the game's musical repetition of the words that are accompanied by the physical
rhythms of a repetitive throwing out and reeling in that bring
the boy pleasure. The two levels of motor-sensory action and
speech are not separate but integrated.

All mammals play, especially young ones. They cavort and
gambol and tumble about. Even pretense is not limited to people.
Anyone who has had a dog has witnessed play fights, and great
apes and dolphins, who recognize their own images in a mirror,
exhibit signs of more sophisticated make-believe. Jaak Panksepp

has his own version of *Spieltrieb,* an instinctual PLAY system in the brain that is fundamentally emotional and social, enhanced by certain synaptic chemistries and depressed by others. Panksepp writes, "In most primates, prior social isolation has a devastating effect on the urge to play. After several days of isolation, young monkeys and chimps become despondent and are likely to exhibit relatively little play when reunited. Apparently their basic needs for social warmth, support and affiliation must be fulfilled first; only when confidence is restored does carefree playfulness return."[41] As Winnicott noticed, some of his patients had to learn how to play in therapy. Before going out onto the *Tummelplatz,* a person (and some animals) must feel safe and recognized.

Compulsive, involuntary repetitions that have no ludic character, the ones Freud also addresses in *Beyond the Pleasure Principle,* are often traumatic in origin. And I think they can be characterized without any reference to a death instinct. They are fully somatized, motor-sensory, and sometimes visual memories without representation in language. Flashbacks are the most dramatic illustration of this. But the symptoms of hysteria or conversion disorder are also conditions unarticulated by linguistic symbols. As Freud wrote in 1895, these are moments when "the body join[s] in the conversation."[42] There is a lot of psychoanalytic and neurobiological work on memory and trauma, which I have addressed in greater detail elsewhere, both in my book *The Shaking Woman*[43] and in a paper forthcoming in the journal *Neuropsychoanalysis.* Let me simply say this: a transference battleground can become a playground under the right emotional circumstances. The holding and containing environments of Winnicott and Bion seem highly relevant here. And, as Freud knew, it is not only profoundly traumatized people who are subject to pathological repetitions in relation to the other or to the analyst, but plain old neurotics, too. My friend Mark Solms, the psychoanalyst and brain researcher who gave this lecture once, says that psychoanalysis is learning to face what you'd rather not know. In my own experience, this is exactly right. It can be painful to look in the mirror, because we are never alone in that image. We are there with our beloveds and our struggles with them. The journey of a therapy is to replace rigid, unrepresented patterns of repressed meaning with freer, more creative and playful meanings that can be articulated in words—to live in repetitions of greater variety.

The fort-da game is a beautiful example of the inherently social and dialogic character of even solitary play, an illustration of the two in one. At eighteen months, the boy is just at the moment of mirror self-recognition. The playground of the child's repetitions is indeed an intermediate space between his desire and the real outside world of others. The illusionary game is transitional because it will vanish from his life, to be replaced by new games and fantasies in further bids for mastery. But these later forms of play are nevertheless built on the oldest cadences and bodily rhythms of preverbal dialogue.

Perhaps the most striking characters of a developing intermediate region are imaginary friends, those transitional beings that rise up in childhood, spend time as important, sometimes difficult members of a household, and then disappear. The phenomenon is poorly studied, because psychologists endlessly stumble over definitions. Do stuffed animals with personalities count? What about the child who becomes the imaginary companion herself, the little girl who, when asked how often she played with Applejack, answered, "I *am* Applejack!"[44] I will give you two examples of imaginary companions I dredged from a tome called *Annual Progress in Child Development, 2000–2001*: "Herd of cows: cows of many colors and varying sizes who were often fed and diapered like infants. Discovered when the father accidentally stepped on one." "Maybe: A human of varying gender whom the child routinely summoned by shouting out the front door of the family house."[45]

The cows and Maybe are characters in fictional worlds that

serve some emotional purpose in relation to the real world out there. The psychological richness of these figments is apparent even from these brief, completely unelaborated descriptions: the cows wear diapers, and the father was so thoughtless, he trod on one! Maybe regularly changes one, the make-believe friend isn't stuck in one or the other, how nice! My sister Liv and I had an enemy, Mrs. Klinch Klonch, a hideous woman who tormented children. The sadistic exploits of this convenient projection gave us hours of delight and a safe reservoir for our own nasty impulses and whatever anger we harbored against our mother. Like Freud's grandson, we were very good children, and I think we needed our sublimated Mrs. Klinch Klonch, the female ogre who gave us a ready supply of hair-raising, but safe, stories.

Even very young children know that their friends and play figments aren't "real." They inhabit Winnicott's and Merleau-Ponty's "potential space," which is not phenomenal reality, the here and now, but an illusory narrative terrain alongside of it. Elaborate story worlds are always the product of double consciousness, of the simultaneity of here and there, I and you. In a paper on impaired play in autism, Somogy Varga says it well: "Play is an inherently intersubjective phenomenon and requires the resonative presence of others."[46] We may not literally *see* the ghosts of those others, but they are there, and their resonance is emotional. The feelings are real. And so, children can frighten themselves with their own pretend stories. Imaginary companions can be mean and tormenting as well as sweet. Once a character has been born on the playground, he or she or Maybe is not always obedient or under our conscious control.

Again we run up into illusion and delusion, health and illness, in life and in analysis. Where are the borders? Winnicott was suspicious of imaginary companions, calling them "other selves of a highly primitive type,"[47] but there is little evidence, as Marjorie Taylor points out in her book on the subject, for any generalized conception of these figments as pathological.[48] For most children, Freud's reality principle remains an active constraint. More revealing are the imaginary friends and enemies of neurological patients, who mistake their mirror images for benign or persecutory others, who personify dolls and toys, invent imaginary children or strangers haunting their attics, who believe their loved ones are doubles or identify their own paralyzed arms as the limbs of other people. As the neurologist Todd Feinberg points out, these delusions are positive symptoms, not negative ones, and they occur almost always in connection with right hemisphere damage. But not *all* right hemisphere lesions result in delusions. No simple locationist theory can account for them, and they cannot be explained away as a simple filling in of absent memories by the intact language areas of the left brain.[49]

Feinberg articulates the connections among these confabulations, the imaginary companions of childhood, and Freud's idea of unconscious defenses. In stark opposition to many of his colleagues, Feinberg, like the psychoanalyst, is interested in the *subjective content* of his patients' curious narratives. Without their personal narratives, their illnesses remain elusive.

After surgery to drain a brain abscess in his right hemisphere, one of Feinberg's patients, JK, claimed that his paralyzed left arm belonged to his brother. The members of the young man's family lived overseas, and he missed them sorely. He told Dr. Feinberg that he had found his brother's arm in a coffin, and its presence on his body brought him comfort. After the delusion remitted, JK explained as he sobbed that his brother's arm had made him feel stronger. When Dr. Feinberg asked him how he regarded his good right arm, the patient answered simply, "OK." Then he explained, "This one [his right arm] doesn't have a story like this one [he then pointed to his left hand] . . . it has a story. Like the one I told you . . . this hand has a background that makes me feel closer to my brother."[50]

It seems to me that in this man's case, his brother's arm occupied a fictional territory between his illness and real life, and that it served him as a transitional object, a metaphorical part for the whole beloved brother. It is not lost on Feinberg that his patients' confabulations bear a strong resemblance to myth, dreams, and literature. But I would like to examine the case with a somewhat different emphasis. JK's right hemisphere injury causes a dysfunction in Freud's reality principle, the regulatory faculty that involves the cognitive control of instinctual discharge, delaying gratification, and facing unpleasant truths, such as: *I am paralyzed on my left side, and I can't possibly have my brother's arm on my body.* The right hemisphere is heavily implicated in both reading affect in other people and regulating, inhibiting it from within. JK and patients like him appear to be in the grip of wakeful dreams. In my own dreams I have found myself with new or radically altered body parts without thinking for an instant: *this is impossible.* Although there is forebrain activity in dreaming, higher cognitive processes at work, the bilateral prefrontal cortex is quiescent.

Freud maintained that there was "a sleeping state of mind"[51] and the dream work is on during the day, too, but not available to consciousness. JK's delusion is reminiscent of dream condensation. "The direction in which condensations in dreams proceed," Freud writes, "is determined on the one hand by the rational preconscious relations of the dream thoughts, and on the other by the attraction exercised by visual memories in the unconscious."[52] Abstract thinking becomes concrete and visual in dreams, and their content is borrowed from memory images. *I am alone and paralyzed; I remember and want my brother. I want his strength and comfort, his love and companionship.* JK's desire is neatly transformed, condensed or compressed, in a transformation of his conscious body image, which is also a case of mistaken identity: *My brother is here with me now. I have his arm, his embracing arm.* There may be a dark side, too: *I wish my brother had a dead arm, not I.* The brother's arm is an imaginary internal construct of an *intersubjective relation,* and the form this fiction takes is *not arbitrary.* The "dead" arm first appears to him in a coffin, after all, the perfect container for a useless, unresponsive limb. The feeling that appears in this Between region of illusion, however, is terrifyingly real. We are looking at grief.

It is a mistake to isolate neurology from psychiatry, the biological from the psychological, and a further grave error to discount subjective experience from illness in general. JK's brain lesion may explain the disinhibition that allows the hallucinatory process of the dream work into daylight, but it does not explain either why it erupts in JK and not in others with similar injuries, nor does it explain the personal content of that eruption. Many forms of dream consciousness occur in people when they're not asleep. The logical sequences of rational thought loosen in reverie, in the hypnagogic visions that precede sleep, in the free associations of analysis, and in the making of art.

Artists and art-making always made Freud a little nervous, but in *The Interpretation of Dreams,* he turns to Schiller, as he did from time to time. He quotes a letter written by the poet and philosopher to a friend: ". . . where there is a creative mind, Reason—so it seems to me—relaxes its watch upon the gates, and the ideas rush in pell-mell, and only then does it look them through and examine them in a mass."[53] When Reason—and, I must add, the whole body—relaxes, ideas rush in and may attach themselves to paralyzed arms or mirror reflections, to the analyst in the room, or to the story or poem being written. And the imagined others or doubles of these fictions are not always good brother fairies. They may be monsters like Mrs. Klinch Klonch. The fairies and monsters take many forms, and they rise up as ghosts of the forgotten past in the transference and the countertransference and in the play of imaginative fiction. They haunt the intermediate region between me and you.

This is where stories bloom, where the confabulations of literature flower like dreams over our wounds and losses in a bid for mastery. And as Winnicott believed, these illusions can paradoxically make us feel real. After Sigmund Freud died, his daughter Anna dreamed of him. In her analysis of her resurrection dreams, she wrote, "The main scene, in the dreams are always of his tenderness to me, which always takes the form of my own earlier tenderness. In reality he never showed either with the exception of one or two times, which always remained in my memory."[54]

Making fictions is something like dreaming while awake. Vague or vivid memories are reconfigured as the artist plays. Imaginary companions appear from unknown regions to keep one company. Like every child, I know that the worlds of my novels are "pretend." My reality principle is intact, but every fiction I write must be emotionally true to sustain its making, to keep my play in motion. The choices are never, never arbitrary, because beneath the words I write, I feel the old music, tuneful and dissonant, my own melodies and rhythms and ruptures that direct the story I am telling, that propel it forward. And every work of fiction is written for the other, an imagined other, to be sure. The novel is dialogical, created by many voices chattering within and rarely agreeing with one another. In psychotherapy, I must also bump up against a real other, my analyst, on the playground where we wrestle with fairies and monsters in the Land of Between, and where I sometimes find myself in the mirror, *transformed*—neither monster nor fairy—but a person who can play harder and more freely.

I met Sigmund Freud and Anna Freud not so long ago—in a dream. I was starstruck, filled with happiness. I shook the old man's hand, and then Miss Freud said to me, "I hope you won't be like Oscar Wilde and overstay your welcome." There is no time for my analysis of this dream, which goes very deep, I can assure you, but I do hope I have neither been too wild nor overstayed my welcome.

2011

LOOKING

NOTES ON SEEING

1. To look and not see: an old problem. It usually means a lack of understanding, an inability to divine the meaning of something in the world around us.

2. Cognitive scientists have repeatedly conducted the following experiment and, without fail, they come up with same results. An audience is asked to watch a film of two teams playing basketball. The observers are given a job to count the number of times the ball changes hands. I have done this, and one has to be very attentive to follow the motion of the ball. In the middle of the game, a man wearing a gorilla suit walks onto the court, turns to the camera, thumps his chest, and leaves. Half the people do not see the great ape. They do not believe that he was actually there until the film is replayed and, indeed, a gorilla strolls in and out of the game. Nearly everyone sees the gorilla if he is *not* given the assignment. This has been named *inattentional blindness*.

3. Writing at my desk now, I see the screen, but this sentence dominates my attention. In fact, my momentary awareness that

there is much around the words distracts me: the blue screen of the computer beyond the white edge of the page; various icons above and below; the surface of my desk cluttered with small Post-it squares which, when I turn my head, I can read, "Habermas 254–55," "Meany et al., implications for adrenocortical responses to stress" scrawled on pink paper (residue of arcane research), a black stapler; and countless other objects that enter my awareness the moment I turn to them. What is crucial is that I don't turn to them. For hours every day, I have little, if any, consciousness of them. I live in a circumscribed phenomenal world. An internal narrator speaks words and dictates to my fingers, which type automatically. There is no need to think about the connection between head and hands. I am subsumed by the link. Were another object suddenly to materialize on my desk and then vanish, I might well have no knowledge of either its appearance or disappearance.

4. Once, in an unfamiliar hallway, I mistook myself for a stranger because I did not understand I was looking in a mirror. My own form took me by surprise because I was not oriented in space. Expectation is crucial to perception.

5. There are days when I think I see an old friend in the street, but it is a stranger. The recognition ignites like a match and then is instantly extinguished when I understand I am wrong. The recognition is felt, not thought. I can't trace what created the error, can't tell you why one person reminded me of another. Was the old friend a subliminal presence in my mind on that particular day or was the confusion purely external—a jut of the chin or slope of the shoulders or rhythm of a walk?

6. We do not become anesthetized to horrible photographs of death or suffering. We may choose to avoid them. When I see

a gruesome image in the newspaper in the morning, I sometimes turn away, registering in seconds that looking too long will hurt me. People who gorge on horror films and violent thrillers do it not because they have learned to feel too little, but because they indulge in the limbic rush that floods their systems as they safely witness exploding bodies. It seems that these viewers are mostly men.

7. We feel colors before we can name them. Colors act on us pre reflectively. A part of me feels red before I can name red. My cognitive faculties lag behind the color's impact. Standing in a room, I look first at the vase of red tulips because they are red and because they are alive.

8. My mother once told me about coming home to find our cat dead on the lawn. She saw the poor animal from many yards away, but she said she knew with absolute assurance that it was dead. An inert thing. An it.

9. Photographs of the beloved dead draw me in. I am fascinated. There is the good, dear face, one that changed over time. It is the picture that preserves the face, not my memory, which is befogged by the many faces he had over the years. Or is it the single face that grew old? Sometimes I cannot bear to look. The image has become a token of grief. And yet, there is nothing so banal as the pictures of strange families. After my father died, I found Christmas cards with photographs of unknown people among his papers—happy families—grinning into an invisible lens. I threw them away.

10. Galvanic skin response registers a change in the heat and electricity passed through the skin by nerves and sweat during emotional states. People in white coats attach electrodes to your

hands and track what happens. When they show you a picture of your mother, your GSR goes up. Meaning in the body.

11. Is our visual world rich or poor? There are fights about this. People do not agree. Philosophers, scientists, and other academics ponder this richness and poverty question in papers and books and lectures. Human beings have very limited peripheral vision, but we can turn our heads and take in more of the world. When I'm writing, my vision is severely limited by my attention, but sometimes when I let my eyes roam in a space, I discover its density of light and color and feel surprised by what I find. When I focus, say, just on the shadows here on my desk, they become remarkable. My small round clock casts a double shadow from either side of its circular base, one darker than the other, a gray and a paler gray. There is a spot of brilliant light at the edge of the darker oval. As I look, this sight has become beautiful.

12. Why is a face beautiful?

13. If an image is flashed too quickly to be perceived consciously, we take it in unconsciously and respond to it without knowing what is happening. A picture of a scowling face I can't say I've seen affects me anyway. Scientists call this *masking*. Blindsight patients have cortical blindness. They lose visual consciousness but not visual unconsciousness. They see but don't know they are seeing. If you ask them to guess what you're holding (a pencil) they will guess far better than people who are truly blind. Words and consciousness are connected. How much do I see of the world that never registers in my awareness? When I walk in the street, I sometimes glimpse a scene for just an instant, but I cannot tell you what I have witnessed until a fraction of a second later, when the puzzling image falls into place: that furry thing

was a stuffed animal, and a little boy was dangling it from his stroller. The lag again.

14. We are picture-making creatures. We scribble and draw and paint. When I draw what I see, I touch the thing I am looking at with my mind, but it is as if my hand is caressing its outline. People who stopped drawing as children continue to make pictures in their dreams or in the hallucinations that arrive just before they go to sleep. Where do those images come from? I dreamed that grass and brush and sticks were growing out of my arm, and I got to work busily trimming myself with a pair of scissors. I wasn't alarmed; it was a job handled in a matter-of-fact way. If I painted a self-portrait with bushy arms, I would be called a surrealist.

15. Some people who go blind see vivid images and colors. Some people who are losing their vision hallucinate while awake. An old man saw cows grazing in his living room, and a woman saw cartoon characters running up and down her doctor's arm. Charles Bonnet syndrome. Just before I fell asleep, I saw a little man speeding over pink and violet cliffs. Once I saw an explosion of melting colors—green, blues, reds, and then a great flash of light that devoured them all. Hypnagogic hallucinations. Freud said dreams protect sleep. At night the world is taken from us and we make up our own scenes and stories. If you wake up slowly, you will remember more of that human underground than if you wake up quickly.

16. Deprived of sight, we make visions. Seeing is also creating.

17. There are things in the world to see. Do I see what you see? We can talk about it and verify the facts. Through my window is the back of a house. One of its windows is completely covered by

a blue shade. But if I tell you I see a flying zebra you will say, Siri, you are hallucinating. You are dreaming while awake.

18. Sometimes artists can make a hallucination real. A painting of a flying zebra is a real thing in the world, a real thing to see.

19. Why do I not like the word *taste* when applied to art? Because it has lost its connection to the mouth and food and chewing. I don't like the way this picture tastes. It's bitter. If we thought about actual tastes, the word would still work. It would be a form of synesthesia, a crossing of our senses: seeing as tasting. But usually it is not used like that anymore, so I avoid it entirely when I talk about art.

20. Looking at a human being or even a picture of a human being is different from looking at an object. Newborn babies, only hours old, copy the expressions of adults. They pucker up, try to grin, look surprised, and stick out their tongues. The photographs of imitating infants are both funny and touching. They do not *know* they are doing it; this response is in them from the beginning. Later, people learn to suppress the imitation mechanism; it would not be good if we went on forever copying every facial expression we saw. Nevertheless, we human beings love to look at faces because we find ourselves there. When you smile at me, I feel a smile form on my own face before I am aware it is happening, and I smile because I am seeing me in your eyes and know that you like what you see.

21. I am looking at a small reproduction of Johannes Vermeer's *Study of a Young Woman,* which hangs in a room at the Metropolitan Museum here in New York. It is a girl's head and face. I say *girl* because she is very young. From her face I would guess

she is no more than ten years old. When I look up the picture in one of my books on Vermeer, I see that there it is called *Portrait of a Young Girl,* a far better title. We should not turn girls into women too soon. She is smiling, but not a wide smile. Her lips are sealed. My impression is that she is looking at me, but I cannot quite catch her eye. What is certain is that she is answering someone else's gaze. Someone has made her smile. She is not a beautiful child; it is her looking that is beautiful, her connection to the invisible person. There is shyness in her expression, reserve, maybe a hint of hesitancy. I think she is looking at an adult, probably the artist, because she has not let herself go. She looks over her shoulder at him. I have great affection for this girl. That is the magic of the painting; it is not that I have affection for a representation of a child's head that was painted some time between 1665 and 1667. No, I feel I have actually fallen for her, the way I fall for a child who looks up at me on the street and smiles, perhaps a homely child, who with a single look calls forth a burst of maternal feeling and sympathy. But my emotion is made of something more; I remember my own girlhood and my shyness with grown-ups I didn't know well. I was not a bold child, and in her face I see myself at the same age.

22. In some of Gerhard Richter's painted-over photographs, he painted over his wife's face and parts of her body. He covered the bodies of his children, too, in snapshots of them as babies and growing children. In these gestures, I felt he was keeping them for himself, keeping the private hidden. Other times, he framed them with swaths of color, turning them into featured subjects. I love those pictures.

23. Mothers have a need to look at their children. We cannot help it.

24. Lovers have a need to look at each other. They cannot help it.

25. Sometimes I like to look at my husband's face in photographs because he becomes a stranger in the pictures, an object fixed in time. Over many years, I have come to know him through my other senses, too—the feel of his skin, the changing smell of his body in winter and spring and fall and summer, the sound of his voice, his breathing, and sometimes his snoring at night. When I look at him in a photograph, my other senses are quiet. I simply see him, and because I find him beautiful, his unmoving face excites me.

26. Looking at pornography is exciting but loses its interest after orgasm.

27. Reading the end of James Joyce's *Ulysses* when Molly Bloom is remembering is erotic because she gives permission, gives up and gives way, and this is always exciting and interesting because it is personal, not impersonal. Isn't it strange that looking at little abstract symbols on a white page can make a person feel such things? I see her in his arms. I am in his arms. I remember your arms.

28. When I read stories, I see them. I make pictures and often they remain in my mind after I have finished a novel, along with some phrases or sentences. I ground the characters in places, real and imagined. But I always remember the feeling of a book best, unless I have forgotten it altogether.

29. I do not usually *see* philosophy—with some exceptions: Plato, Pascal, Kierkegaard, and Nietzsche, because they are also storytellers.

30. Some people cannot make visual imagery. They do not see pictures in their minds. They do not turn words into images. I didn't know such a thing was possible until a short time ago. They see abstractly. They remember the symbols on the page.

31. "I see" can also mean "I understand."

32. There is a small part of the brain called the fusiform gyrus that is crucial for recognizing faces. If you lose this ability, your deficit is called prosopagnosia. It happens that a person with brain damage looks at herself in the mirror and believes she is seeing, not herself, but a double. It seems that what has vanished is not reason but that special feeling we get when we look at our reflections, that warm sense of ownership. When that disappears, the image of one's self becomes alien.

33. I look and sometimes I see.

2010

THE DRAMA OF PERCEPTION
Looking at Morandi

IN AN INTERVIEW WITH EDOUARD Roditi that was published in 1960, Giorgio Morandi said: "I believe that nothing is more abstract, more unreal than what we actually see. We know all that we can see of the objective world, as human beings, never really exists as we see and understand it. Matter exists, of course, but has no intrinsic meaning of its own, such as the meanings that we attach to it. Only we know that a cup is a cup, that a tree is a tree."[1] This is a restatement of a similar comment he made in 1957 in a radio interview: "For me nothing is abstract. In fact, I believe there is nothing more surreal, nothing more abstract than reality."[2] This slightly earlier and more cryptic comment has been quoted by many critics who have written about Morandi, because it seems to reveal something important about the painter's aesthetic position. The question is: What did Morandi mean?

Images are not words, and artists are not always able to articulate what they do or even what they hope to do. Nevertheless, we know that Morandi carefully revised the interview he did with Roditi. Presumably, then, he said exactly what he wished to say, no more or less. Reading the interview is a somewhat comic experience. While Roditi is positively garrulous, meandering in and out of various subjects and bringing up one artist after another, Morandi is terse and often contrarian. He will be led nowhere he doesn't wish to go. *I believe that nothing is more abstract, more unreal than what we actually see.* This is plainly a philosophical statement. We can take it back to Immanuel Kant, who argued that we, human beings, will never get to the *thing* in itself. Seeing is not seeing the real world, but seeing the world through our perceptions of it, perceptions steeped in our meanings and, as Morandi applies it to his philosophy, those meanings are at least in part produced by language: We agree to call that thing a *cup* and that other thing a *tree.* How does Morandi use the word *abstract*? My *Webster's* give several meanings: "**1: a** Considered apart from any application to a particular object; as abstract truth. **b:** ideal, abstruse. **2:** Of words, names, etc. Not concrete. **3:** Dealing with a subject in its theoretical considerations only, and **4:** *Art.* Presenting or characterized by nonrepresentational designs depicting no recognizable thing . . ." My thought is that Morandi is saying that beneath our myriad experiences of the world, under our perceptual images, our language and emotions is something out there, *matter,* which is like *abstraction* in art, a fundamentally unrecognizable reality, which is unavailable to us.

One may ask, should any of this concern us when we look at a Morandi painting? Do we really care about his abstract reality? I think we do, and yet it's important to ground that *caring* in some sense of what happens when we look at a work of art. A painting is there to be seen. It has no other purpose, and we can see it only in the first person. There is no third-person view, no objective *He* hovering above the image looking at it. The first-person experience is an embodied one. I don't only bring my eyes or my intellectual faculties or my emotions to a picture. I bring my whole self with its whole story. The relation then is between an *I* and an *it,* but that *it* partakes of the artist's being as well, his entire being, which is why we treat art in a different way from utilitarian objects like forks, no matter how attractive those forks may be. My position is a *phenomenological* one: looking at art can't be separated from our lived experience of the world, and the image exists in my perception of it. In his essay "Eye and Mind," Maurice Merleau-Ponty quotes Cézanne, "Nature is inside us," and then goes on to say, "Quality, light, color, depth, which are there before us, are there only because they awaken an echo in our body and the body welcomes them."[3] This is the pleasure of art, and doodling elephants and monkeys aside, it is a uniquely human one.

A painting can represent or not represent something in the world, but it is always generated out of the artist's experience of the visible. Morandi's work hovers at the threshold between what I recognize, say, as a representation of a cup, and a quality of alienation in that cup that has lost the illusion of solidity and realness that I may find in Chardin, for example. Morandi loved Chardin, and what the artists share, besides the still-life genre, is that both of them *enchanted* their objects, but in different ways. The magic of Chardin is that the coffeepot and the garlic appear to be representations of ordinary things, and yet, as you look at them, they become emotionally charged to a degree that seems almost supernatural. I attribute this to the gestures in his canvases, which are communicated to the viewer as visible touch. In fact, looking at the best of Chardin's pictures is almost like being caressed. The artist affects us at a deep and wordless level of human experience that goes back to infancy—being held and touched. Paradoxically, this feeling is more potent in Chardin's still lifes than in his images of figures, where the illusion is that we are looking at living, breathing people. Morandi, too, understood that painting the inanimate had extraordinary possibilities, because the very humility of the things represented allows greater room for the artist's expressiveness. But the spell Morandi casts over his objects is different. His bottles, cups, cloths, balls, and various other things he collected and allowed to get dusty and set up before him to paint were not chosen because they are objects of daily human life. Looking at a Chardin still life of a sausage, knife, and bread, I am drawn to the fact that here is food and a utensil, something we human beings use daily. I could have left those same objects out in my kitchen. They summon the absence of the person who cut and ate the sausage and bread. In a Chardin still life, there are human beings just outside the frame. Morandi's groupings of objects do not resemble everyday kitchen scenes. The things he chose are solely for his perception. That is their only utility. In Chardin, I know that a glass of water is for drinking, the garlic for food preparation. In Morandi, a cup is to be seen. I can say, "that's a cup" or "that's a representation of a cup," but I feel a certain uneasiness when I name it. The cup has somehow been denatured of its cupness, not entirely, but partly. *Only we know that a cup is a cup, a tree is a tree.* Language is of course far more than naming; it is a symbolic, intersubjective self-referential system of signs we use to structure a meaningful existence among ourselves. If you and I are standing in my living room, you will suspect I am hallucinating if I tell you there is a frog on the floor and you don't see one, but not if I point to the floor and say *floor,* because we are sharing that entity in our visual field and we both speak English. Language is also internal. We use it to carry on our running monologues or private inner dialogues as we go about our lives.

In Morandi's work, I feel a desire, at least partially, to unhinge the thing from its name, a desire that is closely related to Cézanne. Cézanne wanted to strip perception of conventional expectations, to see anew. Expectation, in its broadest sense, is vital to perceive anything. We see what we expect to see, which is shaped in part by our memories of having seen things before and in part by our brains' innate neural wiring for vision. But we also see what we pay attention to, and we cannot pay attention to everything in an image at once. Anne Treisman, a scientist studying perception, has proposed a sequence for visual perception—a *preattentive* process: we are quickly able to scan a scene when elementary properties such as color, brightness, or an orientation of lines are present that make it possible for us to distinguish figure from ground. This cursory first look has obvious evolutionary value. If your eyes can quickly detect that the tiger is separate from the woods behind him, you are less likely to be eaten. Preattentive vision encodes qualities such as color, orientation, size, and motion. It is then followed by an *attentive* process which proceeds serially and more slowly. An example of Treisman's work in the textbook *Principles of Neural Science* helps illustrate this. If she shows you a painting made up entirely of blue *T*s interrupted by a single red one and asks you to identify the unique element, the red *T* will pop out almost instantly. On the other hand, if she shows you a painting of blue *T*s and *L*s, red *L*s, and a single red *T*, the lone red T will not be apparent to you without a bit of searching. It requires a higher level of cognition to distinguish it. You have to shift your attention from one letter to the next to discover the lone red *T*.[4]

Visual perception is not fully understood. For example, it is known that the many visual areas of the brain specialize in certain kinds of recognition—color, form, movement—but how these various areas or neural pathways in the brain come together to create a coherent image remains a mystery and is often called "the binding problem." What is known is that human beings are *not* passive receptors of the *out there*. Our embodied minds are actively both creating and interpreting what we see. This corresponds to a Morandian vision: *We know that all we can see of the objective world, as human beings, never really exists* as *we see and understand it*. It is also not known how we become conscious of something out there in the world. There is unconscious vision, subliminal information that never reaches consciousness because it is seen too briefly, for example, but even an unconsciously registered image can affect us emotionally. The role language plays in consciousness is hotly debated, but it is safe to say that I cannot speak about something I am not conscious of (although, as Freud has shown, something may pop out of my mouth inadvertently into the light of day—a slip of the tongue that tells you what's going on just below the surface). Nevertheless, I cannot identify a cup as such in a painting without a self-reflective awareness of that object.

Morandi, at points to me, actively investigates the drama of perception, and he plays with both levels of vision—the preattentive and the attentive. He once said, "The only interest the visible world awakens in me concerns space, light, color, and forms."[5] These are what might be called the essentials of vision, but note that he does not mention *content*. The cups and trees he brought up with Roditi, which stand in for his two painterly genres, still life and landscape, are not mentioned. This is because the linguistic identities of the collection of things or the houses and gardens in the natural scenes don't truly matter. It would be preposterous to say that Morandi didn't know he was painting bottles, jars, cups, houses, and trees. He meditated on his still-life objects for years, made a world of them, shifted them around, put them in various lights, and painted them again and again. But if you have ever looked long enough at a *thing,* you will notice that one of the first aspects to vanish is the *word* for the thing. Other qualities come to the fore. I did a test with the Perrier bottle sitting on my desk. First I noticed its green color, the shape of its body and neck standing out against the clutter of my desk. Then I looked for a while at the vague print of its label on the other side. Then the light from my window illuminating its round side suddenly became a form in itself, as did a single ragged spot of light at the object's base. The more I looked, the more I saw. I noticed tiny drops of water inside the round exterior and their pattern, the distorted line of my bookshelf seen through the glass as another shape with another color—a pale green. My attention transformed it. And that was five minutes. Imagine looking at it and some carefully selected cousin objects for years and then painting or drawing them. Even my brief experiment makes it clear that while looking attentively, I focused successively on the various characteristics of the bottle. My visual experience was one of roaming, moving my eyes to discover further qualities. It took time, and as time went on, there was an unfolding of the object in all its variety. And as I looked, the light in my room changed, so the glints, reflections, and transparency of the bottle were altered, too. This happened, and could only happen, in relation to me. As Edmund Husserl puts it in "Perception, Spatiality and the Body," "The same unchanged form has a changing appearance, according to its relation to my body . . ."[6]

Deep concentration on space, light, color, and forms necessarily alienates things from their linguistic identities. *Matter exists, of course, but has no intrinsic meaning, such as we attach to it.* What my cursory attention gleans first, the figure of the bottle in front of my bookshelf, loses its importance as other qualities capture my eyes. After a while the shifting light has changed the thing entirely, creating what is almost another *object,* certainly a visually different one. Morandi's still lifes, particularly his late works, the achievements of a master's eyes, seem to depict the experience of perceptual duration inside a single canvas—that is, his art appears to include the shifts of attention that reveal various qualities of a single thing or a group of things in the narrative of looking, including what *was* with what *is.* The bottle illuminated by the light of a minute ago isn't identical to the light on the bottle now, but the image can carry both. The painting can preserve the memory. And so Morandi creates ambiguity about both the *where* and the *what* in his images. There are many examples of this. When I first look at one of his pictures, I pick out objects against a background. I identify some things by name. My eyes see an object in front of another, but as I continue to look, I imagine that it has receded or that what I identified as a thing may in fact be a shadow. Shapes begin to bleed into one another or appear to push against the object next to it, invading its space. There are deep shaded areas between objects that pull me in and separate them, and other times I'm not sure where one ends and the other begins. A bottle begins to look as if it is teetering on top of another, or a box rests just at the horizon or table line, so the thing and the line merge. It is as if different moments of perception over time have been remembered in the same image. Gottfried Boehm, in his essay "Giorgio Morandi's Artistic Concept," refers to this as "the pulsation of pictorial elements" and notes that despite this illusion of movement, "a calm overall impression keeps reestablishing itself."[7] This is undoubtedly true. My ambivalence about where or what doesn't create chaos or distress in me.

Boehm discovers a paradoxical reality in these images: "In his pictures Morandi allows us to participate in a temporal order that is optimistic and immaterial at the core of its experience. The objects are disembodied as they embody themselves. In the midst of fleeting time the artist is able to create a place with solidity and presence."[8] It is half of the paradox, the sense of the immaterial and the disembodied, which has led me to speculate about transcendent meanings in Morandi.[9] The experience of looking for a long time at one of his paintings can begin to feel as if one is looking at the representations of ghosts of things, not of things themselves, but then it is also true that the objects may reappear again as representations of *matter*. Those fluctuations are also vital to the curious emotional world of the pictures, which I am not at all sure can be characterized as optimistic.

All perception is accompanied by feeling, even if we sense a kind of neutrality or equilibrium about what we're looking at, what the neurologist Antonio Damasio calls "background feelings" that are always present in us as subjects.[10] Good art necessarily has an emotional component, and because emotion consolidates memory, it also helps us to remember a work of art—take it with us in our minds, not an identical copy, but some version of it or recollection of the experience. Henry James articulated this idea beautifully: "In the arts feeling is meaning."[11] Morandi does not produce in me the emotional waves I feel when I look at Chardin, whose work has brought me close to tears. The project is different. But, as with Chardin, the traces of Morandi's brush on the canvases or the stroke of a line in a drawing act on me emotionally and are crucial to the dialectic of stillness and movement which in the end create subtle alterations in mood. Hints of disturbance and imbalance are here, quivers, hoverings, and somber colors that evoke melancholy. Color falls into the *preattentive* visual scheme. Before we can even name a hue, we have felt it as a sensory reality in our bodies. Blue and green affect us differently from red and yellow. As Kym Maclaren argues in an essay on embodied perception, "That the stimuli of short duration produce an effect in persons' bodies before a color is explicitly sensed, suggests that it is our sensitive-perceptual motor body, and not a knowing, thinking subject, that senses colors."[12] Color *acts in us,* and Morandi is a nuanced observer of color revealed by light and its essential instability.

To feel Morandi, it's important to see the actual paintings and not look only at reproductions. And it is also, I think, vital to recreate to some degree the perceptual drama of the studio—to stand and look long and hard at a single picture and see what happens. Apparently, this is what Morandi himself did with his own works even after they were done. According to Janet Abramowicz, who knew the artist, after he had become famous and his pictures were in great demand, he made his collectors *wait* for them. Once he had finished a painting he did not let it go right away. Instead, she writes, he "would hang it on a wall with others that explored the same theme and observe the sequential development of that particular series. At that time he would often write the name of the future owner on the wooden stretchers of the finished painting, but the canvas would remain on Morandi's wall until he felt he had studied it sufficiently."[13] He didn't alter the images; he *meditated* on them.

You may not weep when you look at these pictures, but you will be fascinated by the delineated spaces, the muted colors with the surprise of a yellow or blue, the openings and relations among apparent objects, the wobbles on a fluted form that act on the body like a tremor, solid blocks that begin to vanish into blur, houses that resemble blocks, boxes or blocks like houses, bottles like buildings, dense areas that might be things and might be space, and with continued study, all of this does take on a spiritual quality. *Spiritual* is a difficult word, but I am not using it as a stand-in for the supernatural or God, although Morandi was a Catholic and did go to church. I am thinking of something far more common, which is that if I open myself fully and turn my whole attention onto these canvases for an extended period, if I shut out thoughts about what I'm going to have for dinner, or the book I was reading yesterday, or the fact that my shoes are pinching me, or the comments of fellow spectators, and give myself over to what I am seeing, there will be an accompanying feeling of strangeness and utter muteness, even transcendence, rather like what happens to people who meditate and speak of sensing their deep connections to things in the world, of an empty self, and vanishing boundaries. Indeed, if you look long enough at a single object, you yourself, your "I-ness," will vanish in the fullness of the image you are looking at. I am not proposing Morandi as Zen master, but rather suggesting that the pictures themselves partake of a psychology of vision that occurs when the ordinary semantic meanings we ascribe to things have not disappeared entirely but have loosened their hold, and through an open embracing vision of what appears, the ordinary acquires the attributes of the extraordinary.

Morandi's images do not dissolve into total abstraction, although some of his late watercolors get very close. The artist's flat rejection of metaphysical realism—the idea that we can truly know the *real*—is not the same as saying that we don't see the world, but rather that *what we see is filtered through us*. Subject and object are not so easily separated in this view. I think Morandi's insistence on the *abstract* character of the real is a way to say: *This canvas is my perception, is my reality. It represents what I have actually seen*. From this perspective, Morandi is not clinging to the figurative but acknowledging that figure remains part of his understanding of what had been there for him in its fluctuating temporal reality, and which is now an immutable record or form of that experience.

Abramowicz writes that in 1955 Morandi confessed to her that if he had been born twenty years later, he would have been an abstract painter.[14] Roditi pressed Morandi about abstraction and Mondrian in his interview, but Morandi refused to acknowledge any connection to the Dutchman or his project. But then he was reluctant to be linked to any artist he didn't explicitly acknowledge as important to him, and actively tried to suppress a monograph that had been written about him by his friend, the art critic Arcangeli, because it placed his work in a historical perspective. Whatever the artist's speculations on his fate had he been born later, by 1955 abstraction had had a long history, and Morandi was deeply interested in what his fellow artists were up to all over the world. If he had wanted to cut all links to representation, he would have done it. My belief is that Morandi needed objects of scrutiny, because the act of looking and painting, not the act of painting alone, is the true subject matter of his work.

When I draw a thing in front of me, I have always felt that it is as if I am touching it. My hand traces what I feel is its shape. I am not thinking about where my hand is moving. I am looking and rendering. The two acts aren't separate but one and the same process. The work involves my whole attention. I don't narrate the process usually; it doesn't seem to need words in order to do it. Let us say I am drawing the Perrier bottle; that bottle becomes paramount, completely absorbing. The sight of the bottle and my hand on the paper merge in a single action. And *I lose myself*. As Shaun Gallagher and Dan Zahavi point out in their book *The Phenomenological Mind*, "The body tries to stay out of the way so we can get on with our task; it tends to efface itself on its way to its intentional goal. We do not normally monitor our movements in an explicitly conscious manner, although . . . we do have a pre-reflective awareness of our body in very general terms . . . but this prereflective awareness is not very detailed. I can say that I am reaching out to grasp a cup, but my sense of this is oriented toward the goal or intentional project I am involved in and not toward the specifics of my movement. I can't say very much about how I shape my hand in order to pick up a cup."[15] This is because we have a proprioceptive sense of our bodies, a *body schema,* which does not require explicit consciousness. If we had to think through every gesture, our lives would be a misery. Unlike reaching for a cup, art requires editing and thought as well, but finding the rightness one is looking for and knowing when to stop is a mysterious process and emerges from places in the mind that are often hidden. The result—the art we hang on the wall—becomes the tangible record of that dynamic embodied experience of perceiving and making. *Nature is within us,* said Cézanne. "We speak of 'inspiration,'" wrote Merleau-Ponty, "and the word should be taken literally. There really is inspiration and expiration of Being, action and passion so slightly discernible that it becomes impossible to distinguish between what sees and what is seen, what paints and what is painted."[16]

Morandi's cast-off objects, his bottles, cups, boxes, coffeepots, saucers, and cloths, often asymmetrical and worn, became vehicles in the inspiration and expiration of Being. The humbler, the blanker, the dustier, the more undistinguished the things, the better, because they offered themselves up to the eyes of the painter without context or assigned meanings. He knew he wanted to paint the unknowable—that abstract objective reality—which we have parsed and articulated for ourselves as cups and trees. When I visited the Morandi museum in Bologna, I looked into the small space where the artist's workroom has been reproduced, and was seized by a terrible poignancy. The strangeness of the project became obvious. There was something withdrawn and retentive at the core of this bachelor's personality, and stubborn, too. He did what he did. I looked at his chair, his hat, and the jumble of pedestrian objects that he had carefully gathered and saved to paint. They looked so abandoned, so unremarkable, so irretrievably banal that in that moment they summoned for me only the artist's death, the great gaping absence of the man whose Being had enchanted them.

2008

LOUISE BOURGEOIS

Art is not about art. Art is about life.

L. B.

A TINY, SLENDER WOMAN WITH LONG hair tied back in a ponytail, regal posture, a shrewd expression, and a forceful walk swept through the Pierre Matisse Gallery, an entourage of young men trailing behind her. She was dressed in black, something dramatic, and her presence acted on the room like a bolt of electricity. "Who is *that*?" I asked my husband. "Louise Bourgeois." "Oh, of course," I answered. A couple of years earlier, in 1982, The Museum of Modern Art had mounted a major show of her work. Curated by Deborah Wye, the exhibition brought the seventy-one-year-old Bourgeois, who had been showing painting and sculpture in New York since the forties, into the art world limelight.

That was the only time I saw her in the flesh. After a couple of minutes, she vanished, followers in tow. Although the details may not be perfect, my memory of what I felt as I looked at her is vivid—a mixture of awe, fascination, and amusement. There was a theatrical quality to her sudden entrance, as if she had staged it for our benefit. Louise Bourgeois is now ninety-five and still making art. The Tate Modern will show more than two hundred of her works in an exhibition that opens October 11 and will run until January 20. It's a major retrospective that includes many of her most famous sculptures as well as less well-known pieces that were made during seven decades of intense artistic labor.

The story of Louise Bourgeois's early life has become so enmeshed with her work that many critics have been seduced into biographical or psychoanalytic readings of the art, densely punctuated with pithy pronouncements from the artist, who is also a prolific writer: "My name is Louise Josephine Bourgeois. I was born 24 December 1911. All my work in the past fifty years, all my subjects have found their inspiration in my childhood. My childhood has never lost its magic, it has never lost its mystery, and it has never lost its drama."[1] Or perhaps more tantalizing (at least for someone with an analytic bent): "50 years old be kept in the dark—result rage result—frustration from knowing/10 years old unsatisfied curiosity—rage outrage result rage/kept out/1 year old—abandoned—why do they leave me/where are they/3 month old—famished and forgotten/1 month old—fear of death."[2]

The second of three (surviving) children, Bourgeois began her life on the Left Bank, where her parents owned and operated a gallery. Later, the family moved to Choisy-le-Roi and then to Antony. Her father served as a soldier during the First World War, was wounded at the front, and after his return, the family opened a tapestry restoration studio, where Louise learned to draw in order to assist in the family business. She suffered terribly when her father brought his mistress, an Englishwoman, Sadie, into the house under the pretext that she was the children's tutor, a situation his wife, Josephine, an avowed feminist, tolerated. Sadie stayed for ten years. Louise attended the Lycée Fenelon, and in 1932 studied mathematics for a short time at the Sorbonne. That same year, she cared for her critically ill mother, who died in her presence in September. Bourgeois left the Sorbonne for various art schools. At one of them she had Fernand Léger as a teacher. She knew the Surrealists, but understood they had little use for a woman artist and was frankly irritated by their preaching and antics. In 1938, she met the art historian Robert Goldwater, married him, and moved to New York, where she has lived and worked ever since.

Stories that are told and retold harden. Part of the pleasure we take in fairy tales and myths is that their forms are fixed, but family stories often turn rigid as well. Our narratives about tormented fathers or depressed mothers or suicides or lost money serve to explain ourselves. They order the chaotic and fragmentary character of memory, which is not stable, but dynamic and subject to change. Bourgeois's tale of the family interloper has been reiterated time and again both by the artist and by her critics since she first revealed it in *Artforum* in 1982 under the title "Child Abuse,"[3] but neither it, nor any other story or poetic utterance from her writings, can *explain* her art. The work has its own oblique vocabulary, its own internal logic or anti-logic, its own stories to tell, that resist placing an external narrative, no matter how titillating, on top of it. Its meanings are made in the encounter between the viewer and the art object, an experience that is sensual, emotional, intellectual, and dependent on both the attention and expectations of the person doing the looking.

Before I had read a word about or by Louise Bourgeois, I was fascinated by the emotional power of her work, how it stirred up old pains and fears, summoned complex and often contradictory associations, or echoed my own obsessions with rooms, dolls, missing limbs, mirrors, violence, nameless threats, the comfort of order, and the distress of ambiguity. Bourgeois can take you to strange and hidden places in yourself. This is her gift. What may be deeply personal for her finds its translation in art that is far too mysterious to be confessional. Throughout her long career, however, there are repetitive themes and forms that appear in multifarious guises and mutations. From the paintings first shown in 1947 under the collective title *Femme Maison* to the mesmerizing *Cells* of the nineties, the artist has vigorously reinvented versions of the body/house—as refuge, trap, a bit of both—and she has done it with an eye and mind that interrogates the history of art as well as the human psyche.

The mind and its memories as a metaphorical place, *topos,* is ancient. Freud, too, was fond of a spatial trope—archaeology. Dig and you shall find. Repressed memories. Screen memories. Fantasies. For Aristotle, every memory has two parts: *simulacrum,* a likeness or image, and *intentio,* an emotional color that is an associative link to a person's inner chain of experiences. Word association as a clue to unconscious processes would become an essential part of psychiatry in the nineteenth century, and today brain scientists know that emotion is crucial to memory. What we don't *feel,* we forget. I have come to think of Bourgeois as an artist who roams the antechambers of a charged past, looting it for material she reconfigures as external places and beings or being-places. The house/ women of *Femme Maison* are in and of the architecture that can't hold their huge but vulnerable bodies. The debt to Surrealism is obvious. As in Magritte's *Le Modèle Rouge* (1935) in which boots and feet are one, Bourgeois makes the container the contained. But while the impulse in Surrealism was always toward objectification— turning person into thing—Bourgeois's does exactly the opposite. The inanimate houses come alive.

Her early sculptures, or *Personnages,* first shown in 1949, are thin, life-size rough-hewn wooden figures that have often been cited as an early example of installation art. These abstract tower/ beings or "presences" inhabit a room in relation to one another and to the visitors who come to see them. "They were about people in my mind," Bourgeois said in an interview. Stiff, hacked, and precariously anchored, one expects them to teeter or even topple. When I look at *Sleeping Figure,* I think of someone on crutches. *Portrait of Jean-Louis* is a boy-skyscraper. A work from the same period, the abstract *The Blind Leading the Blind,* with its long multiple legs, feels startlingly like an advancing crowd. But these objects also resemble three-dimensional signs or characters from an unknown language inscribed in space. Like letters, they are stand-ins for what isn't there, tactile ghosts.

Bourgeois's sculptures from the sixties, when she left wood and began to work in latex, plaster, bronze, and marble, look different but reprise her themes. The rigid anatomies and architectures of the fifties seem to have been melted down into organic forms that summon genitalia, internal organs, stones, fossils, caves, primitive huts, as well as the work of other sculptors from Bernini to Brancusi. *Labyrinthine Tower* (1962) is a phallic spiral. The *Lairs*, *Cumuls*, and *Soft Landscapes* are variously disquieting and comforting, suggestive of phallic outcroppings, womblike retreats, and baroque drapery. The suspended bronze *Janus*es are phallic, pelvic, labial, mammary, and ocular. "Oh my God, it's a penis!" becomes "Well, not really, sort of, but it's also . . ." The unstable borders, sliding recognitions, aggressive sexual ambiguity, and visions of the body amputated, in pieces, or sprouting extra parts, evoke a world in which perception is not yet structured by language, a hallucinatory prelingusitic space of primal drives. A nod to Freud's "polymorphous perverse," perhaps? It's not strange that critics have called upon the theories of Melanie Klein, D. W. Winnicott, and Jacques Lacan to explicate the work of a woman who was once quoted as saying, "Psychoanalysis is my religion."

The Destruction of the Father (1974) illustrates the difficulty faced by those trying to interpret Bourgeois's art, because the object and the narrative that accompanies it have become inseparable. The thing looks like a stage with its frame, draped fabric, and internal red illumination. A gigantic mouth or maw with mounds above and below holds at its center cast animal bones, as well as lumps and protuberances. The story, told in first- and third-person versions by the artist, is that "we" or "the children" leap up onto the table and eat the father—an "oral drama." Part Greek tragedy, part *Totem and Taboo*, the exciting fantasy of *eating* Dad may be implicit in what we see, but it is not explicit. Revenge for Sadie? Feminist politics through the language of Kleinian child analysis? These are just two proposed solutions that, however well meant, pinch the work and don't begin to capture its wounded, raw, ambivalent feeling.

The artist's intellectual sophistication, her mordant commentary, and the weight of the theory brought to bear on her work can quickly obfuscate rather than reveal what's in front of us. Even when a visual reference is explicit, as in the *Arch of Hysteria*, critics are quick to jump to conclusions, which are then passed from one to the next. The body in most versions of Bourgeois's arch is male. Art writers have repeatedly glossed this as a feminist inversion of Jean-Martin Charcot's idea that hysteria is an illness exclusive to women. But the nineteenth-century neurologist (with whom Freud studied) firmly believed in, wrote about, lectured on, and treated "traumatic male hysteria." In the Bibliotèque Charcot at the Salpêtrière Hospital in Paris there is a photograph of *a naked man* in the *arc en circle*. I am convinced Bourgeois knows the picture—the similarity is striking. Although the connotations of hysteria then and now are undeniably sexist, and the artist may have wanted to play with that assumption, her use of the image addresses something else: an ongoing fascination with psychic/somatic states, with explosive tension as well as its opposite—flaccid exhaustion and withdrawal.

One version of the arch is part of a *Cell* (1992–93), in which the man has lost his head and arms, perhaps to the saw that stands nearby in the enclosure. Under him, on his bed or covered board, I read the words *Je t'aime* written by hand in red over and over again like an incantation. I love the *Cells*, and there are several in the show. For me, they hold the attraction of forbidden places in my childhood—an erotic tug to see what's *in there*. They both lure and frighten me. They beckon me in and keep me out. Sometimes I can peer through an open door. Other times I look through the cage walls. In *Eyes and Mirrors* (1993) I confront my own voyeurism. In *Choisy* (1990–1993) a guillotine hangs ominously over a marble house, and I imagine it being cut in two. My body. My house. I can't help writing stories for these enigmatic spaces, in which I find both violence and love. They are like mute, motionless narratives, and even when one doesn't know that much of the iconography is personal—the house is a model of the Bourgeois family house in Choisy, the tapestries in *Spider* recall the restoration work of Josephine—its intimacy is palpable. And while the artist makes use of found objects—beds, chairs, spools, perfume bottles, keys, for example—their placement and proximity to sculptures of body parts or abstract forms create an atmosphere of only partial legibility and turn the *Cells* into machines of metaphorical association and recollection for the viewer. I clutch at the fragments of my early memories through the familiar architecture of my childhood house that allows me to locate my experience in space. Without that frame, the memories are suspended in emptiness. But memories change, too. Each time we remember an event, the present tinges the past, which is always also imaginary. The *Cells* gives us enchanted access to that fragile *topos* where memory and fantasy merge.

The most recent pieces in the show are made of fabric, more Bourgeoisian bodies, many of them injured, some of them unhoused or suspended. The rooms have vanished. One of the bed partners in the headless pair of *Couple IV* (2001–2002) wears a prosthetic leg. The *Three Horizontals* (1998), mounted one above the other, like diminishing versions of the same person, are amputees. Their soft anatomies appear to have been torn and mended.

The aching expression on the face of *Rejection* (2001–2002) makes me want to reach into the box, take out the poor head, and cradle it in my arms. I know that these sewn, scarred figures are disturbing, but for me they are also among the most beautiful and compassionate works Bourgeois has made. They are dolls of loss and mortality. I am looking at myself. I am looking at all of us. The artist brings back the *Arch of Hysteria* (2000), this time as a woman. She hangs in the air, her wounds stitched up, but her body alive in its shallow arc. Louise Bourgeois is old, but the vigor of her imagination is clearly ageless. She once said that her sculpture is her body. If I could choose one work from her, I would pick *Seven in a Bed* (2001), a late piece of manic joy—sweet, erotic, and funny. But neither I nor the artist can choose. The body of Louise Bourgeois is multiple and potent. It borrows from and transforms the vocabularies of modern art. It is feminine and masculine, terrified and bold, soft and hard. It speaks in the language of space and form and plays with both recognition and strangeness.

In his essay for the Tate's catalogue, Robert Storr proposes an "unreading" of Louise Bourgeois, the theoretical object.[4] This is wise. I propose that you go to the Tate Modern and look long and hard at the work. After that, you may want to read what has been said by and about this extraordinary artist. And then, you may want to unread all of it, not excluding the words I have offered here.

2007

OLD PICTURES

PHOTOGRAPHS HAVE LONG BEEN SEEN as markers of the past, a way of preserving what *was* in what *is*. Unlike paintings, which can invent a subject, photographs preserve a subject in a *real* moment in time. Despite the fact that well before the era of Photoshop, camera images were manipulated (remember the Cottingley fairies), it is an idea that has had long-standing power. What fascinates me most about photographs are their personal and public uses as tokens of memory and the fact that their efficiency, or lack of it, in terms of seeing and remembering, works precisely to the degree that they are *not* like visual perception and memory in the brain. Photographs are produced mechanically, which means that, unlike painting, they are created outside human perception, but, like paintings, they exist as representations outside our bodies. At the same time, we look at photographs with our eyes. The vagaries of human vision apply to photos just as they do to all other perceived objects.

The visual and the linguistic occupy different sites in the brain. Roger Sperry's famous studies on split-brain patients, people with intractable epilepsy who had their corpus callosums severed to end their seizures, a procedure that separated the language-dominant left hemisphere from the right, illuminate the complexities of perception. By briefly flashing an image on a screen to such patients, Sperry discovered that he could provide information to the right hemisphere that the left couldn't access. For example, he projected pornographic pictures to a female split-brain patient, who blushed and giggled accordingly, but was unable to identify what she had seen or explain why she was embarrassed. Mark Solms and Oliver Turnbull, in their book *The Brain and the Inner World,* sum up the findings in this way: "For someone to reflect consciously on visual experiences, he or she has to recode the visual experience into words. This capacity is lost when the left (verbal) hemisphere is disconnected from the original visual experience."[1]

Perception and its crucial cohort, memory, are complex dynamic systems in the brain and have both implicit (unconscious) and explicit (conscious) features. Although scientists once subscribed to a primitive notion of memory storage—you perceived an object and then lodged it intact in your memory—neuroscientists now believe that when you retrieve a memory, you are not retrieving an original memory but rather the memory you last retrieved. In other words, we edit. Memory changes. It is now obvious that *the brain is not a camera; it is not a computer; it is not a machine.* Despite the fact that new technologies are developing seeing-machines that can recognize people and objects, and many of us work with remembering-machines, our computers, every day, there is little lust for machines that, to use the neuroscience term, *reconsolidate* memories over time, that *unknowingly* rewrite or reconfigure the scenes and faces of the past. Digital alteration is a tool for the conscious, not the unconscious mind.

The "truth" factor in photographs is founded on the notion that the camera, unlike our frail and inaccurate brains, has what

John Berger calls a "supernatural eye."[2] This has been seen as the camera's advantage and was the reason why it was hailed as a great scientific tool—and has proved to be one. When the nineteenth-century neurologist Jean-Martin Charcot wrote, "I am nothing more than a photographer. I inscribe what I see,"[3] he was giving himself a high compliment. Albert Londe, director of the photography department at the Salpêtrière (Charcot's hospital in Paris) called the photographic plate "the scientist's true retina."[4] What Charcot and Londe failed to see was that photography, then still young, had already been codified by conventions, many of them borrowed from painting and sculpture, and that the images they took of the women in the hysteria ward to document what Charcot called the *iconography* of hysteria—a series of frozen, beautifully lit images of its postures, contractions, and seizures— now look both artificial and Romantic. The photography of science was as prey to ideology then as it is now. Whether its subject is a hysterical girl or Martian dust, the machine fixes what it sees and lures the viewer into the feeling that the static image or the bit of moving film is an avenue for retrieval, a way to get the thing or person back.

Every photographed subject becomes a sign of disappearance because it belongs to the past. That's why each family photo, even if it was taken last week, carries in it a quality of bereavement, of loss. In Roland Barthes's meditation, *Camera Lucida,* he confesses that he continues to stare at the picture of his dead mother in the hope that he may discover "what is behind." "I want to outline the loved face by thought, to make it into the unique field of an intense observation; I want to enlarge this face in order to see it better, to know its truth (and sometimes naïvely I confide this task to a laboratory). I believe that by enlarging the detail . . . I will finally reach my mother's very being."[5] Barthes longs to recover something of the living woman and what she meant to him, but as John Berger points out in "Uses of Photography," ". . . unlike memory, photographs do not in themselves preserve meaning."[6]

Berger elaborates by saying that to have meaning, a photograph must be rooted in time and narrative. We surround the pictures with our stories. My father died in early February last year, and since his death, like Barthes before me, I have repeatedly looked at a few photographs of him—one of him as a child with his sister, one of him grinning in his army uniform, another when he was somewhat older, by then a professor, whose hair loss was aggravated by the malaria that plagued him even after he returned from the Pacific, and a last picture of my father when he was dying. Before his death, I did not feel much need to look at these images, but now I do. I look at the photographs of my father because I have assigned them a meaning that is part of my story of him, but the pictures are distinct from my recollections. They are mechanical ghosts, a series of empty phantoms that nevertheless serve as traces of him, the man. Through them, I hope to remind myself of his plural appearances as he aged, because in my memory his faces have merged—the young father, the older father, and the eighty-one-year-old father near death.

Unlike photographs, living memory is exclusive, not inclusive. For example, when I remember an important conversation I had with my father years ago, during which he asked me rather pointedly if I really wanted to become a professor, I recall exactly where the conversation took place: on the lawn in front of my parents' house. It's early summer and the grass beneath our feet is new and green, and I feel the presence of my father beside me and have a vague sense that his expression has a certain kindly earnestness, but his features at that moment, when he was only a few years older than I am now, are lost. Classical theories of memory understood the importance of *place* as an organizing principle of mnemotechnics. According to Cicero, it all began with an episode in the life of Simonides, the pre-Socratic lyric poet, who identified the mangled corpses of people who had been at a banquet when the roof collapsed on top of them because he remembered where they had been sitting. Cicero writes, "He inferred that persons desiring to train this faculty (memory) must select localities and form mental images of the facts they wish to remember and store those images in the localities . . ."[7] My memory of the place and the question my father asked are fixed—the rest is flux. In good Ciceronian fashion, I attached my father's words to a locality and remembered what I wished to keep, namely that my father had no vested interest in my becoming a professor, that he rather wished I wouldn't, and the words he uttered that day became in memory his tacit blessing for my writing ambitions.

This event is part of my extended consciousness, what neuropsychologists call "episodic memory," and the neural networks involved depend heavily on the cerebral cortex, the language zones of the left hemisphere, and particularly on the superstructure of the left temporal lobes. In other words, episodic memory jettisons peripheral information in favor of a reduced but highly efficient version of what happened, which relies strongly on words. The episodic memory then becomes part of what Antonio Damasio calls "autobiographical memory"[8] which is the ongoing narrative of the self. Episodic memory is that which says "I." "I remember . . ." Obviously, a great deal more was going on at the time between my father and me, a foggy emotional and sensual resonance that I retain, as well as forgotten aspects of our talk that I can't summon by saying, "I remember." My father's comments were often oblique and called for interpretation on my part, and that interpretation is not static; it may go on for a lifetime. Had someone taken a snapshot of the two of us that day on the lawn, the picture might have become a ground for memory. I might have included details frozen in the photo that are now lost to me. The image might have become a sign of the conversation, and rather than remaining internalized in my memory, I might have seen myself with my father from a distance as an observer rather than as an actor. I have also attached memories to the wrong places. Not long ago, I realized that an early memory I have from my fourth year was taking place in *the wrong house*. For years I had been seeing that little event unfold in a house that hadn't been built yet. Somewhere along the line, the memory was reconsolidated, and one architecture replaced another. Like many people, I have also mistaken a photograph for a childhood recollection, an inversion that casts light on yet another problem: false memory.

The way I use my father's photographs is intensely private. They are flat, silent tokens of my love for the living man, the man with whom I had a complicated relation for many years, the person I can never resurrect, but who exists for me as an essential part of the narrative of my own life, but they don't function as catalysts for memory. They are aliens, which may in fact interfere with my remembrance of him. They simultaneously fascinate and hurt me because I can't help but think of their kinship to corpses—those shells of nonbeing, the dead.

We necessarily assign meaning to pictures and use them, not only as documents of personal memory, but as imaginary objects to titillate, revolt, comfort, delude, or justify us. In the broader culture, photographs can become signs of collective dreams or traumas. For most New Yorkers, even the most boring shot of the Twin Towers triggers an onslaught of personal memories because we ground or place the image in the story of our lives. If the same shot were part of a montage, like the ones that appeared on television soon after the attack—a firefighter wading through debris, heroic music playing, followed by an inset of an American flag waving in the wind—there is suddenly far less room for private memory. Such a sequence of images is the visual equivalent of a slogan. The words that might encapsulate its meaning appear only as vague abstractions—courage and patriotism. Like a commercial, it is intended to create an emotional response. Our perception is being directed. As David Levi-Strauss writes in his essay "Photography and Belief," "the first question must always be: Who is using this photograph and to what end?"⁹ He also argues that propaganda of this kind works because people believe what they want to believe. This is obvious. Those who are convinced that the earth is flat, that men never walked on the moon, that the Holocaust did not happen, that no Jews died on September 11, or that Saddam Hussein was responsible for the catastrophe on that day are not convinced by documentary films or photographs that "prove" them wrong. But then mass propaganda isn't new, and its most forceful implementation remains repetition: show the same pictures and utter the same words over and over and over again. George Bush successively used this technique in the last American election. The public was inundated with footage of the president repeating the same phrases in front of carefully screened, cheering crowds. And yet, these images did not sway me, and I was hardly alone. Propaganda often reinforces a desire or belief that is already present in the viewer.

A larger question is: Has photography and its uses, both personal and public, altered our perception of what is real and not real? In her famous essay "On Photography," Susan Sontag argues that "the notion of what is real has been progressively complicated and weakened." It is so weak, in fact, that she declares, "It is common now for people to insist about their experiences of a violent event in which they are caught up—a plane crash, a shoot-out, a terrorist bombing—that it seemed like a movie. This is said, other descriptions seeming insufficient, in order to explain how real it was."¹⁰ But exactly the reverse is true. If people summon movies under such circumstances, it is precisely to describe how *unreal* the event felt. Terrifying violence often creates dissociated responses in people, an eerie sense of detachment from the horror, as if they are not participants but observers. The person who, after a car crash, sees herself lying on the highway from above; the soldier who witnesses his buddy's horrific death but relates it as if it had happened to someone else; or the child who, after being beaten repeatedly, acquires the ability to "disappear" from his own pain all suffer from a form of adaptive *unreality*. Pierre Janet, the neurologist and philosopher, coined the term *dissociation* in the late nineteenth century for a psychobiological split within a traumatized person. As van der Kolk and van der Hart, two contemporary researchers on trauma, put it: "Traumatic memories are the unassimilated scraps of overwhelming experiences, which need to be integrated with existing mental schemas, and be transformed into narrative language."[11] More simply stated, some horrible experiences are not taken in as ordinary autobiographical, episodic memories. They are qualitatively different, and in some cases, this results in numbing, or the feeling that you and/ or your surroundings are unreal. Before movies existed, a person suffering from this sensation of unreality might have evoked the theater.

This notion, however, that "the real" has been degraded by our relation to photographic images, that we as a culture are numb to grotesque pictures of war and mayhem, has become a cultural truism, endlessly regurgitated, as if there were no need for further debate. Moreover, the explosion of visual technologies has caused us to lose the ability to discriminate between an object and its copy. In "The Procession of Simulacra," Jean Baudrillard writes, with considerable rhetorical flourish, that we (at least those of us who are citizens of the United States) are living in a culture in which "Disneyland is presented as imaginary in order to make us believe that the rest is real, when in fact all of Los Angeles and the America surrounding it are no longer real, but of the order of the hyper-real and of simulation."[12] It is important to point out that neither Sontag nor Baudrillard would subscribe to naïve realism, the idea that we can truly know external reality. They would agree that human beings gain access to the outside world through our perceptions of it, which is necessarily a limited view of things. And yet, a distinction remains between a life being lived and the mechanical images of a life being lived. Through a complicated evolution of poststructuralist thinking, it became fashionable in some circles to think that people have been entirely remade or "constructed" by our new technoworld, that even our human *needs* have been altered. In an era of reality TV, celebrity culture, and ever-growing digital technologies, has modern life, as Baudrillard would have it, dissolved entirely into simulacra? At the end of his essay he urges readers to stage "a fake hold-up," an action he argues is doomed to failure because "the artificial signs" will be mixed with "real elements." If a police officer believes you are a real robber, he may shoot you. But this would have been true in 1730 as well. Confusion of this order is very old indeed.

There is little doubt that late capitalism relies heavily on an endless parade of images, which, while seductive, are essentially empty and intended to make sure that people consume more and more products. Indeed, Madison Avenue's job is to create needs we didn't know we had. Celebrity means turning a human being into a vacant commodity that can be bought and sold literally as image only, and it can proliferate—be everywhere at once—on the Internet. Reality TV is an oxymoron. Wars are sold (and unsold) to the public through the camera lens. A short list will suffice: Vietnam, the Gulf War, the invasion of Iraq, Abu Ghraib. And photographs have now obtained what Walter Benjamin famously claimed in "The Work of Art in the Age of Mechanical Reproduction" they did not have: aura. An artist's photo, video, or film, despite the fact that it's endlessly reproducible, may command a very high price. It has "cult value." Artists are using digital technology to make art, another tool among many. Baudelaire's diatribe against the idea that photography is not art because it is divorced from dream seems antiquated. All of this is true. It is also true that images affect us; they may even addle our brains with nonsense the way chivalric romance took over poor Quixote. Movies and photographs have entered both my dreams and my fictions.

There is something intellectually exciting about taking an idea and pushing it to its logical conclusion. It is also fun to make grand claims for one's own era, for its singularity, its never-have-we-been-here-before quality, and ironically perhaps, there is visceral delight in pronouncements that things are truly bad now, worse than ever, and that people have become so stupefied by media they have lost all sense of a felt, lived reality. Of course, those who make these claims occupy a special position. They are not duped. They see it all clearly. I am not so confident. I do know I have a routine faith in the reality of my immediate sensory world that I do not have when I watch a movie or look at an image on the Internet, however much I may be caught up in it. At the same time, when I was faced with the catastrophe of September 11 and feared for the safety of my daughter and my two sisters and their families, I had to say to myself, "This is real. This has happened." I also know that after a car accident, as I sat frozen in my seat, and the firemen cut me out of the wreckage with the Jaws of Life, I felt as removed and indifferent and distant from what was happening to me as I ever have. The whole thing felt unreal.

Like many New Yorkers, I do not like to see pictures of the towers on 9/11. A year after the event, I was in a museum in Paris, where I was to give a reading. I had a little time and wandered into an exhibition by the French theorist Paul Virilio, who is known for his speed and accident theories. Projected on the wall was the familiar film of the mass murder in New York.

I felt nauseated and upset and left immediately. That evening at a dinner, my French publisher condescendingly explained to me that Virilio "is one of our great philosophers," certain of course that I had not heard of him. I had, however, known about Virilio for years. I read his work in the eighties, and resisted his ideas. Virilio too believes that "reality" will cease to exist in our hyper-technological age. Personal experience itself, our relation to actual things in the world, are in danger of becoming dematerialized and virtual. According to him, scientific theories of light and speed have now replaced theories of time and space.[13] Vision itself has been industrialized, and we are headed for an apocalyptic future in which these disembodied images will become substitutes for, well, us. The alarm in Virilio's writings is palpable; his voice is pitched high, like a shrill scream. (I venture to say that had he been a woman his fate as a thinker would have been far more uncertain.) The man is serious and knowledgeable, but his ideas have run away with him. There are no brakes on his thought-vehicle as it races toward this horrible science-fiction fantasy.

To be fair, my resistance to his ideas is emotional as well as intellectual. In this, I am no different from other people. Our ideas are born of our emotional temperaments, of unreason as much as reason. It is easy to see how the spectacular character of the 9/11 images, their uncanny resemblance to Hollywood films, and the nearly instantaneous speed of their transmission would appear to be confirmation of these related theories. But there is something terribly wrong with these ideas, nevertheless. Realness, a sense of what is true and present, is a feeling we have, and it is not always fixed. I turned away from the images in the museum because they are *not abstract* for me. Their meaning lies in the personal narratives I have given them. They represent grief. My emotion will not diminish with repetition. Furthermore, looking at the films was not the same as looking through the window of my own house at the smoke rising from the first building after it had been hit, although the question of the real and unreal remains pertinent in this catastrophic context. But it is not pertinent because we have become tools of a technocratic system that has dulled our minds to the degree that we cannot distinguish an actual building from a picture or film of it. Some experiences have a shattering effect on the human organism, so devastating that in order to protect itself, it refuses to acknowledge their reality. Technology has not changed this. The people who suffered from psychic shock after September 11 looked very much like those who emerged from the trenches of World War I.

Particular experience is always part of collective experience. We who were in New York City remember where we were on September 11, and the memories have an almost uncanny vividness, forever attached to a room, a street corner, a garden, the *place* where we were that day. And their clarity is retained by our emotion, what we felt when we understood what had happened. I am convinced that even those who celebrated the carnage remember it with uncommon lucidity. Scientists sometimes refer to this as a "flashbulb" memory. It occurs when the extraordinary happens, when the expectation that is so deeply part of our daily visual perceptions is thoroughly disrupted. The memory of ordinary daily events falls easily into conventionalized visual categories that often blur together. Surprise and shock create a sharpening of pictorial recollection.

I am glad that I do not have a photograph of the car my husband, our daughter, and our dog were in that day we crashed. I never saw the ruined Toyota, but my husband did, and he said he could not believe that we had come out of that squashed, deformed vehicle alive. If such an image existed, it would have little meaning for other people, except perhaps as a warning to drive defensively. For me, however, it would remind me of a reality a part of me denied. It would also serve as an objective confirmation of the accident: *I really was in that car.* My perception of the picture would be complex and variable, and dependent on my mood. I am well aware that thoughts like these—ambiguous and meandering as they are—hold little attraction for most people. It is certainty that seduces many of us—the brash and/or scolding declarations that new technology has permanently and profoundly altered human beings, has made us dimwitted, or turned us into appendages of our machines. Sontag, Baudrillard, and Virilio are thoughtful advocates of this view. It is advanced by countless other far more debased and popular voices in books, newspaper articles, blogs, and in the media generally, many of them propped up by the "latest" brain research. These writers either misrepresent the science they cite or, if they represent it accurately, do so without any critical distance because they simply don't understand it well enough to judge it.

I think it is useful to remember that in the nineteenth century the inhuman speed of train travel and its inevitable consequence, accidents, ushered in a new illness: railway spine. John E. Erichsen, a respected surgeon who published a book on the subject in 1866, declared that ". . . in no ordinary accident can the shock be so great as in those that occur on railways . . ."[14] The idea is pointed: falling from a bridge or off a horse or going down in a storm at sea might shock you, but railway accidents are particular in their horror. The technology that had made train travel possible also created a unique, modern pathology that was much debated in the medical profession and heavily covered in the popular press. The mysterious affliction, which was often physically undetectable, was a testament to the fact that human beings had become the helpless victims of their own ingenious invention. As a chapter in medical history, railway spine is a complicated and interesting phenomenon, but for my purposes here, it may simply stand as a striking echo of contemporary ideas about the frightening changes wrought by our own new versions of speeding technology.

The truth is people *like* to believe these chilling ideas. They speak to their fears, and there is something exciting and enjoyable about being safely afraid. Paradoxically, for many (those in the New York art world who leapt on Baudrillard's simulacra theories, for example), embracing this line of thought had the stimulation value of going to a science-fiction movie about copies of human beings growing in pods or replicants running around a wrecked city. And, like so many theoretical positions, it exempts those who advocate it: *They,* not I, have lost their hold on reality. Some skepticism might be in order here.

Pictures have always been steeped in the cultural ideologies of their time, and our perception of them is necessarily shaped by these historically mutable fictions. It is also true that often we cannot articulate what we are seeing, and some aspects of an image may have a subliminal effect on us that we will never fully understand. Indeed, an unconscious perception may shape us in ways we will never know. As part of our visual universe, photographs and films are subject to the vicissitudes of perception and to memory, desire and emotion. They gain or lose meaning, feel familiar or alien, real or unreal, depending on who is looking at them. But these meanings and feelings are often diffuse, difficult to categorize, and rarely simple.

2005

DUCCIO DI BUONINSEGNA AT THE MET

Ever since I saw his *Maestà* in Siena in 1980, I have been haunted by the images of Duccio di Buoninsegna. When I heard that the Metropolitan Museum of Art in New York had acquired a painting by the Sienese master, I couldn't wait to see it. *The Madonna and Child*, painted in tempera and gold on wood, is a small work, 27.9 by 21 centimeters. Its provenance dates only to the late nineteenth century, but scholars have assigned the work an approximate year: 1300. A small, sober baby sits in his mother's arms and looks intently into her eyes. Although she is turned toward him, her eyes don't meet his. She seems to be looking inward. The lines of her molded brows and the turn of her small, delicate mouth create an expression that is at once sorrowful, resigned, and tender. This picture, like all devotional objects of the time, was a means to gain entrance to the sacred narrative, not through an intellectual understanding of dogma, but through emotion. In the classic fourteenth-century work *Meditations on the Life of Christ*, Pseudo-Bonaventure exhorts his readers to feel the story, to imagine "the very young and tender mother" on the flight into Egypt, the "wild roads, obscure, rocky, and difficult," and then to contemplate the little boy who is with them. "Be a child with the child Jesus," he writes. The successful image was one that facilitated empathy.

Seven hundred years later, Duccio's painting remains one of powerful feeling. Why? Although its composition preserves the abstract character of a Byzantine icon with idealized figures who inhabit the gleaming nowhere of a gold background, and the unusual detail of a parapet below the two removes them even further from the viewer's space, the emotional resonance between this mother and her infant is recognizable as profoundly human. The two bodies are linked through gesture—the baby clutches the veil near his mother's face, while her fingers hold the hem of his red robe. But the real story lies in their facial expressions, in their eyes, in the exchange that takes place between them. What neurobiologists are now telling us—that the mother's face, especially her eyes, is a primary source of visual stimulation for an infant and that the gaze patterns between mother and child are essential to the latter's forebrain development—simply confirms what most mothers already know: you have to look at your baby. Duccio's Madonna has withdrawn her eyes for a moment to think, but the child looks directly into her eyes as if waiting for her to turn back to him. The quiet sadness in her face implies what the viewer knows and must anticipate: the suffering of the Passion. And yet, beyond the Christian narrative is the ordinary one. Every child who grows up leaves its mother, and no child can be protected from the sorrows of the world. The fact that the image is so simple and unburdened by the details of a particular place enhances its stark subject matter—the love between mother and child. The spectator becomes witness to the essential dialectic of what it means to be human: I become myself through the eyes of another.

2007

KIKI SMITH
Bound and Unbound

YEARS AGO, I SAW A Kiki Smith exhibition somewhere in
New York City. On the gallery floor were several sculptures
of women who looked as if they were staggering forward. In
memory the figures are black, and gleaming red chains of glass
beads fall from between their legs. I recall that the blatant reference to menstruation took me aback, and I asked myself whether
I, sophisticated urbanite and art viewer, remained influenced by
the lingering taboo against depicting the menses. On hindsight,
however, what interests me is the memory itself: the fact that a
version of those figures stayed in my mind with a potency I
could not have predicted.

As I looked at the works in the Smith retrospective at the
Walker Art Center in Minneapolis, the recollection of the bleeding women continued to haunt me. Those sculptures were not in
the retrospective, but I noticed that many of the pieces had a
strong emotional impact on me. Depending on the object, I felt
uncomfortable, sad, anxious, calm, pitying, tender, sympathetic,
and several times I actually burst out laughing. This broad range

of feeling interested me because many artists have what I think of as a consistent tone: sober or witty, tragic or comic. In Kiki Smith's art, on the other hand, thematic unity is coupled with a striking affective diversity.

Because so much of Smith's art refers to bodies, I began with the problem of anatomies. One need only think of the immense variety of the human form in various tribal arts, waxworks, effigies, death masks, mannequins, votives, icons, Greek statuary, and dolls to understand that perception of the body is not a given, but a drama of perception coded in time and culture. The energy of Smith's work is in part derived from looting traditions of representation and then altering them for her own purposes. The longer I looked at her work, the more I became convinced that hers is an art of shifting borders, an art that disrupts divisions, categories, separations, and definitions of our own bodies in relation to the world around us. The fact that her bodies and parts of bodies, human and animal, in two dimensions and three, are rendered in a profligate array of materials—fabric, paper, beeswax, bronze, hair, porcelain, latex, glass, aluminum, pewter, gold, wood, feathers, jewels, Plexiglas, pigment, and amalgams thereof—infects the spectator's vision with the sense of touch. As I walked through the show, I continually imagined what it would be like to commit the forbidden act of reaching out and caressing the works.

A number of pieces refer directly to anatomy as a science and to the old business of dissection. Body parts are sometimes depicted as discrete units: an untitled plaster and pigment hand (1980), *Teeth* (1983), and *Glass Stomach* (1985). *Nine Tenths of the Law* (1985) made me think of the familiar anatomical charts found in doctor's offices, but Smith's chart defies pedagogy. It blurs not all but some of the nine forms beyond recognition and suggests similar shapes, not inside the body but outside it—stones, leaves, plants. The superimposed legal phrase forces the viewer into a wry consideration of what it means to *own* one's body and includes the darkly comic implication that our organs and parts become isolated only in morbidity or death. *Tongue in Ear* welds the two named parts in a simultaneously repellent and humorous rendering that made me think of the strangeness of human eroticism. There are "pieces" of people and animals throughout the show: *Inner Ear* (1992), *Tailbone* (1993), the beautiful crystal breast called *Little Mountain* (1993–96), the abstract *Skins* in cast aluminum (1992), the frightening *Daisy Chain* of a bronze head and limbs connected by a steel chain, as well as *Lowbow*, fumed glass drops that resemble sperm (1999), *Animal Skulls* (1995) and *The Cells—The Moon* (1996) in bronze that explicitly binds the two named entities as metaphors of one another.

But the piece that made me pause, then laugh, and then further ponder the theme of bodily fragmentation was the untitled work (1987–90) of twelve uniform silver jars in a line, elegantly labeled: *semen, mucus, vomit, oil, tears, blood, milk, saliva, diarrhea, urine, sweat, pus*. Each container designates a liquid corporeal waste. In short, what we leak, secrete, excrete, ejaculate. All of them emanate from an opening in the body and cross its threshold. They are literally the stuff of our borders. Penis, mouth, eyes, nipples, anus, urethra, skin are all porous. Where the body begins and ends, what we find innocuous and what we find repugnant are ideas shaped by culture. In Smith's list, all the liquids, with the possible exception of tears, are subject to one level of taboo or another in our world. As Mary Douglas points out in her book *Purity and Danger,* ideas about pollution vary. "In some [cultures] menstrual pollution is feared as a lethal danger; in others not at all. In some excreta is dangerous, in others it is only a joke. In India cooked food and saliva are pollution prone, but Bushmen collect melon seeds from their mouths for later roasting and eating."[1] What is at stake is not germs but order—a symbolic structure with its myriad meanings that determines our perceptions of what is and what isn't *us,* what we cast off as not-I-anymore. Why does urine, or any other secretion, cease to belong to me the moment it hits the air? Why does it cease to be *mine*?

All liquids, of course, are shapeless unless they are contained. They seep into the ground or evaporate and become part of the atmosphere. By neatly isolating and *containing* body fluids in lovely silver jars, each labeled with the name of what it holds, Smith offers us a wry commentary on language and identity. Words, after all, create the linguistic categories, which help dictate the separation of one thing from another. Openings and leaks in any structure are a threat to the neat outlines we construct for all beings and things and how we distinguish that person or object from what is around it. Broken and running boundaries destroy the clarity of form. Although humor is notoriously difficult to explicate, I think my chuckle when I saw this piece was generated at least in part by its beauty, the row of gleaming jars with their elegant old script designating pus or diarrhea was comic, not only because I often laugh to dispel disgust or uneasiness, but because the whole piece exposes our huge investment in symbolic containment and the anxiety about ambiguity that lies beneath it.

Symbolic divisions and categories fix what is by nature unfixed and unnamed. Smith plays relentlessly with the problem of flux in a given system. For example, exactly what constitutes a whole and what a part? Are her male and female *Uro-genital Systems,* for example, wholes or parts? In anatomy they may qualify as discrete systems, but in the living body they are merely fragments of a functioning whole. And what is one to make of the fact that these systems are bronze and summon nothing so much as archaeological finds, relics of a lost civilization and belief system? The empty bronze *Womb* (1986) resembles a vessel or bowl from a "dig" and simultaneously unearths a host of container associations, including small coffins or tombs. Smith's work functions as an associative engine, in which one reference summons another, and then another, often shuttling back and forth between the internal and corporeal and the external and societal. The effect is to create doubt in the viewer. I like to doubt what I'm seeing because it inevitably generates multiple meanings and ambiguities that refuse to rest in a single unified totality, and this, I think, is why I keep looking.

Several years ago, I was asked by German *Vogue* to participate in a series in which an artist in one field talks to an artist in another. I thought of Kiki Smith. She agreed to it, and we had what became a printed conversation. At one point during our dialogue, I asked her about the influence of dreams on her work. She said that in the past there were times when she'd have a dream and then get up in the morning and "make it." Although I wasn't expecting an answer quite so direct, her answer didn't surprise me. We all know that dreams do not follow the laws of waking life, that in our dreams familiar cognition is suspended, and things happen that could not happen in the world. Although the physiology of sleep remains highly controversial, and the biological reason for *why* we sleep and dream remains unknown, it seems clear that certain "higher" functions of the brain, including monitoring and inhibition of the self, are missing from dreams. In a fundamental way, we are freer in oneiric space than we are when we navigate the world as fully conscious human beings. The constrictions of waking logic do not apply when we sleep.

Smith is only one of many artists to borrow from the language of dreams, and whether or not any of the works in the Minneapolis show were generated by a specific dream does not matter. I have always thought that making art, whether it's visual art, music, or fiction, is a form of conscious dreaming, that art draws from the boundlessness, brokenness, merging identities, disjunctions of space and time, and intense emotions of our unconscious lives. I often dream of familiar people who have unfamiliar faces. My body is subject to innumerable mutations— I've grown fur and extra eyes. My ears and lips have drooped, my hair has fallen out, my stomach bulged, and I've bled gallons. Such transformations are rampant in Smith's work. Three powerful pieces in gampi paper and methyl cellulose (two untitled from 1988 and 1989 and one called *From Hear to Hand*—1989—as well as the papier-mâché work *Hard Soft Bodies* from 1992) summon for me the strange anatomies in dream space, its dismemberments and mysterious phantoms. The seemingly weightless work of a partial female body, from the waist down, that hangs in midair and dangles an infant from an umbilical cord, is at once awful and poignant—a birthing ghost.

Unconscious imagery—the stuff of dreams—is often coupled in Smith's work with references to Catholicism: the votive in particular. Votive objects are offered to a holy site either to give thanks to a sacred figure for salvation from a perilous event or to make a plea for healing. An ex-voto painting, for example, might depict a shipwreck with the saved person bobbing above water. The countless votive limbs that hang from church ceilings, especially in Latin America, are mounted in the hope of a miraculous cure for the injured part. As David Freedberg points out in his book *The Power of Images*, the desire for verisimilitude plays an important role in the creation of votive objects. Wax, papier-mâché, clay, human hair, and clothing are all employed to make sculptural images as lifelike as possible. Smith's *Nuit* from 1993 makes overt reference to votive limbs. The scarred legs and arms dangle from the ceiling on mohair threads that hold blue stars, signs of the heavens. Her extraordinary whole figures in wax, bronze, and paper from the nineties also evoke this sacred form of representation. The suspended woman and man who spill milk and semen, the seated woman whose back is raked with long thin cuts, the flayed *Virgin Mary,* the shackled and bestial *Mary Magdalene,* the black *Lilith* with her startling blue glass eyes, and the doubled-over hanging woman with real (horse) hair, her arms held in a position that resembles the crucifixion, are all variations on the Christian theme of the wound and suffering. Smith's figures, however, are by no means identical to votive works; they draw on the religious imagery in order to reinvent the mythical narratives. Both her *Mary Magdalene* and *Virgin Mary* radically alter traditional Christian representations of these women in favor of a blunt acknowledgement of their feminine physicality. At the same time, neither of these images engages in ideology, winking coyness, or parody. Their sincerity is precisely what gives them their raw emotional charge.

The controversial *Tale,* shown at the Whitney Museum of American Art's 1999 exhibition, *The American Century: Art and Culture 1950–2000,* was not included in the Minneapolis show, but it serves as a vehicle in my argument that Smith relentlessly investigates liminal zones, especially the vulnerable corporeal territory between inside and outside, a threshold which when pressed hard enough begins to shift and alter both our vision and our understanding. *Tale* (1992) is a wax sculpture of a woman on all fours with a long "tail" of excrement behind her. Her buttocks and upper thighs are smeared with feces. The work so offended Philippe de Montebello, former director of the Metropolitan Museum, that he called it "simply disgusting and devoid of any craft or artistic merit" in *The New York Times.*[2] I mention this, not because I want to engage in the culture war, but because after a century of art insurrection—Surrealism, Dada, Duchamp's readymades, Warhol's adaptive commercialism—a representative of a major art institution felt called upon to defend himself (and presumably museums in general) from a representation of the turd.

To my mind, however, *Tale* is not intended to shock the viewer. Like the other bodily expulsions depicted in Smith's work, feces have cultural and psychic meanings. In stark opposition to the divisive, retentive bottles, *Tale* creates a continuum between body and body product, merging the two in a single form—a tail that functions as a visual "missing link" to our mammalian forebears. The human/animal connection is one passionately explored by the artist in many works, and is, of course, real. The oldest part of the human brain in evolutionary terms is sometimes referred to as "the reptilian brain." At the same time, the fecal mess in *Tale* violates what we think of as *civilized* codes of cleanliness and summons a period of infant oblivion, when we had to be washed by others. Literal "wallowing in shit" is also seen in some forms of psychotic regression. The piece is emotionally complex—both deeply disturbing and, with a little distance, rather funny. The pun, tale/tail, acts as the verbal equivalent of the many shape-associations the artist exploits in her work. The tail's length implies extension in time as well as space. Syntax allows for the imaginative movement of the "I" backward and forward in time, and such complex linguistic forms are not shared by other species but are specific to human beings. We are the only ones on the planet who tell stories.

The tales that preoccupy Smith are the ones we share—the organizing narratives of religion and folklore. The multimedia work *Daughter* (1999) refers to Little Red Riding Hood. In the fairy tale, a child is devoured by a wolf, disguised as a *maternal* figure, the grandmother, and then released from the beast's belly by the huntsman's ax. The story recapitulates the universal narrative of pregnancy, birth, and ultimate separation when the umbilical connection between mother and baby is severed. Smith's heroine is part wolf. She stands in her red cape and looks up at the (adult) viewer with an expression both innocent and alarmed, her face sprouting the hairs of the one who ate her. As in a dream, two figures are combined in one, but here the familiar story about maternal engulfment and release has also collapsed into a single body, which *tells* what has happened. *Rapture* (2001) graphically shows what is hidden in *Daughter*: a woman steps out of the opened belly of a wolf, and *Born* (2002) continues the birth theme with a woman emerging from a deer. The intrinsic strangeness and magic of fairy tales is reinvigorated in Smith's piece because it addresses the truths that make children want to hear the stories again and again. We were all once inside a woman's body, were part of that body, were born and cut from it. Umbilical connections, both overt and subliminal, recur repeatedly in her art. The paper *Virgin Mary* (1990), *Puppet* (2000), *Getting the Bird Out* (1992), *Black Flag* (1992), the womblike *Revelation* in paper with handwritten text on a long narrow scroll (1994), and *Bird and Egg* (1996) all include cords, strings, streamers, and threads that dangle from bodies or bind one form to another. The acts of binding, knitting, tying, and stringing together are means to repair or piece together what has been broken and cut. This is also the work of story that welds disparate elements into a whole and is essential to memory and to the construction of what we call a "narrative self."

To look at Kiki Smith's work is to enter a borderland where the articulated lines between inside and outside, whole and part, waking and sleeping, human and animal, "I" and "not I" are often in abeyance. It is territory of shifting associations and metamorphoses, both visual and linguistic. These fertile links, though not always conscious, create a ricochet effect in the mind of the spectator that may dart from the minute to the cosmic, the abject to the sacred in a matter of moments. I think these imaginative transformations account for both the strength of my feelings when I looked at the exhibition and the fact that the pieces linger in my mind. Like those bleeding women I saw years ago, they refuse to leave me. Emotion plays a vital role in memory. Indifference is the swiftest road to amnesia, and in the end, the only artworks that matter are the ones we remember, and the ones we remember, it seems, are the ones we felt.

2007

THIS LIVING HAND

—see here it is—
I hold it towards you.
      John Keats

WHEN I DRAW SOMETHING OUT there in the world—a table, a person, a tree—it is as if I am touching it. The pencil, pen, or chalk serve as an extension of my arm. My eyes see the object and my hand seems to move over its contours as I work. I do not need to tell myself what I am doing. In fact, words are often outside the immediate experience of drawing. I don't speak to myself about "representation" or "likeness." I don't even have to name the object I'm drawing. Theoretically, someone could place an object in front of me that I had never seen before—a mysterious piece of machinery, say, or the organ of a being from another planet—and my hand would move on the paper, wholly oblivious to the thing's linguistic identity, as I continued to see it and explore its appearance. When I draw I do not see everything about the object all at once. I see more over time, and my hand responds to that visual "moreness"—a shadow under a nose, a patch of light on a vase, a wrinkle in a particular organ. Drawing is an embodied motor action: my roaming eyes, my arm, and my hand, but also my breathing, my heartbeat, my thoughts, and my mood are part of a coordinated response to my perception of an object. It can only happen through me. I am sitting in a particular place, looking at a particular thing; if I move, it will appear different. If it moves, it will also change. In the final drawing, the artist-viewer and her seen object are no longer distinct individuals. As M. M. Bakhtin argues, an aesthetic object is a "realized event of the action and interaction of creator and content." Subject and object merge.

My emphasis on the experience of drawing is to insist that it has a proprioceptive character, not just a cognitive one—that it is part of the mostly unconscious system of our bodily motions. Drawing, like riding a bike or driving, is learned, but once learned, the artist no longer has to be consciously aware of every movement. All children draw. Holding a crayon comes early. At first they scribble, fascinated by the marks they leave on paper, and then they begin to represent their own worlds or imaginary worlds schematically (a yellow ball with lines coming out of it as a signifier for the sun). Whether children's drawings have a universal quality that mirrors human development (as Piaget believed) or not is still a matter of controversy. The urge to do it appears to be a universal form of human play, but postscribble representations cannot be free of cultural meanings and conventions. Our visual perception is never solitary but steeped in an intersubjective, shared reality.

In June of 2008 I found myself deep inside the Niaux caves in Southern France, face-to-face with a bison, whose burning eyes I can still feel radiating into me. By no means the oldest cave drawings that have been found, these images are nevertheless about 12,000 years old and were startlingly "realistic," a word I use advisedly to mean that I had no problem whatsoever identifying the image in front of me as a bison. The creature's broader religious or aesthetic meanings for the people who created the pictures, however, are lost to us. What remains are the traces of human gestures, ones that I found deeply familiar and not at all alien. The particular artist who drew that animal created an illusion of aliveness that approached the frightful. Whether it depicts something out there in the world or something inside the artist, including abstractions, the image a viewer encounters is brought about through another person's movement, a tactile, sensory rendering that brings movement with it, if only because these strokes are the product of a particular living being. Whether I am looking at a rendering of an open skull by da Vinci or a portrait of Jean Genet by Giacometti or a late drawing of a shoe by Philip Guston or the abstract rock drawings of the Hopi, I am aware of another mind and body, a "you" in relation to my "I."

And I apprehend the artist's image on paper as a communicative act, the mute expression of something known to her or him. My perception of the lines, the shading, the figures or things is created between me and it. And what I see there is also felt, not only for its content, but as an artifact of the living hand that once moved over an empty space and has left behind the marks of that intimate encounter.

2009

TRUTH AND RIGHTNESS

Gerhard Richter

WE ALL HAVE PHOTOGRAPHS AT home, pictures of our babies who become children and then adults, our parents and siblings, our husbands and wives, our friends, our vacations. They lie in boxes or are organized in albums or languish in a computer file. Over time, they become markers of our mortality, small windows onto earlier moments in our lives, some of which are remembered, some not. These images are suffused with personal meanings. My parents as teenagers. My child as a newborn. At her sixth birthday. At eighteen. My young husband before his hair turned gray. My father, now dead. But there is nothing so banal as the snapshots of other people's families—strangers who stand on a mountaintop grinning or pose on the beach or hold up their infants to the camera. Landscapes documented by the family photographer, eager to record a moment of awe, are often worse—as dull and interchangable as postcards. Every once in a while, there is a felicitous shot, a well-framed instant that even an outsider can admire, but it is rare. The family photo is a document that stands in the place of memory: the mechanical alternative to the faces, views, and events that shift and blur in the mind that strains to recall them.

We don't use these pictures the way we use art, if we can be said to *use* art at all. For me, a work of art must be an enigma. It must push me into a position of unknowing or else I find myself bored by my own comprehension. I don't write about art to explain it but to explore what has happened between me and the image, both emotionally and intellectually. The act of looking, after all, always takes place in the first person. I see the object, but the very act of seeing it breaches the divide between me and it. At that moment aren't subject and object bound together in a unified loop of perception?

Gerhard Richter's history of using or referring to photographs in one way or another is long and complex, but whatever he does with an actual photo or the idea of a photo, it always feels reinvented. Looking at these small painted-over pictures, the size of snapshots I could shuffle through like cards in my hands were I ever to hold them, I thought: *They're so beautiful.* What beauty is is anybody's guess; it's a response to what we see, some of which may be a genetically programmed attraction to symmetries, to light and color; the rest, no doubt, is learned. But I found myself entranced by the colors of both the paint and the picture underneath it and, as I continued to look, I felt wistful, sad, amused, mystified, amazed, and sometimes overcome with a feeling of poignant loss. A couple of times I laughed out loud. I was always fascinated. Why?

Before their transformation, these were the artist's personal photographs, some of them of his wife and children. In many of them, the intimacy between photographer and subject is apparent. There are also landscapes and cityscapes. There are houses snapped from the outside and the inside. There's an airport with a plane. There are windows and doors and parts of rooms, a few of which include Richter's paintings in the background, looking a little distant and dull, not anything like reproductions in a catalogue, but which made me think of his own blurred canvases. All in all, what I can see of the "before" pictures isn't so different from the rather pedestrian photos I've taken myself. These glimpses of the ordinary snapshot that lies behind, below, between, or above the paint are essential to the cumulative emotional effects of these works. I recognize their ground as part of a vast sociology of picture taking, the passionate documentation of private life most of us engage in to one degree or another. The photographic instant in time: I see a girl lying on the floor of a room playing with a dog. She is wearing red tights and gray, red, and white striped socks. A red and blue object protrudes into the frame at the lower right corner. The shutter clicked *then*. I see her *now*. The cliché "capturing the moment" comes to mind: the illusion that time has frozen, and I can take back the seven-year-old, the eight-year-old, the child of the past, but it is always and only her flat representation in a little rectangle that I am left with. That is why every photograph, especially of people, simultaneously summons presence and absence. What happens when these images of what *was* are painted over? Their meanings change.

There is nothing arbitrary about Richter's painterly intrusions. Above his daughter and dog is a swath of paint in colors that resonate with the child's clothes—red, blue, greens, and touches of white—that lowers (or lifts) itself like a curtain over them, as if the picture has become a stage set. There are also a few tiny drips of red to the right of the figures, which remind me that my theatrical notion is a fantasy. In this particular picture, the essential subject matter of the photo—the interaction between child and animal—is revealed, not hidden. The painted section, however, changes my relation to the figures. Although my reading of the two retains an everyday, familial quality, the artist's strokes intensify my interest in what's happening by reducing my frame of vision, but also by turning the action into part of an artwork, an alteration that is almost ludicrously profound. It instantly catapults the image into another tradition, another mode of seeing which is placed inside the long history of painting. A painting doesn't "save" a moment in the world. It isn't a document recorded by a machine, but the trace of someone's lived experience that may or may not represent *things* in the world.

Strictly speaking, all of Richter's interventions are nonfigurative. They all resemble an abstract painting that finds its home inside the photo's rectangle. The painted gestures, however, generate a host of meaningful associations that play with or against the image that lies beneath them—curtains, veils, walls, waves, snow, foliage, grasses, leaves, flames. The mind is a glutton for meaning, for making sense of things that may escape it, for resisting ambiguity, for naming. I smiled when I saw three winter landscapes: a hill of snow with a row of pines against the sky; a mountaintop with patches of snow; a group of skiers. They are all sprinkled with red paint, and those flecks become snow, an enchanted snow perhaps, but snow nevertheless, as if these pictures were slightly daffy Christmas cards. It doesn't matter that the color is *wrong,* that no one says "as red as snow." Verisimilitude is not at issue. Visual poetry is. As Paul Éluard wrote, "The earth is as blue as an orange." Some of the beach photos are given what I came to think of as the wave treatment. A great form of blue, turquoise, gray, green, and white rise up over a woman and child. Her face juts over its edge against an intensely blue sky, her legs partly visible beneath. All we see of him is the top of his head and another bit of his skin below. The artist's intervening hand has created a thing in the scene that connotes, but doesn't denote, *water.* And by partly hiding them, the fluid shape has made the figures more intriguing, no longer the painter's wife and son exactly, but creatures of an artistic imagination, transfigured by an embodied thought.

"It is by lending his body to the world that the artist changes the world into painting," Maurice Merleau-Ponty writes in his essay "Eye and Mind."[1] It is the motion of a man's body, his arm, his hand with its tool that has come between me and the recorded image of a mechanical eye—an eye that takes in all that enters its frame. This is not how I see. As with all human beings, my peripheral vision is poor. I have to move my head to take in what's at the far corner of the room. I see what I attend to. I miss things. And after the moment has passed, I remember what mattered, not all the flotsam and jetsam I don't care about. Memory is emotional. I may remember my own daughter tussling with our now deceased dog on the floor of a room in our house, but I would not remember the schoolbag beside her unless it had some feeling attached to it. The camera, however, takes it in. I can't help but feel that Richter's *motion*—that is what it is, after all, the trace of a gesture or gestures—in these pictures make them more true to human feeling and to our visual experience.

I am only too aware that this is not a reading dear to a number of contemporary art critics, who have turned the artist into a rather cold business indeed, artist as supreme ironist and theorist of art. It is undeniable that Richter refers to genres, to periods, to art, to his own art, and to *things* in the world, that he uses the viewer's expectations and then often subverts or complicates them. He is thoughtful and intelligent about his own work, but it seems to me that his statements are often misconstrued. In his essay, "Landscape as a Model," Dietmar Elger quotes Richter, "When I look out of the window, then what I see outside is true for me in its various tones, colors, and proportions. It is a truth and has its own rightness. This excerpt, any excerpt you like for that matter, is a constant demand on me, and it is a model for my pictures." Elger refers rather vaguely to this articulation as "an intellectual concept."[2] I don't understand that characterization. This is a phenomenological statement with all that implies, the intellectual, emotional, physical experience of a man looking out at the world beyond a window. *What I see is true for me.* This truth is not the truth of science, of an objective view. It is not the camera's truth, nor is it an altogether private or solipsistic vision. I, too, can sit at the same window and point to a house we both see. That house can be shared, but the eyes of the painter will feel the demand of *rightness* in a way that I won't.

The demand of art is always also the demand of the world, a demand of truth (with a small *t*). When I write novels, I am always thinking to myself, "No, that's wrong. That's a lie. Get rid of it." And then I go further, more deeply into what I'm making. I find the rightness, and *I know*. But what is that knowing? I am living in a fictional universe with invented characters and imaginary stories, and yet the force of truth is compelling. It has nothing to do with realism. Magic can be true and right as well. In her paper "Towards the Source of Thoughts: The Gestural and Transmodal Dimension of Lived Experience," the cognitive scientist Claire Petitmengin addresses the terrain of this rightness. She calls it "a prereflective dimension of subjective experience," an internal zone which is both gestural and rhythmic, the terrain of "felt meaning." The question is, when I'm working, how do I know that a turn in the story or a conversation between characters is *right*? Why do I choose one word over another? Petitmengin cites the simple example of searching for a word. ". . . A few minutes ago," she writes, "I was looking for the word 'to distil.' I had an interior, global sense of it, very difficult to describe, and at the same time, very precise, because when a word with a close meaning came to my mind ('to ferment'), I instantly rejected it."[3] This recognition that we have come upon the right thing takes place every day in our conversations, when we write, draw, paint, do research, but it is rarely discussed or studied. Something appears. It isn't yet a thought or a word or a created image. It is there beneath what may later be articulated as a word, a formula, or the stroke of a brush. As Petitmengin points out, the vocabulary used to describe this strata of experience comes from a number of "sensorial registers: visual (shape, shadow, fuzzy, etc.), the kinesic and the tactile (vibration, pulsation, pressure, density, weight, texture, temperature, etc.), the auditory (echo, resonance, rhythm, etc.) and even the olfactory or the gustative."[4] These are metaphorical ways of grasping internal gestures, often not yet differentiated, categorized, or made distinct but *felt* nevertheless. This is the world of Richter's "right and true" and of the "demand" made on him by his visual experience.

I do not mean to suggest that making art is unreflective or without intellectual content. All the artist knows is brought to bear in the work itself, but some forms of that knowledge remain hidden. They live in corporeal memory, which struggles toward a representation that feels right—verbal, musical, or visual. In an interview with Robert Storr, which was included in the catalogue for his retrospective at the Museum of Modern Art in 2002, Richter responded to a question about hierarchies of subject matter in painting by saying, "I never knew what I was doing. What am I supposed to say now? Now I could lie here, like I am on an analyst's couch, and try to figure out my actual motives with the help of others and make sense of them. Is that what we want to do now?"[5] It is the ongoing torment (as well as narcissistic pleasure) of artists to be interrogated and analyzed. Sometimes one answers directly; other times, to avoid what feels like a personal intrusion or a blanket assumption, one escapes altogether. Nevertheless, *I never knew what I was doing* does not strike me as an insincere response. Richter's joking reference to psychoanalysis acknowledges the ambiguities that inevitably arise when one is called upon to interpret one's own work. He resists answering *why* because part of the *why* simply cannot be understood.

I see a bald baby. I know it is the painter's son, Moritz, who is now considerably older than he was then. This small person has disappeared. His head and shoulders and one hand are visible.

The rest of him is hidden behind a white barrier I can't identify. He is looking up, his eyes narrowed, his mouth open in an expression of unmitigated joy. Perhaps he is greeting a beloved person. He is not looking at the photographer but beyond him. To either side of the infant and touching his face there is paint that seems to fly—streaks of brilliant airborne colors that make me feel more joy, as if the marks soar to the rhythm of the child's feeling. The spatial metaphor is *up*. An instant of wild happiness represented in a photograph becomes a work of art that expresses an internal movement—an ecstatic flight toward something or, more likely, someone. The relation between the abstraction and the photo don't create a tension in mood. The child's face isn't hidden but displayed; its likeness to "a great shot" many of us have stumbled upon at one time or another of our own children remains intact, which means that a certain humdrum "cute, happy baby" quality is still present. And because it isn't *my* baby, a picture from my own private life, my response is colored by the faintest hint of alienation that complicates the image and draws me closer to the curiously inert character of family pictures, even when they depict high emotion. Without the painted intervention, the image would die.

The dynamic between photo and paint becomes one of revelation and concealment, of seeing and blindness, of playing one dimension against and with the other, and of creating ambiguities between them. Where does the paint end and those leaves and branches begin? The colors of the photographed skies, of grasses, of buildings, of clothing blend or contrast with the paint, which opens, closes, or shrouds my view as I peek into the image that is given a new and startling sense of depth by the intervening strokes. The paint's texture—rippling, striated, dabbed, layered, creates an illusion of motion that I can feel in those not yet articulated registers of my being—a sense of quiet, turbulence, a sweeping or ebbing. But I am also reading the pictures, creating an associative chain of thoughts about what is happening. I see Richter's wife, Sabine Moritz. Her lowered head is visible, and she has an intent but relaxed expression, and I am able to make out that she is nursing an infant. The jumping veil of red, white, green over her body and the baby doesn't cancel the subject matter but elevates it beyond an ordinary maternal act and inevitably conjures a reference to the many Madonna and Child paintings I've seen, but also the painterly interpretation of covering seems to repeat opening the private to the public. There is a dialectical tug at work between these two realms. The faces and bodies of people dear to the painter appear and vanish or reveal themselves only as obscured presences, or even ghosts, and there are also people and places I cannot recognize because they are strange to me. That they are in some way *personal* is implicit in the very idea of the underlying photograph: he was there. He took a picture of that. But it can't be explicit for me as a viewer who comes to the gallery to see them. My recognition comes from a familiarity with the underlying form itself, which has then been utterly reconfigured or abstracted by the intrusion of the imaginary—a fictive act of motion and color that is both right and true.

2009

ANNETTE MESSAGER
Hers and Mine

SOME PEOPLE REMEMBER THEIR CHILDHOODS well. They remember what it felt like to play and pretend. Others don't. Their childish personas have vanished behind clouds of amnesia. Still others, some of whom are artists, continue to play and pretend all their lives. The French artist Annette Messager is still playing hard, as is evident in the Hayward Gallery's retrospective of her work *The Messengers* (March 2009), the first major show of her work in England. When looking at Messager's art, I have always felt a strong pull back to my own early life, to my reveries, fears, cruel and kind thoughts, magical feelings, and fantasies that were part of play; not organized play or sport, but unhindered free play.

"I'm the captain of a pirate ship. You be the kidnapped sailor."

"No, *I* want to be the captain."

"Okay, we'll take turns."

The deep absorption of making something.

Scissors and glue and pieces of cloth.

Drawing eyes and mouths and bodies.

Dolls and figures and stuffed animals that talked to one another in different voices. They also hugged, kissed, hit, spanked, and sang.

The funeral my sister and I gave for a dead sparrow we found in the grass. The theater and ritual of that funeral. The pleasure we took from acting the parts of solemn mourners.

Wondering if my dolls came alive at night.

We all lived in that fertile, labile world once, and in Messager it returns to us with force. I am not saying that her work is unsophisticated or that many artistic influences are not present in it, or that her pieces are in any sense infantile, but rather that the impact they have on the viewer is connected to the universality of play.

In *Playing and Reality,* Winnicott wrote, "It is in playing and only in playing that the individual child or adult is able to be creative and to use the whole personality, and it is only in being creative that the individual discovers the self." Winnicott is talking about a capacity in all human beings, which requires relaxation and openness, and it is only in this state that people find what we call *selves.* Winnicott's conception of a "self" is not rigid or even whole. He argues that the search for a *me* happens in "an unintegrated state of the personality," or during what he calls a "desultory formless functioning." In other words, when we play freely, there is a loose and unstructured quality in us that allows for exploration and discovery. This truth, I think, goes to the core of Messager's art, which is born of play toward identity, or rather identities, a play which is never finished. Of course nobody becomes a self alone. It happens only in relation to others and within a specific culture and language. Messager's work is also born of a resistance to her specific language and culture. Throughout her career, she has usurped given vocabularies and scrambled them to create new meanings, a process of articulation, disarticulation, and rearticulation. The word *articulation* must be employed in its double sense because in these artworks its meaning is verbal and anatomical—to articulate, to join segments together, in words and bodies, and also to disarticulate, to dismantle and take them apart. (One of her works is entitled *Articulated-Disarticulated*. Neither her wordplay or purpose is buried.) It is possible to argue that everything Messager has made is forged out of an intense dialogue with received ideas, familiar narratives, myths, and rituals. She does this, in part, through language, but also through her choice of materials and their manipulation. For example, she has frequently used knitting, embroidery, fabrics, stockings, veils, fishnets—all connected to femininity—in contexts where the association is both retained and subverted, sometimes with caustic precision. A simple but chilling example can be found in *My Collection of Proverbs* (1974). Onto each simple square of linen, the artist embroidered an old French saying, each of them about women: *Quand la fille nait, même les murs pleurent.* (When a girl is born, even the walls weep.) Centuries of misogyny are given expression in needlework, "woman's work" now elevated to "art."

Messager was born in Berk-sur-Mer in northern France in 1943. Her father was an architect passionately interested in visual art, and both her parents encouraged their gifted daughter. In the early 1960s, she moved to Paris, where she still lives and works. The Hayward show takes in almost four decades of her art, and the spectator is able to follow the evolution of a woman whose production, broadly speaking, has become both larger in scale and more dramatic as she has aged. In the art of the seventies, the viewer will find *Annette Messager: Collector, Artist, Handywoman, Practical Woman, Trickster, Tinkerer, and Peddler.* "I didn't have any titles, so I gave myself some," she is quoted as saying in the catalogue. "In so doing I became an important, clearly defined person. I found my identity through the wide variety of these characters." Roles of becoming, becoming roles, playing a role, and fictive selves are central to this first decade. The collector gathers words and things. She tries out various signatures in *Collection to*

Find My Best Signature and portraits, *How My Friends Would Draw Me*. She collects photographs, sewn objects, notes in her albums. She cuts out marriage announcements with photos from newspapers and pastes her own name over the bride's, leaving the images untouched. The Practical Woman sews, knits, and hangs fabric on the wall. The drawings of the Trickster show her "terrifying" sadomasochistic adventures. This is a period of trying out and trying on various personas through multiple fictional biographies, a time of identifications and classifications *in the third person*, a view of her selves as if seen from the outside. That's *Annette Messager,* and that and that and that. The viewer participates in the artist's ongoing search for a perceiving subject by way of multiple objects. In these years, the feminist message inherent in the movement toward an "I" is overt. The usual female categories have to be reshuffled, rearranged, renamed, made ambiguous, and sometimes *inverted*. In *Approaches*, she shows a series of photographs of men's crotches. (Women look at men, too.) In *Man-Woman,* we see a photograph of a woman's naked body with a penis and testicles drawn onto it, a carnival-like borrowing of phallic power that empowers/plays with/jokes about art—*look, all I have to do is draw one!* By the 1980s, the third-person *she* has given way to the first-person possessive pronoun, which is used in the titles of a number of her series: *My Trophies, My Illuminated Letters, My Little Effigies, My Wishes, My Wishes with Penetration*.

This shift in perspective from outside to inside allows for a deeper register of play with stories, signs, and characters, not exclusively identified as *me,* but rather as *mine*. I do not mean to overdo this change in position or to imply that it ends the restlessness of the work because now there is a fixed subject or singular artistic self. I don't believe this. Rather, I think that in the eighties Messager's gaze turned toward other mysteries, and she began to draw from older pictorial traditions. In a series of exhibitions— *Varieties, Clues, Les pièges à Chimères, Chimèras, Effigies, Veils, My*

Trophies, My Wishes, My Handiwork, as well as in other series, the cryptic image and sign replace the collector's boxes and categories. Every series holds multiple references. In *Clues*, I feel as if I am looking at ideograms that contain messages: a razor blade, an eye, a knife, a mouth. Writing and picture merge. The "chimeras" take the shapes of things that nevertheless feel like hieroglyphs. A pair of scissors contains a distorted face; a key holds another. It is as if the viewer is being offered a dream vocabulary. The bodies in these works are usually in pieces—eyes, ears, hands, feet, noses, buttocks—but these are hallucinatory, Surrealist disarticulations, rather than ghoulish or violent ones.

Messager also mines the very old, popular world of the votive image. Historically, vast numbers of these representations were of body parts, especially of hands and feet, which people brought to churches in hope or thanks for a divine cure. The votive is not only low art; from early on, it carried a subversive quality—two facts which, no doubt, must have appealed to Messager. In 533 The Synod of Orleans formally objected to the practice, maybe because it had pagan origins, and in 587 the Counsel of Auxerre forbade it. These wooden or terra-cotta body parts were often suspended from the ceiling in churches, a crowd of loose limbs that dangled over the heads of the faithful. In ex-voto paintings, an inscription usually accompanies the image. I saw many of these small pictures by amateur artists in Mexico. I especially recall one of a boat tossed by huge waves. Beneath it were words of gratitude to the Virgin for having saved the believer from drowning. In *My Wishes* (1990), framed photographs of body parts, male and female, along with colored handwritten texts, hang together from strings—a direct translation of the ex-voto tradition. The mechanical representations of photography replace the sculptures and paintings. These wishes also continue her theme of blurring the sexes, here in a jumble of disparate corporeal bits and pieces, including genitalia.

The multiple allusions to sanctity, miracles, and wishes both mask and remind us of mortality, the deaths we hope to ward off, delay, hide from, or forget. A funereal feeling, a tone of mourning and memorial run through many of these pieces, most poignantly in her *histoire des robes, History of Dresses,* where the garments are displayed like fabric bodies in their cases/coffins, often with a sign or label. One says: *trouble.* But by claiming the fetish, the effigy, the ex-voto, and the child's toy as her own, by embracing these as building blocks, as the "letters" of her visual vocabulary, Messager also acknowledges the eternal potency that these representations, symbols, and rites have over us. They have a force that sways not only children and those peoples anthropologists once called "primitive," but all of us. We know that art is not alive, and yet it has a strength that acts on us subliminally as well as consciously. In his book *The Power of Images*, David Freedberg addresses the aura that haunts us when we look at representations, but which, he argues, sophisticated, educated people have been taught to suppress or ignore. "We too feel a 'vague awe' at the creative skills of the artist; we too fear the power of the images he makes and their uncanny abilities both to elevate us and to disturb us. They put us in touch with truths about ourselves that can only be described as magical, or they deceive us as if by witchcraft." Messager takes the viewer into worlds that are variably enchanted and demonic, beautiful and sinister, or all of these at once, and she does so with increasing intensity and confidence as the years go by.

In the nineties, the toy stuffed animal enters Messager's work as a *character,* a newer version of the taxidermy birds (literally stuffed animals) she used in her early series, *Boarders* (1971–1972), in which she created an aviary of creatures on moving vehicles and then strapped to metal tables, works that mingle poignancy, tenderness, as well as hints of sadism, of the sort children indulge in when they release their anger and frustration onto dolls. The taxidermy birds and animals take their place with the children's

296 LIVING, THINKING, LOOKING

toys in works such as *Fables and Tales* (1992), which includes tall stacks of books that squeeze piles of the soft creatures, while perched on top of the volumes are the once living animals, wearing masks or blindfolds. Animals are the speaking beings of fables and fairy tales most of us began reading when we were very young, stories that lured us with their magic and their cruelty. I shall never forget my horrified fascination when, at the end of the story, birds flew down and picked the eyes out of the heads of Cinderella's stepsisters in one version of that classic tale. Messager populates her work with these soft characters and stuffed corpses to great effect. They are ambiguous beings who refer to the narratives we already know, as well as the hidden stories we cannot fully divine but only guess at.

Variations on the mask theme come and go, along with their multiple associations and underground narratives that summon carnivals, masquerades, robbers, S & M games, and torture victims. The adorable toy merges with the dangerous effigy, the celebratory with mourning. Spikes and spear forms appear with their allusions to ceremony, ritual, and revolution. And colored pencils enter Messager's stage, pencils reminiscent of daggers, needles, porcupine quills, or teeth, depending on how they are used. These piercing forms contrast dramatically with the plump and vulnerable fur and flesh of the animals or the faceless humanoid forms Messager calls *replicants* in an homage to the movie *Blade Runner*. The artist's tools metamorphose into weapons: aggressive, defensive, and protective. But these pencils, like many of her objects, are also visually witty, almost comic, an ingredient in Messager's personal and self-reflexive art adventure. Her instruments for drawing and writing become metaphors for both armor and attack, and yet, they remain pencils.

"What we are driving at is this: that with each performance we are playing a serious game, that the whole point of our effort resides in the quality of seriousness," Antonin Artaud wrote in an essay on the Alfred Jarry Theater. Messager's work has developed into a form of theater, a spectacle of playing in earnest, of the deadly serious game, which has nevertheless kept its relationship with the pretend. Multifarious, sometimes kinetic elements are assembled to create paradoxes and ambiguities, as well as to combine menace with fun. In a late work titled *Casino,* first shown at the Venice Biennale in 2005, Messager borrows Collodi's familiar children's story *Pinocchio* and his mendacious little hero with the mobile nose in a visual narrative that employs an alphabet the viewer has come to know—bolsters, birds, beaks, suspended masks, and nets. The nets in *Casino* remind us of the puppet's miserable sojourn in the circus after he is turned into a donkey, but they (and all the recurring nets in her work) also function as a visual pun on the artist herself: *Annette/a net,* one she has pointed out in several interviews. In some way, *Pinocchio* serves as the perfect myth for this particular artist and the story of her own art, in which she is both puppet and puppet master. The naughty wooden trickster, who just wants to have fun and who is magically transformed from one thing into another over the course of his journey, recapitulates Messager's deepest theme— the vulnerable, mutable, plural being whose grand theater plays with words and pictures toward a self-ness. A friend quotes Messager in the catalogue as having once said, "My own me is mine." By walking through this exhibition, that *me* will become yours, too.

2009

NECESSARY LEAPS
Richard Allen Morris

THE FIRST TIME I SAW a group of paintings by Richard Allen Morris, I knew I was looking at tough, smart, and sophisticated canvases that were made because the artist *had* to make them. It is difficult to explicate what it means to *see* this need in the space of a rectangle that you can hang on a wall, but I gleaned it from Morris's work right away. The desire to make art is both a physical and an intellectual urge—the translation of lived experience into something else, a thing outside the body of the artist. All good art is marked by this compulsion, and it is often the mysterious quality that distinguishes strong works from mediocre ones. When an artist's goal is simply to produce a poem or a symphony or a novel or a painting, the work is shriveled and dead even before it's born.

That first viewing happened on a Wednesday in November of last year. I had been asked to curate an exhibition for the CUE Foundation, a nonprofit organization with a gallery in the Chelsea district of New York City. It was established to show the work of deserving artists who for one reason or another had remained beyond the notice of the New York art world. And it was my job to choose an artist for the exhibition, so I began asking painters and sculptors and art editors about possible candidates. Among the people I asked was my friend, the painter David Reed, and it was David who laid out several small canvases he owns by Morris on a table for me to see. At the time, I had never met Richard Allen Morris. I wrote to him, spoke to him on the telephone, and then almost five months later flew to San Diego to visit him in his downtown studio.

Because I had never curated an exhibition before, I was nervous, but the mild-mannered, articulate man who met me at the door immediately put me at ease, and as he showed me one work after another, we talked for the next four hours. I asked Morris when he had decided to become a painter, but he couldn't cite the moment his life turned toward art. Painting had always fascinated him, he said, even the kitschy images of the American West he was familiar with as a child. He recalled two pictures, which hung in a pool hall in Torrington, Wyoming, the "cowboy town" where his family lived during his high school days. One depicted dogs playing poker and the other a stag jumping over a log. But he also remembered Clement Greenberg's piece on Jackson Pollock in *Life* magazine in 1949 and the overwhelming impact the works reproduced in its pages had on him. For the young Morris, Pollock's drip paintings kicked open a door that would never close. And yet, when the artist finished his stint in the navy on an aircraft carrier during the Korean War and docked in San Diego in 1956, he didn't move to New York City, the feverish center of Abstract Expressionism, and when Los Angeles became a city with a burgeoning art scene, he didn't move there either. He remained in San Diego and stayed in touch with every turn in the wider art world through books, magazines, and catalogues. For years he has been cutting out reproductions of work by artists he admires from magazines and pasting them into blank books so that he can return to them at any time for

sustenance. The artist's mental residence then has often been at
odds with his physical one. Although he has had many shows in
the San Diego area and an exhibition in 1999 at the Chac-Mool
Gallery in Los Angeles, his debut in New York came after his
seventieth birthday last April. It took only a few minutes with
Richard Allen Morris, however, before it became obvious that his
ambitions for a "career" have taken a distant second place to his
ambitions for the work itself and his ongoing need to make art.

During my conversations with him, I came to understand
that the man whose work had caught my attention was a repository of thousands of works of art from the distant past to the
present. The immense size of this inner catalogue has given Morris a startlingly rich vocabulary for his own work and an uncanny
ability to loot, reconfigure, revise, and anticipate art history for
his own purposes. In our conversations he mentioned, among
others: Giotto, Rembrandt, Vermeer, Giacometti, David Stone
Martin (as an influence on Andy Warhol), Ben Shahn, Joseph
Beuys, Gerhard Richter, and Earl Kerkham, an artist I had never
heard of. He also referred to classical Japanese painting and to the
masks used in Noh plays. His relation to other artists, he told me,
isn't "scholarly," but "hit or miss," and he compared his glean-
ing of information from other works of art to a "detective
agency," a metaphor I particularly liked. Indeed, Morris's vision
has a Holmesian quality, a kind of radiant focus on what is essential to the case—the minute details that other spectators usually
ignore. For example, he mentioned a painting of a girl in the San
Diego Museum attributed to Rembrandt, but Morris is less interested in the provenance of the canvas than with a spot just above
the girl's eye, near her eyebrow. In the same museum there hangs
an oil sketch of a woman by Robert Henri, not a very good piece,
Morris told me, but the rendering of her brooch had held him
like magic. Isolated, the brooch becomes a vehicle for thought,
and then for gesture.

His own paintings are given the same scrutiny, and pictures he deems failures often become parts of new work. For example, strips torn or cut from old canvases reappear in *For Cy Thomsby and Geoffrey Young* (1979) and in the crosshatch strips of the untitled work from the same year. The delicate inner frames of the three untitled works, one from 1974 and two from 1987, play with a parallel idea—turning a single work into an arena of multiple four—by cutting up a picture without scissors. The aesthetic and pragmatic are often ingeniously combined in Morris's work. He uses what he finds and what he has near him in his ongoing project of prolific and ingenious production. He once created an entire show from chewing gum—premasticated by the artist himself, who had to take a two-day hiatus during creation to rest his weary jaw. *Gum Map* (1996) is a product of that noble chewing. Many years earlier, during his time on the aircraft carrier, a vessel he described as the size of "a small town," Morris became known as the man who would happily take over unfinished paint-by-number kits that bored sailors had abandoned. These became the foundations for new works by Morris, who painted over and altered them at will. When his time in the service ended, he carried the reinvented paintings home with him in a cruise box.

Much of Morris's art is small, and when I asked him about it, he explained to me that the size of many of his pieces is due to the fact that most of his studios have been small. A number of his early paintings, some of the heads, for example, are large, but the increasing restraints caused by an ever-growing body of work and cramped space have meant that his canvases and constructions have shrunk over time. His studio is now filled to bursting with nearly fifty years of labor. Morris has literally painted himself into a corner. In recent months, the limits on his space have become so severe that he no longer has the elbow room to paint and has been drawing only. As with a canvas, when he isn't satisfied with an ink drawing, he sometimes cuts out a felicitous detail and pastes it into a blank book. These abstract cutouts are tiny. Most of them are no bigger than a small marble or the eraser at the end of a pencil. He explained to me that his plan for these miniature forms was eventually to enlarge them by means of a projector and use them as models for much bigger pictures. I was intrigued by this idea for the future because I had already re-marked to myself that even Morris's tiniest paintings feel strangely large. Not a single work I've seen, and I saw many during the two days I spent with him at his studio, had a diminutive, reduced, precious, or pinched quality. Any number of his small canvases could be blown up many times and lose nothing in the expan-sion. I think the secret lies in the boldness and complexity of his colors and gestures—the tension between freedom and constraint that is always present. In Morris's work littleness is not the point. It is the result of necessity.

Sitting on the steps in his densely packed studio, I became a witness not only to a man's oeuvre over time but to the geogra-phy of a particular imagination. Richard Allen Morris has done figurative and abstract canvases. His work includes collages, ready-mades, and constructions. He has used words inside a painting and has employed a variety of canvas shapes: classic rectangles, circles, and long, narrow bars—both vertical and horizontal. There are works that butt out of their frames like *Vagabond's Joy* (1983); pieces with three-dimensional elements in them, such as *Wet Paint* (1962) and *Blue Black* (1963), as well as a double canvas that must be mounted in a corner, *Untitled* (1967). Morris re-ported to me that a reviewer in California once accused him of "being all over the place." To my mind, the man in question was suffering from what might be called a provincial and prejudicial case of critical blindness. While it is true that many artists make careers from a single idea and repeat it with minor variations until they die, there are *no rules* for making art. Moreover, I can't think of a single philosophical reason why sameness should be valued over variety or incremental changes over great leaps. Gerhard Richter, an artist Morris and I agreed we both admire, continues to explore a host of possibilities in his painting. Like Richter, Morris is unafraid to experiment, and like Richter, Morris creates work that is, despite its variety, the product of a singular, restless, and probing imagination.

Whether figurative or abstract, the work inevitably has wit, which Webster's defines as "the keen perception and cleverly apt expression of those connections between ideas which awaken amusement and pleasure." When he names a painting, the title works with or against his images to poetic and sometimes comic effect. The yellow canvas from 1963 is called *Blue Black*. The paint-encrusted rail from 1999 bears the name *Fearless Chemist,* and another round canvas from the same year forces the viewer to consider what self-reflection means with its title: *Mirror.* In purely visual terms, however, Morris's wit appears in his tendency to plunder a known vocabulary and then give it an idiosyncratic turn or blur. The portraits of heads from the sixties and early seventies are works animated by reference: the haunting Expressionism of *Philo* and *Stone* (1968); the cartoon imagery of Pop Art in *Brenda* and *Nigel* (1969) and in the face of Alfred E. Neuman lifted from *Mad* magazine (1968). There is also the melting abstraction of a canvas like *Chuk* (1970); and the weird power of *Cal* and *Argor* (1968) that reminded me of ancient totems. And yet, despite their allusions, none of these images is a straight borrowing that creates pastiche, and not one of them can be situated firmly into a single artistic mode or moment. They feel like cultural masks—at once ironic and frightening. Their wit is derived from the tension created among the ideas present in these versions of a standard art historical practice—the portrait as bodiless head.

Although Morris abandoned painting pictures of heads, he has been making what he calls *Transformations,* filling blank books with cutouts from art magazines. The process is simple and, as he explained to me, necessarily fast. He removes the heads from reproductions of paintings and sculptures of the human body, and then in a single swift gesture, in which there is almost no lag between the thought and the motion of his hand, he assigns an existing body a new head. The results are comic, striking, strange, scary, lovely. They are also revealing. After closely examining the *Transformations,* I understood that Morris's choices were as much about harmony as juxtaposition, and that this art historical game (I recognized many of the paintings and sculptures used in the changes) speaks to the work as a whole, which reshuffles the known into the unknown.

The guns to which the artist has returned during his career both as images in painting and as collage constructions partake of a similar reinvention. He described them to me as "a cross between children's toy and African fetish." These guns are, of course, fictions. They don't shoot. They are vehicles through which the mythic meanings of firearms in the culture are unearthed: as symbols of war and the American West, as the omnipresent appendages to good guys and bad guys in the movies, and as signs of phallic masculinity. From the snub-nosed *Gun for Tess* (1965) that uncannily prefigures Guston's late pictures to the sinister nail-spiked *Prince,* Morris's guns can't be easily interpreted. They conjure both real and fake weapons, the battlefield and the cinema, power and impotence. At the same time, because all of them look very different from actual weapons, they tease the border between iconic representation and abstraction.

In the nonfigurative works, to which most of his years as an artist have been devoted, Morris also draws on a variety of formal ideas: constructivism in *Off Red* (1961); abstract expressionism in the thick, lush density of *Sunday in Paint* (1991); and a primary minimalism in *Hop, Skip and Jump* (2003). Despite the role of allusion in the art, Morris has never been an artist hog-tied by self-consciousness or forced reference. He returns to forms that move him. The complex black-and-white figurative spaces of early works like *Hero* and *Art International* are revisited in abstractions such as the untitled work from 1979. The ideas present in the skinny portrait, *Argor*, in which the soft geometric planes of a man's face are squeezed into near abstraction, recur over the years in Morris's penchant for the long thin canvas. The totemic quality of *Argor* returns as well. The first time I looked at the startlingly beautiful and haunting canvas from 1988—two bars of unequal size, one whitish yellow, the other blue-gray, on an ochre background—I thought immediately of sacred tribal signs, perhaps an echo of images and colors I remembered from a book on Native American arts, but I'm not certain. The apparent simplicity of the composition becomes more intricate as you continue to look at it. The two neat bars are colored with immense subtlety, and their ragged painted edges with their suggestive striping have an eerie effect on me. It's as if they are continually triggering a memory I can't retrieve, as if I'm looking at a sign of something once known but now lost.

Morris is aware that even the most abstract images conjure people and things, that the mind insists on these links, and his forms play with the viewer's desires. A title such as *Find It* speaks directly to this omnipresent wish in the spectator. Even without its title, *To Read* (1976) suggests the white haze of foreign script on a yellow page. The untitled work from 1999 also evokes a yellow page with brilliant lines of pure color squeezed straight from the tube, and the double corner canvas summons a book opened to pages of cryptic text glowing in neon color—the hieroglyphs of an unknown story. And yet these paintings aren't rigidly coded. They aren't riddles to be solved once and for all. My book, for example, may be another person's landscape. But however ambiguous the allusions may be in a canvas, however simple or complex its composition, every color, line, stroke, or swath of paint feels necessary to the work as a whole.

"I've improved over the years," the artist told the San Diego art critic Robert Pincus, who quoted his statement in the *San Diego Union-Tribune* on April 14, 2002. "That's an absolute thrill. Sometimes painting seems effortless now and that's an amazing feeling. My eye has improved." Morris has a great eye, an eye trained by an ongoing hunger to do and to make. The more you look into his spaces, the more you see, and that is the single test of all art. It must allow the viewer time to wonder or it vanishes into the dullness of the immediately apparent and the readily understood. In short, it dies. Richard Allen Morris's work is terribly alive. His paintings and constructions are a testament to over forty years of solitary creation, an enduring narrative of rigor, fierce intelligence, humor, and joy.

2005

MARGARET BOWLAND'S
THEATRUM MUNDI

ONE NIGHT, LYING IN BED on my way to sleep, I was think-ing about Margaret Bowland's paintings, and this sentence came to my mind: *Bowland stages confrontations*. This felt right to me, but its rightness must be explained. I believe every encoun-ter with a work of art is dialogical, that is, what happens when someone looks at a canvas or sculpture or any object that an-nounces itself as art is created between the viewer and the thing viewed. Art partakes of the intersubjective because we do not treat it as just a thing but as an object imbued with the traces of another living consciousness. In figurative art, this intersubjec-tivity, this dialogue between viewer and image, is heightened. Not only do we encounter the artist's intentionality as expressed in the work before us, we gaze at a representation of someone like ourselves, another human being. There is a form of mirror-ing at work.

From birth, infants treat other human faces with particular attention. A face is viewed differently from an inanimate object. Babies respond to a photograph or simplified drawing of a face, as well as to the mobile features of a living person. They prefer anatomically correct renderings to scrambled or distorted faces. Newborns are not predisposed to like cubist portraits. Discoveries in infant research have demonstrated that even before we become self-conscious beings, we mirror and participate in the actions of others. Looking at a depiction of a person in a work of art necessarily activates this mostly unconscious attraction and connection. It is precisely this face-to-face human drama that Margaret Bowland uses in her work. The viewer finds herself caught in a visual dialectic that is enacted on multiple levels— from the simple desire to continue looking at a beautiful face to the complex reading of imagery each one of these pictures demands. They are dense with particular cultural and historical references as well as more ambiguous allusions, ones that, variously, give pleasure and disturb. The static reality of these canvases opens into an emotional tumult created by the spectator's need to understand what she or he is actually seeing.

The question, "What am I looking at?" should never be posed casually. Perception is a tricky business, one laden with expectations, both conscious and unconscious. This is an inescapable state of affairs. We all come to a work of art with thoughts and feelings, as well as with a history of experiences that have shaped our vision, both personal and cultural. Each one of us can, however, struggle against our own prejudgments by adopting a phenomenological attitude. After looking long and hard enough at a work of art, I have often seen what I couldn't see before. Examining Bowland's oil canvases and pastels in this exhibition, I began to understand how her work both exploits and undermines our expectations. We are confronted with multiple images of a single person. She has been rendered by the artist with such technical refinement we participate in an illusion of her reality, but she has been placed inside an iconography that demands to be deciphered.

The model for all of these works is the same child, Janasia or

"J.J." Smith, a girl who is now nine years old. She inhabits the world of what I like to call high middle childhood, the era before even a breath of puberty has blown over her body, the time Freud called "latency." She is beautiful. What beauty is remains mysterious, but this child's face is beautiful, and I was immediately drawn to her large eyes and delicate features. We look at faces first. But in many of these images the brown skin of the girl's face has been whitened, dusted with a powder or masked in white makeup. The story of race in the United States and our legacy of slavery make her white face startling, if not shocking. Her fake pallor instantly summoned its opposite for me—blackface—the necessary ingredient of minstrel shows, in which a bewildering mixture of hatred for and envy of black people mingled to create the first wholly American form of theater adopted from black music. There were black minstrel troupes, too, who also performed with blackened faces. Indeed, the recurring white masking in Bowland's images evokes myriad forms of the theatrical: Japanese Kabuki and Noh players, the white-faced clowns of the circus, and the high artifice adopted by members of the eighteenth-century French court with its powdered wigs and eggshell-colored makeup, directly referred to in Bowland's canvas *Party*, in which our child in white wig, with posture suggestive of the court servant, holds out a black-and-white Hostess cupcake, a quintessentially American second-half-of-the-twentieth-century mass-market treat, while behind her on the wall hangs a painting that pushes the viewer into still another period. The picture inside the picture is a *noirish* canvas of a car and the headless body of a man in forties garb.

Skin, surfaces, artifice, art, signs, and objects that have become symbols—we are looking at works of art, but within each work we are lured into a drama of contradictory appearances. What am I looking at in *It Ain't Necessarily So*? The child, in white face, is wearing a bikini, a garment designed to cover only female breasts, buttocks, and genitalia, but this girl has no breasts, an observation that becomes poignant when the viewer notices that the top of her bathing suit is twisted to one side. She is posed with her arms outstretched; one of her hips juts to the side; and one foot rests on the other. Despite the "itsy, bitsy, polka-dot bikini" and the potential eroticism of her posture, she exudes no sexuality. She stands inside an immense, opened watermelon—that icon of a specifically American racism —on the skin of which is written the title of the famous Gershwin song (about not taking the Bible literally) from *Porgy and Bess*. The text is not fully visible, but is not difficult to read. Behind the melon is a huge, menacing kitchen knife and, in the background, the seductive suggestion of more text—further letters or hieroglyphics that might be deciphered were we only able to see them better.

Bowland's mastery of painting technique is on display in the rendering of the girl herself; this is not a slick photographic realism but a painterly, visual realism that draws on centuries of figurative representation in the West. The watermelon is subject to a somewhat different treatment; it is not "realistic," after all, this gigantic melon and its seeds; it is fantastic, supernatural, a thing of our collective cultural nightmare. Although it is not known how watermelon became associated with black people in the United States, the fruit was featured endlessly in racist trading cards, postcards, figurines, and countless knickknacks for decades. A Victorian trading card from the 1890s for Sapolio Scouring Soap is exemplary: it depicts the head of a smiling black girl inside an opened watermelon. Grinning with satisfaction seems to have been an intrinsic and defensive part of the racist message. And let us not relegate such horrors to the past. In 2009, the mayor of Los Alamitos, California, Dean Grose, sent out an e-mail card of the White House lawn as a watermelon patch. The caption: "No Easter Egg Hunt This Year." (The aptly named Grose was forced to resign, but has received Republican endorsement to return to public office and is seeking your contributions.)

It Ain't Necessarily So borrows overtly racist imagery and complicates it—evoking iconic American music composed by a pair
of white Jewish brothers for an opera about black people based
on a novel about a black man, *Porgy*, written by a white man. The
thematic material of the painting mingles race with childhood
and femininity. We continue to romanticize childhood, a legacy
of the nineteenth-century notion that early human life is a time
of unspoiled innocence. Children and women were tightly linked
in science and popular culture as pure, desexualized beings. This
pivotal idea of innocence became the hallmark of the period's
sentimentality and its condescension to women. It is no accident
that the fight for women's rights was waged simultaneously. In-
fantalization was also, of course, a tool of racism. In the United
States, the childlike "happy darkie" was essential to the argument
for slavery, despite the fact that this creature of white fantasy was
belied again and again by the reality of slave sabotage, insurrection, and violent uprising. Fear sharpens stereotypes.

A few passages from an article in *Dwight's Journal,* November
15, 1856, I found in an anthology *Jazz in Print: 1859 to 1928,* edited by Karl Koenig, offer a gloss on this complicated history, a
history Bowland forces us to recognize: "The only musical population of this country are the Negroes of the South . . ." the
author tells us. Musically, the white North is a desert. "Even the
gentler sex who ought to have most of poetry and music, seem
strangely indifferent to it." The Negro, however, is a "natural
musician" and "the African nature is full of poetry." Codes of
thought, frames of reference, ideologies that shape us and produce a train of associations that become part of the iconography
of Bowland's work. Janasia wears a crown of cotton in *The Cotton Is High*. The extraordinary beauty of the girl with her steady
gaze and erect posture stands in stark opposition to what we know
is the brutal landscape of the plantation and enslavement. The
crown of cotton is also a crown of thorns. The artist forces us to

look, to confront what many white Americans would rather forget. The nearly nonexistent public discussion of reparations for slavery in this country is an indication of the degree to which this is true.

In *Somewhere Over the Rainbow*, a work which refers again to American popular music and a film about dreaming another world, Oz, Janasia stands, scissors in hand. In this canvas, Bowland visually quotes Kara Walker's cutout images of the Antebellum South. Walker, like Bowland, has used racist forms to critique and explore the violence inherent in the images themselves as well as the history that created them. Some black artists, however, attacked Walker's use of stereotypes as demeaning to black people and pandering to whites, to a white art world in particular. None of this is simple. What is certain is that references to race and to racist imagery remain dangerous in public discourse of all kinds. This was Walker's angry response to her critics: "What you want: negative images of white people, positive images of blacks?" As the cliché goes, life is not black and white. Oppression deforms people; it does not, in general, make them better. And it is no guarantee of moral purity. Like Walker's, Bowland's work explores the fantasy that is race and its attendant cultural pollution. Each of these artists, one black, one white, unlocks a door and looks in on the monster that is us.

Such courage is rare, however, and a cult of both authenticity and repression has grown up around these discussions. In one of my novels I have a black character, a young artist named Miranda, who was born in Jamaica. Race and slavery are themes of her art and of the book itself. No journalist I spoke to nor a single reviewer, either in America or Europe, with a single exception, mentioned Miranda or her art or race. The man who did was a white Italian married to a black woman from Jamaica. I guess he felt he was on safe ground. My question is: What is the imagination if it is not becoming the other?

As the allusions thicken in Bowland's art, so does the ambiguity. The black child of these works is not only whitened; she is variously adorned in the paintings with all manner of feminine frippery—lace and ribbons and full skirts—the stuff of sexual difference. How else can we distinguish children of that age if we don't brand them with their sex from birth—in pink and blue and dresses and pants? In *Murakami Wedding*, the little girl, in flower girl attire, occupies the center of an elaborate still life that includes balloons, a wineglass, china plates, a silver spoon and fork, a basket and rose petals, the ladder back of a golden chair. Weddings remain a fetish in our culture—the enactment of "every little girl's dream"—a theatrical but also anachronistic event, with its virginal *white* symbolism and paternalistic "giving the bride away" as she moves from the stewardship of one man to that of another. The wedding in contemporary America may be thought of as *the* extravaganza of ordinary life, a ritual ceremony in which the bride becomes a momentary celebrity in a culturally scripted fantasy of femininity.

Again and again, these works articulate and then rearticulate the phantasms of crippling, simplistic ideologies, the fictions we live by. In *Someday My Prince Will Come,* Janasia and another girl, both untouched by white makeup, but dressed up in finery, stand in front of the bottom of a canvas, in which a black man, rendered in a cartoonish style, lies wounded or dead in this painting within a painting. The title (notably a song from the Disney movie *Snow White*), the somber girls, the image of a fallen man—together these make me unutterably sad. It is merely human to long for another person, to desire love and company, but romantic fantasies of love fulfillment, of princes and knights and heroes in films and songs and romance novels are, quite simply, corrosive. Girls are supposed to wait. Penelope waits. Waiting is a state of passive anticipation: "Someday . . ." The children look bored. Waiting is boring.

The reference to still life or *nature morte* in *Murakami Wedding* is pointed. Bowland "arranges" the girl along with the other objects in an elaborate, gorgeous, highly artificial evocation of the aftermath of a nuptial celebration. In Baroque still life, the remains of a meal on a table were depicted as a kind of study in chaos, an oxymoron that perfectly fits the form. These leftovers in the Dutch and Flemish paintings of the period were cautionary; their theme was *vanitas,* a reminder of our mortality—the ephemera of this world and its pleasures will vanish. But we also find in Bowland's canvases an allusion to the theatricality of Baroque painting in general and the period's idea of *theatrum mundi,* the world as stage, that resonates powerfully with the artist's ironic references, textual and visual, to popular plays and music. Unlike the low genre of still life, the high genre of Baroque figurative painting was meant to break down the barrier between viewer and viewed, an illusion achieved by both technique and scale. The body of the spectator and the bodies on the canvas create a mirroring reality because the painting stages a form of corporeal mutuality. Through this device, Bowland allows the viewer no escape. She binds her spectator to the hallucinatory dream world of the canvas.

Standing in front of *It Ain't Necessarily So,* I look directly into the girl's eyes. She gazes back at me without any obvious emotion. Her expression is one of solemn attentiveness. It took me a while to understand that she is actually larger in the painting than she is in life. She is not nine-year-old size, but adult size. The scale of her body makes it literally impossible for me to *look down* on her. I am prevented from feeling the ordinary and comfortable condescension an adult has for a child. There is something in this girl's face that resists the burden of both the trappings of gender—the silly bikini on her sexually immature body—and the broadly racist imagery in which she is so unmistakably framed. I am returned to the essential face-to-face reflection, the

I and *you* dialectic of human exchange, the sense of seeing someone who is like me, not *other*. In work after work, I am confronted by this child's dignified selfhood, neither fully open nor
entirely closed to me. Who is she? I wonder. Is it the absorbing
intensity of her gaze that has taken me in? Is it her posture? Who
am I really looking at? The artist's immense skill has rendered a
personality, a *being* rather than an icon of a being, a defiant personage who shines through the riddled texts and myriad cultural
signs of the *theatrum mundi* that surround her. In the pastels, which
suggest forms of black-and-white photography, the girl's face becomes a consuming focus; it is hard, very hard, to look away.

Margaret Bowland's work orchestrates a visionary theater of
difference, of differences that have cut so deeply into our cultural
images and discourses, have become so critical to identity, that
they may begin to seem natural rather than unnatural and artificial. It is crucial to remember that both skin color and sex have
been defined and redefined in various ways over the course of
history. In Bowland's work, icons of the past and present are
merged in the simultaneity of the canvas. And they may be read
as dreams can be read through their relation to waking reality.
The frightening constructions and constraints of race and
gender—the lies of difference that have infected us—are also
truths because their brutal divisions have entered us, become us.
And sad to say, many of them are unconscious or suppressed. Do
not be mistaken: there is rage in these pictures. But there is also
the mute dialogue of human mirroring—the natural magic that
occurs between us.

2011

WHY GOYA?

I LIKE TO IMAGINE," CHARLES Baudelaire wrote about Goya's *Los Caprichos,* "a man suddenly faced with them—an enthusiast, an amateur, who has no notion of the historical facts alluded to in several of these prints, a simple artistic soul who does not know a thing about Godoy, or King Charles, or the Queen; but for all that he will experience a sharp shock at the core of his brain, as a result of the artist's original manner, the fullness and sureness of his means, and also of that atmosphere of fantasy in which all his subjects are steeped."[1]

I continue to feel this jolt to my brain when I look at particular works by Goya, despite the fact that I have come to know them well. The drawings for and prints of *Los Caprichos, The Third of May,* the Black Paintings, especially *Saturn Devouring His Son,* the drawings for and prints that comprise *The Disasters of War,* as well as some of images in the *Disparates* series and late drawings, all deliver this blow. Interestingly, they are all works the artist either asked to paint (*The Third of May*) or made for himself after his serious illness and subsequent deafness. For me, they remain images so powerful they hurt.

Baudelaire called Goya "an always great and often terrifying artist." He also called him "modern," and many have echoed that thought since.[2] After visiting the Goyas in the Prado in 1932, the art critic Bernard Berenson commented, "Here in Goya is the beginning of our modern anarchy."[3] David Sylvester pronounced Goya "a forerunner" of modernism.[4] Fred Licht[5] and Robert Hughes[6] have both argued that Goya brings something radically new to art. Time and again, Goya has been seen as prescient and anticipatory, a prophet of what was to come. In his opera *Facing Goya,* a complex work about scientific theory and its sinister uses in the twentieth century, the British composer Michael Nyman includes the line: "Goya saw Hitler before Hitler saw Goya"[7]—a temporal reversal that succinctly captures the notion of the artist as visionary. Over the years, Goya's work has been copied, quoted, and reinvented regularly. His influence on Delacroix, Manet, Redon, and Picasso is well known, but Goya thrives as a touchstone for contemporary artists as well, people for whom the word *avant-garde* signals a long-lost past. Composers like Nyman, but also poets, novelists, photographers, filmmakers, along with visual and comic artists, repeatedly acknowledge Goya as a master whose work addresses current social and political realities. Marching with hundreds of thousands of other demonstrators in New York City to protest the policies of the Bush administration at home and abroad before the 2004 presidential election in the U.S., I saw raised high above the crowd ahead of me, not far from a placard with the notorious photograph of the tortured hooded figure from the Abu Ghraib prison in Iraq, two reproductions from Goya's *The Disasters of War.*

Why is it that Goya's images of hacked and cut bodies, of torture, rape, cannibalism, executions, flying demons, and voracious monsters in drawings, paintings, etchings, and lithographs inhabit the present with such screaming urgency? Why do these pictures that Goya created out of his own roiling imagination and his

personal experiences in a ravaged Spain two hundred years ago
continue not only to move and frighten us, but also to *shock* us?
Long after the invention of photography, which, after all, can
document *actual* carnage, suffering, and horror, Goya's pictures
of subjects both natural and supernatural remain undimmed in
their power, so much so that the work of serious photographers,
such as Don McCullin, a man who has documented war, famine,
and illness, is inevitably compared to Goya's.[8] John Berger compares the light in Goya's *Disasters* to "film shots of a flare-lit target
after a bombing operation,"[9] and Gregory Paschalidis in his essay
"Images of War and the War of Images" echoes others when he
claims that the prints of *The Disasters of War* made by a witness of
war are a "prefiguration of the close link that the technical image
was to develop with the representation of war . . ."[10]

At the same time, it has become an intellectual commonplace
to argue that images of violence, both fictional and real, are ubiquitous, that our television and computer screens have become
arenas of spectacular horror and that we viewers are the desensi-
tized consumers of the glut of pictures that assault us every day.
Susan Sontag summarized this position in her well-known essay
On Photography: "Photographs shock insofar as they show something novel. Unfortunately, the ante keeps getting raised— partly
through the very proliferation of such images of horror."[11] For a
theorist like Jean Baudrillard, image-making has evolved to a
point where the *real* has been entirely submerged by simulacra.[12]
Paul Virilio articulates an apocalyptic vision of technologies sub-
stituting a virtual reality for an actual one, a state that leads to "derealization."[13] The force of these arguments is that human beings
are being fundamentally changed by the images they see.

It is significant that when Sontag refuted her earlier thoughts
on photography in a second book, *Regarding the Pain of Others*, she
singled out Goya as an artist whose vision of atrocity is unprecedented. "With Goya a new standard of responsiveness to suffer-

ing enters art."[14] Although she gives a quick overview of the lack of background in *The Disasters of War,* and the use of captions, she does not address what this new standard is or how it works. Similarly, in his discussion of *The Third of May,* Robert Hughes states that Goya's illuminated martyr is one of the "most vivid human presences" in art. "In an age of unremitting war and cruelty, when the value of human life seems to be at the deepest discount in human history, when our culture is saturated with endless images of torment, brutality and death, he continues to haunt us."[15] Both Sontag and Hughes feel what Baudelaire felt. They experience the same shock he gave to his imaginary viewer, and that electrical connection takes place *between* the viewer and the image seen. The spectator's emotional response is essential to understanding both Goya's potent images and their continuing influence on working artists.

Art historians often step around feeling, presumably because it is too ambiguous and subjective to be dealt with in a dignified manner, but consciousness without feeling is a pathological state that impairs normal functioning and intellectual judgment.[16] Goya has frequently bewildered scholars who look for rational patterns, schemas, and coherent meanings in his work, as if once a logical key is discovered, all will be revealed. But as Nelson Goodman points out in *Languages of Art,* the cultural insistence on a divorce between cognition and emotion results in an inability to understand "that in aesthetic experience the *emotions function cognitively.* The work of art is apprehended through the feelings as well as through the senses. Emotional numbness disables here as definitely if not completely as blindness and deafness."[17] Feeling is essential to perception and meaning. If modernity or postmodernity truly meant humanity (or Western humanity) had developed anesthesia to pictures, especially violent ones, through overexposure, then why would we respond to the same subjects in art? Goya's work would have little relevance for us, could not be held up as a "standard," and wouldn't be found on protest placards. And, although it is often overlooked when the artist is summoned for ideological purposes, Goya included images in *The Disasters of War* that are not first-person documentary drawings. The owls, bats, and bestial/human combinations he employed in *Los Caprichos* also make their appearance late in the *Disasters*. The monstrous creature sucking the breast of a dead woman in number 72 with a caption that reads "The consequences" is surely an indictment of war, but not a "realistic" depiction of it. The fact that the artist could not actually have seen this monster as he claims to have seen the events in number 44, "I saw it," doesn't undermine its emotional power. Similarly, the Black Painting of *Saturn Devouring His Son,* a mythological subject, isn't made innocuous because it depicts a Roman god.

Images move us because we enter into an imaginative relation with what is depicted, and the neural foundation for this dialectical encounter is a topic of ongoing scientific research. The truth is that people have strong responses to images even when they are well aware that they are looking at a representation, not the real thing. In the forties, the neuroscientist D. O. Hebb demonstrated that primates in general respond with fear and avoidance to representations of bodily fragmentation—a model of a severed monkey head in this case.[18] Cognitive and brain researchers who study emotion regularly use pictures and videos in their experiments. For example, a research group at the University of Florida concluded (not surprisingly) that their subjects had the strongest physiological responses to pictures of mutilation and attack. An additional finding of interest to art studies in general and to Goya's drawings and the images of *Los Caprichos* and *The Disasters of War* specifically is that it made no difference whether the participants saw the pictures in color or gray scale.[19]

The discovery of "mirror neurons" in the ventral premotor cortex of monkeys has created waves of speculation both in and beyond the neuroscience community that this system can account for everything from language to empathy. [20] The human equivalent of this dialogical/reflective system is now being studied. Very recently, David Freedberg, an art historian at Columbia University, collaborated with Fortunato Battaglia, a neurologist and neuroscientist at New York University, to experiment with viewers looking at a part of a painting (the expulsion of Adam and Eve from the garden in Michelangelo's *Sistine Chapel* ceiling). Simply looking at Adam's defensive arm gesture in the painting engaged the same neurons in the cortex that are engaged when the gesture is enacted.[21] Another study discovered that people viewing facial expressions of pain in photographs engaged the same cortical areas involved in the direct experience of pain.[22]

Although the full meaning of this research is far from understood, it casts light on the affective power pictures have *on* and *in* the viewer. A good deal of our engagement with images is processed unconsciously, and what we come to feel consciously is not under our control. To some extent, this is simply a matter of content—pictures of broken and bloody bodies will stir primal defensive reactions that a landscape won't. On the other hand, neural imaging and cognitive studies haven't the subtlety to explain why pictures with similar content can feel so different. Rubens's noble Saturn taking a bite out of his cherubic little boy as he stands on an incline, scepter in one hand, with drapery decorously hiding his genitalia, doesn't frighten me nearly as much as Goya's horrible painting, which both fascinates and repels me. And this is despite the fact that Rubens's god and child are rendered according to the conventions of Baroque realism, infant flesh gleaming, aging sinew and muscle defined. Goya's monster-god seems to come roaring out of the darkness into the viewer's space as he clutches the waist of a small, headless, sexually ambiguous, and anatomically impossible corpse. This grown-up child is smeared with blood, its stump of an arm inside the howling jaws of the cannibal. Although the painting has endured hardships, what remains of it is enough to terrify anyone.[23]

But what am I seeing? Why does Goya's work feel so much more threatening than Rubens's? Is it only because the later work has smashed the old rules and left the idealized neoclassical body of the past behind, as Fred Licht, Janis Tomlinson, and others argue? This is certainly true, but I've seen many bodies of all kinds in art and this one still startles me. I am not used to it. In my last novel, *What I Loved,* the narrator, Leo Hertzberg, an art historian, goes to an exhibition to see the work of Teddy Giles (an artist I made up) whose work includes bodies made of polyester and fiberglass that are dismembered, ripped open, decapitated, and smeared with fake blood and a photograph of the artist holding a remote control device. Leo comments:

> The show repulsed me, but I also found it bad. In the name of fairness, I had to ask myself why. Goya's painting of Saturn eating his son was just as violent. Giles used classic horror images presumably to comment on their role in the culture. The remote control was an obvious allusion to television and videos. Goya, too, borrowed from standard folk images of the supernatural that were immediately recognizable to anyone who saw his work, and they were also meant as social commentary. So why did Goya's work feel alive and Giles's dead? The medium was different. In Goya I felt the physical presence of the painter's hand. Giles hired craftsman to cast his bodies from live models and then fabricate them for him. And yet, I had admired other artists who had their work made for them. Goya was deep. Giles was shallow. But then sometimes shallowness is the point. Warhol had devoted himself to surfaces—to the empty veneers of culture. I didn't love Andy Warhol's work, but I could understand its interest.[24]

Leo, whose opinions about art are *not* identical to mine, is nevertheless befuddled by the same question: Why does one work feel powerful and another empty, despite the fact that they both describe horror? Later in the novel, Giles buys a valuable canvas made by Leo's painter friend, Bill Wechsler, shoves a fake body through it, and displays it as an artwork. I finished my novel in August of 2001. It was published first in England, France, and Germany in January of 2003. Later that year, Dinos and Jake Chapman exhibited a set of *The Disasters of War* that they had purchased and altered by drawing gas masks and puppy and clown heads on the victims. They called the piece *Insult to Injury*. Whatever one may think of this work, the brothers were able to startle their audience, just as my invented New York City artist, Teddy Giles, startles his. My fictional premonition suggests only that turning an admired work of art into another work of art by defacing the former was in the art world air, and I smelled it. (In an atmosphere where self-mutilation and experiments in pain have entered the gallery, it hardly seemed a revolutionary step.)[25]

The question of emotional power remains, however. Unlike their life-size sculpture of the figures in the plate from the *Disasters* with the caption "Great Deeds Against the Dead," which is a remarkably tepid work (and that may be the point), *Insult to Injury,* partly because it includes so much of Goya's original work and partly because it masks the victims, is genuinely disturbing. I suspect that the Chapman brothers' ongoing obsession with Goya is connected to the blow Baudelaire described as inevitable for any viewer of *Los Caprichos*. In interviews, Jake and, to a lesser extent, Dinos Chapman are prone to a grandiose, peculiar, academic prose that borders on parody. For example, "We take the 'monstrous' to describe a noumenal or vampirical sublime which preys upon corporeality in moments of aesthetic bliss." Their commentary is sprinkled with piecemeal allusions to psychoanalysis, philosophy, and technology, and they often quote tag phrases from authors without citing their sources: "speed and image" (Virilio), for example, or "the spectacle" (Debord). They evoke Freud's essay "Mourning and Melancholia" and then say, "psychosis suggests superconductive discharge because it is uninhibited."[26] What emerges from this soup of references is a kind of excited adolescent nihilism and a voyeuristic interest in extreme states during which ordinary perceptual borders collapse. No wonder Goya has become a supreme object of their fascination.

Although their direct allusions to and changes made to the *Disasters* are well known, they have borrowed more than that from Goya. Their sculpture, *DNA Zygotic,* which includes children with genitalia sprouting from their faces, makes use of the age-old associations (mouth/vagina, penis/nose), not by any means unique to Goya, but which, considering their obsession, may well have been inspired by the two drawings that were part of the evolution of plate 57 "The Lineage" in *Los Caprichos*: "He Puts Her Down as an Hermaphrodite" from the *Madrid Sketchbook* and a drawing for *Sueños,* both explicit renderings of genital faces that appear from between the legs of a masked woman being examined by a scribe, and the drawing for Capricho 13 also in the *Madrid Sketchbook,* which features a monk with a long penis for a nose. In an earlier essay on *Los Caprichos* I have written in detail about Goya's treatment of corporeal openings in the plates— mouths, anuses, and genitals in particular—as vulnerable to both reversal (heads in place of genitals) and monstrous transformations.[27] In the Chapmans' *Tragic Anatomies,* a female figure sprouts two heads, a deformity also found in Goya (*Disparates*), and in *Zygotic Acceleration* the brothers weld a group of children into a single body.[28]

The Chapmans' attraction is to the delirium in Goya's work, the explosive, feverish, and unrestrained. In an interview, Jake

Chapman said that Goya is an "artist who represents that kind of expressionistic struggle of the ancien régime, so it's kind of nice to kick its underbelly. Because he has a predilection for violence under the aegis of a moral framework. There's so much pleasure in his work."[29] There *is* pleasure in Goya's extreme images; his rendering of sadistic joy is direct, not censored or disguised. Castrating, raping, and mutilating the bodies of other people are not activities done reluctantly, without desire, and they are not activities we as human beings have left behind us. It is no secret that violence can create the paradoxical state of feeling more alive, and it is precisely this emotion that permeates the savage Goya in pictures both natural and supernatural—the two are not and should not be isolated from one another. As Baudelaire also pointed out, "the line of suture" between human being and beast or monster in Goya cannot be found.[30]

The drawing called *Saturnine Sorcerer,* which clearly anticipates the image of Saturn in the Black Paintings, shows a grinning cannibal who has the leg of one of his children in his mouth. The satisfaction derived from cruelty of various sorts often reappears in Goya's work: the genial smile of the tall thin man in plate number 69 "Blow" of *Los Caprichos,* for example, who swings a child in the air, buttocks outward to release a great gust of wind, or the infamous grin of the soldier in plate 36 of the *Disasters.* In an etched re-creation of the theme of that same plate, the Chapmans replace the soldier with a two-headed figure and the dead Spaniard with one marked by a swastika, all drawn in the style of a seven-year-old on a densely filled background. The twinned figure has an erect penis. As Goya did with himself in *Los Caprichos,* the fraternal team as two-in-one inserts itself into the familiar image to take the place of Goya's perpetrator/voyeur, a frank acknowledgment of the potentially erotic relationship between artist and his own violent, abject, or pornographic image, a relation that necessarily implicates the spectator, if only for *look-ing*. My rather staid art historian, Leo, admits that many of Goya's drawings affect him like an aphrodisiac:

> I kept turning the pages, eager for more pictures of brutes and monsters. I knew every one of them by heart, but that night their carnal fury scorched my mind like a fire, and when I looked again at the drawing of a young, naked woman riding a goat on a witches' Sabbath, I felt that she was all speed and hunger, that her crazed ride, born of Goya's sure swift hand, was ink bruising paper.[31]

If the Chapmans mean to condemn a critical language that hopes to domesticate Goya's images by wrapping them in a "greatness of the old master" mantle and then turning a blind eye to their profound ambiguity or their variously titillating, horrifying, and shaming effect on the viewer, then their small-scale re-creations and interventions (the larger works simply feel innocuous) have the effect of both glossing and returning us to the wild feeling of the original works.

The Chapmans' use of and commentary on Goya, however, is circumscribed. Their work has force when the viewer feels an infantile, amoral, irrational happiness in making things and their pleasure in kicking ingrained pieties in the pants, a frisson they clearly feel but cloak in post-humanist theoretical ideas that insist on their political impotence and their place in the art market as willing commodities. Irrational joy and a spirit of insurrection exist in Goya as well, but in the Spanish artist there is a broad range of emotions that include pathos, rage, and empathy. Although we can't know exactly what Goya saw during the Peninsular War, he obviously witnessed *enough*. It seems unlikely that the artist wandered about the countryside with a sketchbook as gruesome events were taking place in front of him. What he saw, heard about, and felt were realized afterward on paper and then in the plates. All conscious perception requires attention, and memory of that perception is both selective and mutable, but it is clear that emotion, especially strong emotion, keeps memories alive.[32] In a situation of fear or threat, people become hypervigilant and focused. There is no leisure in such looking, a fact that contributes to explaining why horrifying memories often lack the contextual detail of ordinary autobiographical memories.[33]

Many writers have cited the lack of detailed backgrounds in the plates of *The Disasters of War* (a schema also used in *Los Caprichos*). A comparison of drawing to etching often reveals further simplification and reduction of particulars for the final version. The drawing for plate 60, "There is no one to help them," includes the suggestive outlines of figures to the left of the distraught figure who stands at the center of the image and the outlines of trees to the right. In the plate, these have been eliminated. The bodies now *conform* to the shape of the hill. The sky is pure abstraction, a cloud of light surrounded by darkness; the position of the living mourner's hand that was below his chin in the drawing is now pressed to his face; and what remains visible to us is part of his opened mouth contorted in grief. His unheard cry becomes the searing focus of the picture. Similarly, in the drawing for plate 22, "All this and more," an illuminated sky and visual information in the far left of the drawing are dropped for the etching: the sky is blank, and the ground follows the lines of the corpses with only a hint of buildings to the right. The spectator is given an *emotional* landscape. All peripheral information is dropped except as visual shorthand—the line of the sky or a building or a tree. Furthermore, the bodies seem to merge into one another and into the ground itself, and the viewer sees them as if he is above them, despite the fact that this makes no rational sense according to the rules of perspective. In the drawing for plate 63, "A collection of dead men," the bodies are more fully articulated than in the later etching, where one cannot decisively locate where one body begins and another ends. They are war's refuse—and will bleed and rot and decay into one another and into the earth. Goya used these same techniques in *The Third of May*. The corpses lie tangled together, and locating all the limbs of the dead isn't easy. The spectator looks *down* on them, but *up* at the soldiers, as if he occupied two places at once.[34] This double vision, if you will, binds the viewer in empathy to the kneeling figure at the mercy of his *looming* executioners who will soon join his *fallen* comrades.

An argument can be made that Goya's exclusions and multiple perspectives heighten his viewer's perception of the terrible events he depicts in a way that is emotionally true. Terrifying events, if we don't forget them altogether, may be retained as potent visual fragments or simply a rush of overwhelming and involuntary feeling—the shuddering horror of the flashback—not as full, detailed images that can take their place inside a coherent narrative. According to a scientist researching post-traumatic stress disorder, they are "organized on a perceptual and affective level with limited semantic representation, and tend to intrude as emotional or sensory fragments related to the original event."[35] Photographs of the same events Goya renders would allow the viewer to *see everything* caught inside the frame and could not include a vertiginous perspective. The more inclusive, rational, and mechanical image is ultimately weaker as a representation of both the experience and its memory.[36]

In my research, which included informal conversations with artists in different fields whom I knew already or was able to contact, forays onto the Internet, and reading or looking at Goya-inspired works of varying quality from all over the world, it became clear to me that it is the private, deaf artist, the man who showed us violence and dreams, who feeds the contemporary imagination and begs for artistic dialogue. Had he died from his illness in 1794, Goya would not exert the influence on art he does now. The visual re-creations and literary texts on or inspired by *The Disasters of War, Los Caprichos,* and the Black Paintings are numerous. There are well-known works, such as Sigmar Polke's haunting take on Capriccio 26, *This Is How You Sit Correctly,* and the English painter Cecily Brown's hallucinatory homages to Goya. "I have loved Goya," she wrote to me in an e-mail "since I first saw a reproduction of *Saturn Devouring His Son* when I was a child. At art school I loved *The Disasters of War* and *Caprichos* best, and in a way still do. I have worked indirectly from Goya reproductions many times, and twice made 'copies,' though neither ended up looking anything like the originals . . . I have also openly ripped off 'The Sleep of Reason,' especially in my black paintings." Kiki Smith, the American artist, was also first impressed with Goya as a child. Her aunt had a set of "the bull-fighters" on her wall. "Of course," she wrote me, "*Los Caprichos* and *The Disasters of War* are influential to me—most directly in the prints that I have made with hand-dropped aquatints." Art Spiegelman, whose *Maus,* a comics version of his parents' internment in Auschwitz during the Second World War, changed the way people regard the genre, also reworked "The Sleep of Reason." He cited the profound influence Goya has had on those working in graphic art, a line that runs from Goya through Otto Dix and George Grosz to the present. But there are many less well-known artists who have also turned to Goya. An exhibition organized by the University of California at Berkeley called *In the Light of Goya* included artists like Victor Cartagena, Rupert Garcia, and Sue Coe, all of whom, despite the show's title, took inspiration from the dark Goya.

In the literary arts I found numerous Goya tributes and tales, from a full-blown adventure novel *Les Fantomes de Goya* by Jean-Claude Carrière, to a series of very short stories written to accompany *Los Caprichos* by the American science-fiction writer

Michael Swanwick. Again and again, it's the strange and brutal Goya that writers summon. Lawrence Ferlinghetti's poem, "In Goya's Greatest Scenes We Seem to See," includes the lines: "they are so bloody real/it is as if they really still existed/And they do . . ."[37] The famous Voznesensky poem "I Am Goya" addresses the sufferings of Russians in the Second World War, and the Dutch poet Stefan Hertmans's book *Goya as a Dog* refers to the poor canine in the Black Painting. In 1986, the Serbian author, Ivo Andric, published his *Conversations with Goya*. The narrator imagines meeting Goya in Bordeaux, where the artist spent his last years. The painter does most of the talking:

> All human movements spring from a need to attack or defend. That is their fundamental, for the most part forgotten, but instinctive cause and stimulus . . . Every artist who wants to paint what I have painted, is obliged to portray an action which is a collection of . . . many movements, and this concentrated movement must inevitably betray the stamp of its true origin, attack and defense, fury and fear.[38]

It is clear that Andric, who in his youth was part of the Young Bosnia movement and spent years in prison after the outbreak of the First World War, sees Goya as a spiritual comrade. The painter had seen the beast in human beings, as had Andric.

> I saw principles and systems which looked more solid than granite disperse like mist . . . and form into unshakeable, holy principles, more solid than granite. And I asked myself what was the sense of these changes, what was the plan they were following, where was it all leading? And however much I looked, listened and wondered, I found no sense nor plan nor aim in any of it.[39]

The roads back to Goya are many, but they inevitably pass by way of "the sleep of reason"—*non-sense*—which is why Goya's commissioned art, his portraits, religious paintings, his work for the royal tapestries, or even his early treatment of supernatural subjects, are much less often referred to in contemporary art. Despite the explication and emphasis on Goya's Enlightenment sympathies by historians, artists have little use for these readings, however insightful. Like Baudelaire's sympathetic but ignorant art lover, they respond to the *extreme* images of Goya, in which dreams and war merge to spew forth monsters so hungry and alive they appear unlikely to be quashed by any form of reasonable discourse. The Enlightenment faith in a rational order, its encyclopedic yearning to contain all things within defined categories, also produced its opposite: a fascination with the grotesque—the chaotic body maimed, insane, and distorted. Therefore Goya's preoccupation with terrible bodies isn't unique, and this historical frame leads to speculations such as Janis Tomlinson's that the Black Paintings may have been a fashionable phantasmagoria to spook the artist's guests.[40] I don't deny that this is possible, but what artists seem to understand that scholars often don't is that whatever Goya may have *thought,* however much he sympathized with his *Illustrado* friends and opposed the superstitions of the Spain he inhabited, however much he was a bourgeois man of his time, the power of his awful images belie and overwhelm any such designation. They burst the category.

It may simply be that artists know they don't control their work. When you paint or write or compose, things happen that you don't understand. I have often felt that writing fiction is connected to dreaming, a state of altered consciousness, during which material I didn't know was there begins to assert itself, to take over, which may help explain the bizarre feeling I have had on occasion that a text is writing itself. Far from being Romantic claptrap, this phenomenon is rooted in the now-indisputable fact that most of what the brain does is unconscious, that most of memory, perception, and emotional processing takes place beneath our awareness. As Freud knew, it's under there, and sometimes it comes up.

The consuming artistic interest in Goya's hallucinatory and violent works, *Los Caprichos* and *The Disasters of War* in particular, is a tribute to the "sharp shock at the core" of the brain delivered by these works, as well as the uncomfortable mirroring effect they establish between spectator and image. Despite its satirical intent, the vertiginous, gleeful, demented quality of *Los Caprichos* cannot be *contained* by moralizing commentary. Its greedy beasts and goblins have an intimate, disturbing quality I recognize from my own dreams. In his poem "Capriccio for/about Goya" the Bulgarian poet Konstantin Pavlov describes this queasy relation in his final lines:

> *Ah, it's the smile that makes it so revolting,*
> *makes it perverted*
> *and mad.*
> *I feel sick with a revulsion*
> *as never before.*
>
> *As if babies with beards and mustaches*
> *were kissing me lasciviously.*

The speaker cannot keep his distance; earlier in the poem he says, "[the terror] courts me and flirts with its own image."[41] He is tainted, as if he has been molested by impossibly mature infants. The prepositional ambiguity in the poem's title "for/about" signals his suspicion; is this an homage or an indictment?

Although the tone is altogether different from *Los Caprichos*, the frankly depicted sadism in some of the plates of *The Disasters of War* has a fascinating as well as a repulsive aspect, one that plays on the feelings of an uneasy witness, torn between seeing and not seeing. The caption *No se puede mirar* "One [or we] cannot look at this" (plate 26) is the same text given to a drawing (#101) of a torture victim in the *Sketchbook Journal*. And yet, Goya *made these images*. Their sole purpose is to be *seen*. The caption refers to the picture itself and to the implied *real* brutalized body it represents. In her poem cycle "Musée des Beaux Arts," Debora Greger describes the ambivalence inherent in looking at hurt bodies in these lines on Goya from the poem's third section, "The Art of War."

> Nothing dared stand,
> Not even the light.
> It lay collapsed on the muddy boots.
>
> It crawled up to the knees. It peered
> Into the hands,
> The faces gone dark.
> I looked away. I looked back.[42]

My uneasiness when I look at these pictures doesn't vanish because I have seen too many unspeakable images, nor do the complex emotions evoked by them—the instant shock to my limbic system that comes from seeing a broken human body, the accompanying guilt and shame I feel for my fascination, which mingles with my empathy for the victim, whether he or she is imaginary—in an image or text—or documented in a photograph.[43] In the real world, we look, too. People gather to watch fires burning, ogle beheadings on the Internet, just as they used to rush to public hangings. On 9/11 my sister ran north with her seven-year-old daughter and hundreds of others away from the burning towers behind them, and just before she reached their

street, she said to my niece, "Okay, now turn around and look."
They did. "I don't know why," my sister told me. "I just did it."

My sister also remembers running past a man who had
kneeled in the street to vomit. Like Goya's man in the *Disasters*
who spews over a pile of corpses, his body rejected the horror he
had seen. On the battlefield, in a ruined city, when bombs fall,
when buildings collapse, and subways explode, reason disinte-
grates along with bodies. "With or without reason" reads Goya's
caption for the second plate of the *Disasters*. It ceases to matter.
There is a hallucinatory quality to the actual experience of disaster as well, a sense of unreality that psychiatrists call disassocia-
tion. Victims may feel remote and dreamlike. Some have the
uncanny experience that they are hovering over themselves in
out-of-body experiences. In *Disasters* 36, the hanged man in the
foreground is echoed by two dangling comrades behind him.
They are suspended in a curious receding landscape in which the
ground itself appears to float. In Goya, plural human realities
coexist and overlap. We see the reality of nightmare and the nightmare of reality united by senselessness: the terrifying *Nada* inscribed on a slate by the half-buried, gaping figure in plate 69 of
the *Disasters*.

The ambiguities of Goya the man can't be resolved. His legacy, however, is defiantly vigorous, and his artistic offspring
continue to multiply. Although the mournful meditations of Ivo
Andric and the bad-boy, post-Nietzschean works of the Chapman brothers have little in common, they were both generated
by looking at Goya, and they were made in response to the shock
they felt when they looked at the unbridled men and women and
beasts and monsters he unleashed onto his pictures. Goya may
well have been the first "modern" artist, but his images will out-
live the modern and the postmodern and whatever comes after
it, because instinctual "fear and fury" aren't characteristic of any
particular age, nor are violence, loss, grief, madness, and dreams.

Context, vocabulary, ideology, and technologies all shift with time and surely play an important role in shaping our collective consciousness, but the Goya that continues to sustain art in its myriad forms is a person who felt the anarchic, unspeakable depths we carry within us and was able to make us recognize them. We find ourselves looking in a mirror. In Goya, we are the monsters.

2007

EMBODIED VISIONS
What Does It Mean to Look at
a Work of Art?

HUMAN BEINGS ARE THE ONLY animals who make art. I have heard stories of painting elephants, drawing monkeys, and typing dogs, but despite the complexities of pachyderm, simian, and canine cultures, visual art is not central to any of them. We are the image-makers. At some moment in the narrative of evolution, human societies began to draw and paint things, and it is safe to say that the act of picture-making is only possible because we have the faculty of reflective self-consciousness; that is, we are able to represent ourselves to ourselves and muse about our own beings by becoming objects in our own eyes. This ability is distinct from what has been called prereflective self-consciousness, that immersion in everyday experience that we do not have to reflect upon to perceive, the smell of the basil on the kitchen counter, the warmth of sunlight through a window, the feel of my body in a chair. I am not *unconscious* of myself as I sit in that chair, surely, but I can sit comfortably for a long period without meditating on what it means for me to be sitting there, and I can stay quietly in place without having a mental picture of myself as Siri the Sitter. This form of subjectivity is a given of our experience. William James called it "the outward looking point of view" as opposed to what happens when we "think ourselves as thinkers."[1] Edmund Husserl understood that even when we don't think ourselves as thinkers, there remains a form of self-knowing, "To be a subject is to be in the mode of being aware of oneself."[2] Although I can't be sure, I suppose that my old dog, Jack, had a prereflective sense of himself, a feeling of Jack-ness, a bodily me-ness that allowed him to know that he was too warm or cold or hungry and needed to do something about it. But let us say that while I am in the same chair I get it into my head to do a self-portrait of myself in the chair, and I fetch a pencil, paper, and a mirror so I can see myself and begin to draw. The idea expressed in the words—*I'll draw me*—entails a splitting of myself into both subject and object, and this self-reflective distance is an essentially human adventure.

But what lies beneath this reflective faculty—mirroring and recognition—is not unique to people. Elephants, dolphins, some of our fellow primates, and certain birds recognize themselves in the mirror. Dogs do not. At around eighteen months, it happens to children. Long before Jacques Lacan wrote his lecture on the mirror stage in 1949,[3] the researcher William Preyer, who worked in Germany, published a book called *Die Seele des Kindes* (1882), in which he argued that before a child is able to use the pronouns *I* or *me,* she has a sense of self and that mirror self-recognition is a crucial aspect of her development.[4] But prior to mirror self-recognition is mirroring behavior in infants, which appears to be innate. Babies as young as an hour old have been photographed imitating the facial expressions of adults.[5] Their reflecting behavior seems to be an automatic response to the face of a fellow human being. Newborns do not have reflective self-consciousness. Hegel was surely right when he argued in *The Phenomenology of Mind,* "While the embryo is certainly, in itself, implicitly a human being, it is not so explicitly, it is not by itself a human being (für sich) . . ."[6] This being there "for itself" arrives later in life, but it is preceded by earlier forms of intersubjectivity. Winnicott reconfigured Lacan's mirror stage to include the mirroring looks between mother and child that are crucial to the baby's growth.[7] More recently, neuroscience has shown that these exchanges affect the way the infant's brain develops.[8] We find ourselves first in the eyes of our mothers, and we continue to have strong reflective responses to the expressions on the faces of other people long after we have grown up and ceased to imitate their facial gestures. The faces of others affect our moods, something that has been seen over and over again in what cognitive psychologists call "masking" studies. People are presented with images of faces frowning and angry, or friendly smiling, for example, but so briefly they cannot consciously register the images. Nevertheless, the subliminal pictures influence their responses to the questions that follow. Even though the face is not consciously perceived, it can affect a person's thoughts, memories, and feelings.

The discovery of human mirror systems in neuroscience underscores what many psychologists and philosophers have long postulated about the dialectical relation between self and other, and this unconscious neuronal firing is at work in human beings whether we are looking at a real person, at a photograph of a person, or at a painting of a person.[9] Furthermore, these shared systems that match an action and the perception of the same action are also involved in prediction, in what the movement is for. All of this takes place un- or subconsciously. The mutuality that happens between people is indisputably real, and it cannot develop in isolation. What becomes an *I* is embedded in a *you*. We are inherently social beings and our brains and bodies grow through others in the early dynamics between a child and his parents, but also within a given language and culture as a whole.

My argument here is that the experience of looking at visual art always involves a form of mirroring, which may be but is not necessarily conscious. This is fairly obvious to us when we look at a portrait or at any human figure—we see something *like* ourselves there—but it is also present when we look at a representation of a thing or at an abstraction. The reflective quality is there because we are witnessing what remains of another person's creative act, and through the artistic object we find ourselves embroiled in the drama of self and other. This back-and-forth dialectic between spectator and artwork occurs despite the fact that a painting, sculpture, or drawing is also just a thing, an object like any other in the material world. It may be a canvas with oil or acrylic paint on it or wood or stone or a paper with some charcoal markings or fiberglass or rubber or any other material. It can last for centuries or burn up in a fire, but it is fundamentally different from the chair I mentioned sitting in earlier. It has no purpose other than to be looked at and thought about. It is not a tool. We can't eat with it. Art is useless. I am well aware that with architecture, for example, this becomes murky. I also know that Picasso decorated some plates I'd be afraid to eat off of and that some designers of furniture have made objects I personally find more beautiful and even more interesting than certain works of art, but I am bracketing my discussion here to objects without utility. A famous example of a fundamental transformation from practical thing to art object is Duchamp's urinal. Once it became *Fountain,* nobody, to my knowledge at least, ever took a pee in it. Ripped from its context in the ordinary world as a repository for human waste, turned upside down, and signed "R. Mutt," it metamorphosed into a mysterious art object thickly wrapped in layers of cultural irony.

Although works of art are things, they are also strangely alive, animated by a mysterious power, and this thought brings me round to Friedrich Schelling and to his thinking about art. He too recognized that works of art are particular, finite things, subject to the laws of all objects. Nevertheless, art cannot be finally *determined* or pinned down, because for Schelling works of art were the result of a fusion between the unconscious creative energy or "drive" in nature and the free conscious efforts of the artist, and therefore something in the artwork always remained hidden: its unconscious roots. Unlike other philosophers, Schelling did not oppose Nature and Spirit. He was a monist, not a dualist, who believed that the world was made of a single dynamic stuff— nature and intellect are one and the same, but they represent different stages in the development of that force—intellect and self-consciousness become possible in the human being when he is able to reflect upon himself.[10] It is not necessary to embrace the whole of Schelling's philosophy or his Romantic idea of "genius" to acknowledge that he identified something essential about art. Although I'm convinced he would have been appalled by Duchamp's urinal, not even that scandalous ready-made can be said to have been created from purely self-conscious cognitive activity. Where do thoughts come from, after all? There is an underground to thought, a place of incubation we have little access to. And just as no artist brings only an idea to his art, no viewer perceives art only through his intellect, not even if he is staring at the urinal or at Joseph Kosuth's *One and Three Chairs*. I can articulate several sentences about Kosuth's three kinds of chairs, which I believe would be true, but there is more to my experience than those sentences. I also have a physical relation to the three chairs, one that is immediate and felt, and I have a keen sense of the artist's dogmatic presence and his desire to overturn old notions of the aesthetic. I may sympathize with this, but the man standing next to me might find himself irritated. He might say, "That's not art. I could have done that." But there is always an emotional component that is part of a viewer's response to the work, and what generates that emotion is not easy to understand, describe, or quantify.

Art requires an artist, and that artist is, or was, a living, breathing human being with an embodied self that functions both consciously and unconsciously within a larger world of meanings. For some reason that person is driven to make art. This urge, one I have, is not explicable to me. I am aware of an urgent need to write, to make something, to push forward, but where it comes from or why I have it is unknown to me. Most of what I am at any given moment is hidden. We have explicit memories—the ones we can pull forth at a moment's notice—but also implicit ones that may return as an association to something else or remain forever buried. For Freud, making art was a *sublimation,* a kind of translation of fundamental human drives, for him sexual, that were then turned into something else. It is not hard to see the influence of earlier philosophers on his thought—Schelling certainly, but also Schopenhauer, with his will to power, the blind force that drives human beings. I think the German word *Trieb,* or drive, rather than instinct, as it has been translated into English, describes this push best. All animals have drives, most notably to survive, but making art is not about survival, despite the fact that many artists feel that if they couldn't do their work, their lives would lose meaning.

Art, it seems to me, must be distinguished by a kind of *intentionality.* Franz Brentano, his student Husserl, and the French philosopher Maurice Merleau-Ponty all used this word, and it is now essential to the vocabularies of people working in phenomenology, as well as to Anglo-American analytic philosophers. For Brentano intentionality was a characteristic of all mental acts. He described it as "reference to a content" or "direction toward an object."[11] Although Husserl disputed aspects of Brentano's definition, he also mostly employed the idea of intentionality as a conscious directedness. Merleau-Ponty, influenced by Gestalt psychology and neurology, had a far more embodied notion of intentionality, one that included a prereflective intentionality, a motivational force toward something that is not necessarily self-conscious in that thinking-ourselves-as-thinkers way. For

Merleau-Ponty the sphere of lived intentions was much larger than conscious thought.[12] Long before research unveiled a subliminal neurobiology of intentionality, Merleau-Ponty included it in his theory. Works of art exhibit traces of this embodied intentionality. In drawings, the feeling of the hand that once moved on the page is present. When looking at a painting I am often deeply affected by the remains of the artist's gesture or the sense of his motion now stilled—in a Jackson Pollock action painting, for example, or in a work from Gerhard Richter's series *Sinbad*. Not only do I feel the movement of the lacquer on the glass, I want to start dancing. This sight, with its colors and the now stopped motion, affects my limbs as if I were listening to a rock-and-roll song. But even when there is no trace of the artist's hand, brush, or movement, intentionality is present, albeit in a more cognitive form, in an upside-down urinal or a simple chair. It is this quality that turns an "it" into a form of a "you."

Producing art includes a drive to make something, an embodied *intentionality*. But art is not possible without intersubjective human experience because art is always a gift made for another, not a specific other, but a generalized other person who is asked to read or listen or look. Art necessarily establishes a relation between the artist and an imaginary reader, viewer, or listener; it is inherently dialogical. Therefore, *all visual art implies a spectator*, even when that other is part of the self, the viewing self, as was the case with Henry Darger, one of the so-called outsider artists. When he died in Chicago in 1973, he left behind him the immense illustrated saga of the Vivian girls, over fifteen thousand pages of narrative and several hundred watercolors that include hermaphroditic girl armies and their often violent adventures. He was his own voyeur.

The artist presses something of himself out into the world—the fantasies of a man bruised forever by his childhood. Darger's mother died when he was four. Then he lost his crippled father, and the boy, deemed defective, was sent to a mental institution, from which he escaped when he was sixteen. In his art, he created an epic of children enslaved by sadistic adults, a narrative of suffering and insurrection that finally ends in triumph. And the story and the pictures are at once of him and not of him. Darger was an urban hermit. It is doubtful that he spent much time in art museums, but his pictures draw from visual representations he knew well: advertisements, comics, and illustrations from children's books. I am using Darger as an example, but what I am going to say is true of every artist, for this is where inside and outside collapse. No artist lives in a vacuum, not even Henry Darger. The perceived world becomes part of us in memory, but we are also immersed in that world. Much of what we take in becomes part of our vast implicit understanding of things once it is learned, becomes the body's knowledge, and this knowledge can't be separated from our engagement with people and things in our particular environment.

When I am drawing my self-portrait I do not think about where my hand is on the paper; it moves because I know how to move it. My hand responds automatically to what I am seeing in the mirror. I don't rehearse drawing any more than I relearn how to ride a bike every time I jump on one. I might mourn my skills and wish I were Leonardo da Vinci, but what I am able to do is present in my hand's motion. Living is movement. Thoughts are in motion, and when I think, my body thinks too. While writing I find the words not only in my mind but in the feeling of my fingers on the keyboard. When I'm stuck, I stand up and walk around the room, and walking often jogs the sentence loose. There is a powerful connection between vision and motor-sensory circuits in the brain, and visual perception cannot be separated from our knowledge of the world gained through our movements in it.

We are proprioceptive beings. Broadly, proprioception, which comes from the Latin word *proprius,* meaning *one's own,* is our ability to sense the position, orientation, and movement of our bodies and its parts in space. Much of the time we simply don't have to think about this; it is unconscious. As with so many things we take for granted, it is only when this sixth sense doesn't develop or is lost to injury that its absolute necessity is made clear. Children with a defective proprioceptive sense may fall down or intentionally bump into walls and doors to get a better idea of where they are. People who suffer a brain injury and damage this faculty cannot feel where their bodies are in relation to a chair, for example, and will have to actively evaluate their spatial relation to it in order to sit down.

If you are throwing up your hands and saying, "But what does this have to do with art?" my answer is that every encounter with a work of art is an embodied, subjective one. Our phenomenal experiences of Duchamp, Kosuth, Richter, or Darger are not objective, third-person experiences. I don't fly out of my body and my personal story when I stand in front of Duccio's *Madonna and Child* at the Metropolitan Museum. What happens happens between me and the image. Even in science there is no such thing as perceptual neutrality.[13] This doesn't mean that looking at art is a solipsistic experience either or that any response is as good as another. I can imagine flying out of my body and examining the picture from another perspective, say as an old childless man, but I know that my excursion is not real. I can also use my learning about painting in Siena at the turn of the fourteenth century to inform my vision. We cannot help but be part of our language and culture, which shape our beliefs about how things are. And we all engage to one degree or another in consensus-making, and intersubjective consensus precedes us. Nevertheless, we all have a genetic makeup—some scientists call it temperament—that will be expressed through our environments. The temperamentally sensitive will be more vulnerable to shocks and blows than the temperamentally robust. This applies to art as well. Our temperaments in tandem with our personal stories as we grow as human beings will affect our responses to a painting and become part of the dialogue.

We are born into meanings and ideas that will shape how our embodied minds encounter the world. The moment I walk through the doors of the Prado or the Louvre, for example, I enter a culturally sanctified space. Unless I am an alien visitor from another galaxy, I will be permeated by the hush of greatness, by a sense that what I am going to see has the imprimatur of those in the know, the experts, the curators, the culture-makers. This idea of grandeur made physical by big rooms, rows of paintings and sculptures, affects my perception of what I am going to see. An expectation of greatness is apt to be part of my perception, even if I consider myself unprejudiced and am not aware that my view of a work of art has been subtly altered by *where* it is.

Art's meaning is created at every level of our experience. Sensing color, for example, appears to be prereflective. Red, green, or blue will affect us—we will feel their impact—before we are even able to name the color. As the Gestalt theorists argued, we will also distinguish foreground from ground prior to a recognition of the objects on that ground. This has been called "preattentive" vision.[14] A large work of art will immediately strike us, as will a very small one, before we can articulate largeness or smallness because, if our proprioceptive sense is working, we will engage with its size instantly, before we can meditate on it. And, I think what we see has emotional or affective value, not after we have contemplated the object and named it, but in the earlier subliminal stages of vision. In an article "See It with Feeling: Affective Predictions during Object Perception," L. F. Barrett and Moshe Bar argue that before an object has even been identified, we respond bodily to its perceived salience or meaning through past experience. Depending on the prediction about the thing's value, our breathing, muscle tension, heart rate, stomach motility, as well as vague or potent sensations of pleasure, anxiety, or distress will be present. Merleau-Ponty referred to this kind of expectation as a stereotype.[15] Barrett and Bar write, "When the brain receives a new sensory input from the world in the present, it generates a hypothesis based on what it knows from the past to guide recognition and action in the immediate future."[16] Aside from the fact that the authors turn the brain into a subject, which is rather silly, their point is well taken.

A vivid and conveniently prolonged example of stereotypic ways of seeing can be seen in something that happened to my husband, Paul Auster, and which he included in his novel *The Book of Illusions*. He was walking our now-deceased dog Jack down a street in Brooklyn one misty night, and in the blurred light of the streetlamps saw a small blue object glowing on the sidewalk. Pleased and curious, he leaned over to investigate. It was a stone, he guessed, or a piece of cut glass, or perhaps a moonstone or sapphire fallen out of a ring or necklace. Part of the passage from the book reads: "And so I started to pick it up, but the moment my fingers came into contact with the stone, I discovered that it wasn't what I'd thought it was. It was soft, and it broke apart when I touched it, disintegrating into a wet, slithery ooze. The thing I had taken for a stone was a gob of human spit."[17] Needless to say, disgust quickly replaced pleasure. Our earlier motor-sensory experiences order our vision and become predictors of what we are going to see when we pay close attention to the object. This is why when blind people recover their sight physiologically—their primary visual cortex is functioning normally—they nevertheless cannot "see." Years of perceptual learning that create expectation and orientation are missing and their vision is chaotic, blurred, and incoherent.

Looking at a work of art engages this prereflective expectation of its value—of pleasure or disgust or boredom and their bodily concomitants. But this is usually instantaneous, and once one has stopped to look properly at a work of art, forms of reflective consciousness are also brought to bear. Indeed, almost all writing about art takes place at this level of the experience. We read about the historical period of the painting or sculpture or about the artist's biography or about what x-rays reveal about its creation or perhaps a complex theoretical argument about the avant-garde or capitalism and the art market. If I know, for example, that Kosuth was interested in Ludwig Wittgenstein, especially the *Tractatus Logico-Philosophicus,* this information will affect how I "read" his chairs, just as knowing about Darger's childhood changes his work. The *Tractatus* and years of boyhood spent in a mental institution are part of the intersubjective and linguistic fabric that clothes my perception as I think about what it is that I am actually seeing.

Despite significant advances in research on the visual areas of the brain, there is a lot of disagreement about *how* we actually see. It is known, for example, that there are as many as thirty areas in the brain dedicated to vision, that some of these areas or rather neuronal networks appear to be for specific functions: color, motion, depth perception, etc. Interestingly, there is also a part of the brain in the temporal lobe crucial to face recognition, the fusiform gyrus. Face recognition is a particular neurological event, and it too can be lost. But none of these discoveries constitutes a theory of vision. There are still many scientists and philosophers who cling to a computational model of perception. We are like computers with serial inputs and outputs, and our brains operate according to logical rules. In this view, seeing is largely passive. All we do is receive images from the world that are then represented like reflections in our brains. Another view, one I find far more compelling, is a phenomenological one. We are not computers, and we are not just brains. We have bodies that move in space and we have emotions and a vast unconscious, and our perceptions of people and things are active and creative. It has become increasingly clear that a large part of the dynamic patterns of neural connectivity in our brains is not predetermined genetically. They are not static but are shaped by our behavior and our motor sensory and cognitive experiences. Learning changes the brain, and its plasticity continues throughout our lives.

Despite the scientific zeal to atomize experience, to break it down into comprehensible bits and pieces, this approach often results in a frozen view of reality. In recent years, parts of the scientific community have been influenced by the phenomenology of Husserl, and, more important, by Merleau-Ponty, to challenge a paralyzed, purely third-person view of perception. Neurobiologists such as Humberto Maturana and the late Francisco Varela,[18] the cognitive scientists Shaun Gallagher[19] and Claire Petitmengin,[20] as well as philosophers such as Alva Noë[21] and J. J. Gibson[22] argue for an enactive theory of perception founded on our motor-sensory abilities and have embraced a whole-body-in-relation-to-its-environment understanding of vision. Although there is no unified front and there are many disagreements among them, my reading of these thinkers has led me to the position that viewers are not merely passive reflectors of the out-there, but embodied creative seers. Two researchers at the Max Planck Institute, Andreas Engel and Peter König, articulated the position well in a paper called "Paradigm Shifts in Neurobiology: Toward a New Theory of Perception": "What neuroscience has to explain," they write, "is not how brains act as world-mirroring devices, but how they serve as 'vehicles of world-making.'"[23]

Let us take a very simple example of active visual perception. One day last spring, I was walking down the street with my daughter, Sophie, in lower Manhattan. She had just moved into a new apartment a few blocks away, and we were shopping for household objects to put in her new place. The sun was shining.

The sky was blue, and we walked along arm in arm. I felt like singing. I looked up, saw a sign and read: HAPPY ORTHO-DONTICS. I turned to Sophie and said, "Look, isn't that the craziest name for an orthodontist's office?" I pointed to the sign, but when I looked again, it said: KARPOV ORTHODONTICS. This simple error is illuminating. My misreading was subliminal, active, and creative. I projected my emotional state onto the text and proceeded to garble the letters. Similarly, it has been shown that clinically depressed people respond to pictures of neutral, unemotional faces in a far more negative way than people who are not depressed. Mood acts creatively on our perceptions.

The first time I saw Zurbarán's *Lemons, Oranges, and a Rose*, which is in the Norton Simon Museum in Pasadena, California, I had a very strong reaction to the picture, and I stood in front of it for some time. It's neither tiny nor huge: 60 by 107 cm. Its size did not overwhelm me, but I had no feeling of its being diminutive either. Its colors are vivid but muted against a dark background. I cannot track the initial unconscious milliseconds of my response to the picture, but I know the image hit me instantly and bodily, and had some person been there to measure the activation of my sympathetic nervous system that had sped up my heart rate and increased the sweat levels in my skin, he would have pronounced me in a state of heightened emotion and attention.

Why? How can four lemons on a silver saucer, oranges in a basket, a rose, and a teacup filled with water sitting on another silver saucer create such a physical charge? Naming the contents of the painting gets us nowhere; it is simply a banal recitation of ordinary things. And if I arranged these objects for you on a table, I could make a lovely still life. There would be a pleasant contrast of colors for the eye, but the visual experience would be very different. First of all, the real fruits, china cup, and flower would exist in three-dimensional space and have a backside that could be explored. Part of your perception would be that you could, if you dared ruin my construction, pick up a lemon or an orange and eat it. I could declare it my artwork, and it would be one. But you would never *see* the objects in my piece as this work by Zurbaran *sees* them. They appear to be in hyperfocus, to be more defined, more perfectly clear than things in the world, despite the shadows. It is as if we have improved our normal vision with specially made glasses, and the objects are illuminated by a light that represents no time of day or light source we could ever name. We do not imagine a window or candle somewhere in the room lighting these objects. The initial "pop" of this picture is not because we are experiencing realism or naturalism, but precisely the opposite. They are fictions in a fictitious world, an imaginary elsewhere that has opened up before our eyes. We recognize every thing in the painting, but each of these objects is forbiddingly removed from any idea of use or consumption, not because they are painted but because of *the way* they are painted. They are enchanted by the artist's intentionality—a force that is prereflective and reflective, one that I engage with as a distinct presence of another human being, albeit the ghost of that other, that absent *you*.

The longer I looked at it, the stranger and more mysterious the image became. The words *lemons, saucer, oranges, basket, teacup,* and *rose* detached themselves from my experience as I tried to pin down what was happening and discovered that I couldn't, or rather, that whatever I said to myself seemed inexact. After that initial startle response, my nervous system quieted down and the stillness and silence of both the things represented (lemons and oranges are not animate) and of the medium itself (painting does not move in a literal sense) acted on me like a balm, and I fell into a kind of reverie typical of art viewers, an active, ongoing, shifting, physical, mental response to what I was seeing, one that included emotion—but which one? A form of awe, I would say, a sense that the world we live in with its fruits and cups and tables and chairs and animals and people becomes increasingly alien the more closely it is examined. It is a feeling I often had as a child and still have from time to time, and on occasion it is accompanied by a strong lifting sensation inside me, as if I am rising up and out of myself. This Zurbarán brings me back to that emotional state, and so a part of my response to the picture is an active projection or, to use the psychoanalytic term, a form of *transference* of my memories and my lived past onto the painting. This transference is subtler than my misreading of KARPOV ORTHODONTICS but is nevertheless a related phenomenon. Subject and object, *I* and *you,* begin to collapse in my viewing. What part is the Zurbarán picture, and what part is the spectator?

When I saw the painting for the first time, I did not know that the objects in the work are symbolic offerings to the Virgin Mary, that lemons are an Easter fruit, that the rose signifies love, purity, and chastity, and the table an altar. I read that later. It did not fundamentally change my feelings about the picture but rather added to what I had already felt in an undogmatic way— that there is something unworldly about the things I see here, that they are objects suffused with transcendent feeling. Much scholarship about art is in the business of explaining these sorts of meanings: the oranges and their blossoms signify the renewal of life. Other academics write long discourses about technique to explain how a work was made, and there is high theory about art as well, the philosophy of art. In my reading of these philosophers I ran across this:

O is a work of art-e = df O is an artifact and O functions to provide for aesthetic appreciation.[24]

This is part of a much longer analytical argument, in which James C. Anderson gives the reader a definition of art. Every definition is under siege, and there is little agreement. I have no problem with logical formulas as a way to get at meanings and, in the course of his essay, Anderson modifies this definition to include a second qualifier as a subcategory of appreciation: "art self-conscious art,"[25] but what interests me here is the way "aesthetic appreciation" appears in the formula. The words imply an abstract viewer, a general appreciator, and that something happens in that "appreciation," but the particular embodied dynamics of appreciating are missing, although Anderson suggests that even disgust can be subsumed by the word *appreciation*. I am not saying that Anderson is necessarily wrong. I am offering here an addendum to theories that have left the drama of creative perception and embodied feeling out of the discussion about art, theories that have largely forgotten that art lives in a viewing subject, in the person who stands in front of whatever the thing is and looks at it, sometimes appreciatively, sometimes not. We might ask how much appreciation does it take to make a work of art. Why do we appreciate art at all? Why do I love the Zurbarán picture? Why am I not alone in loving it? Where and how and when does that love I feel take place? There is no art without the imaginary, and the imaginary is not a given; it arrives at a moment in human development, and it begins in play.

All mammals play, especially young ones, but imaginative play—taking on other roles, being the mother or the father or the baby, building sand castles, making mud pies, drawing a house with a big sun shining over it—belongs to human children and the ability develops over time. Vygotsky argues that in early childhood "there is a union of motives and perception. At this age perception is generally not an independent but rather an integrated feature of a motor action. Every perception is a stimulus to activity."[26] This comment resonates well with my earlier discussion about our proprioceptive, motor-sensory abilities that underlie our visual perceptions of things. Children learn through their active exploration of space, which in time develops into a sixth sense. Around the age of three *pretending* begins. In imaginative play, the child detaches the usual meaning of a thing, *stick,* for example, and gives it another significance, *horse.* The new meaning *horse* determines the child's action—galloping across the floor with the stick between his legs. That gallop has been severed from the ordinary meanings of what he sees around him. Dogs romp and play with each other, but they do not indulge in the fantasy of another world. And where does pretending happen? It occurs in an imaginary space that exists side by side with actual or real space. This human flexibility to be two places at once is a function of understanding time and symbolic representation. Because at some moment in my childhood, through my acquisition of reflection—in mirroring and then in language—I developed the ability to remember myself in the past and project myself into the future. I can leave my immediate circumstances and pretend that I am elsewhere or that I am someone else: the old man looking at Duccio, for example. I can imagine myself in the third person and as someone who is not me. Without this there is no art.

Merleau-Ponty writes, "In the case of the normal subject, the body is available not only in real situations into which it is drawn. It can turn aside from the world . . . lend itself to experimentation, and generally speaking take its place in the realm of the potential."[27] Art happens in this potential space—I would say fictional space of human life, the world of play and its transformations, which Vygotsky refers to as a "realm of spontaneity and freedom."[28] And it always involves some form of intentional motion outward into the other and otherness, not necessarily a specific place or person but an active *seeking toward them.* In *Remembering, Repeating, and Working Through* (1914), Freud uses the word *playground* in connection to the transference, that mysterious fluctuating space between patient and analyst, which he also calls "an intermediate region" where "almost complete freedom" is possible.[29] Winnicott elaborated on Freud's playground as the essential space of creativity: "This area of playing," he writes, "is not inner psychic reality. It is outside the individual, but it is not the external world."[30] Its origins are deep and bodily. They begin in the first relations between child and mother, in mirroring, in our physical explorations of space and our ability to posit an imaginary zone of experience, which Winnicott also refers to as "potential space."[31] This is the ground on which art lives. It is also where appreciation happens and where love can happen.

When we come to a work of art, we are not only witness to the results of another person's intentional play in his or her fictive space, we are free to play ourselves, to muse and dream and question and theorize. As spectators, we too find ourselves in a potential space between us and what we see because perception is active and creative, and artworks engage us, not just intellectually but emotionally, physically, consciously, and unconsciously, and that relation, that dialogue may be, as Schelling believed, finally indeterminable. But when we love a work of art, there is always a form of recognition that occurs. The object reflects us, not in the way a mirror gives our faces and bodies back to us. It reflects the vision of the other, of the artist, that we have made our own because it answers something within us that we understand is true. This truth may be only a feeling, only a humming resonance we cannot put into words, or it may become a vast discursive statement, but it must be there for the enchantment to happen—that excursion into you that is also I.

2010

NOTES

Variations on Desire: A Mouse, a Dog, Buber, and Bovary

1. Quoted in Mary Carruthers and Jan M. Ziolkowski, *The Medieval Craft of Memory: An Anthology of Texts and Pictures* (Philadelphia: University of Pennsylvania Press, 2002), 7.

2. Jaak Panksepp, *Affective Neuroscience: The Foundations of Human and Animal Emotions* (Oxford: Oxford University Press, 1998), 144.

3. Ibid., 144.

4. Martin Buber, *Between Man and Man* (New York: Macmillan, 1965), 11.

5. Gustave Flaubert, *Madame Bovary*, trans. Alan Russell (Baltimore: Penguin, 1965), 71.

6. Ibid., 325.

7. D. W. Winnicott, "The Relationship of a Mother to Her Baby at the Beginning," *The Family and Individual Development* (London: Routledge, 1995), 15.

My Mother, Phineas, Morality, and Feeling

1. Antonio Damasio, *Descartes' Error: Emotion, Reason and the Human Brain* (New York: HarperCollins, 1994), 44

2. A. R. Luria, *Higher Cortical Functions in Man* (New York: Basic Books, 1962), 256.

My Strange Head: Notes on Migraine

1. Francis Crick, *The Astonishing Hypothesis: The Scientific Search for the Soul* (New York: Simon & Schuster, 1994), 3.

2. A. R. Luria, *The Man with a Shattered World: The History of a Brain Wound*, trans. L. Solotaroff (Cambridge, MA: Harvard University Press, 1972), 42.

3. "Varieties of Religious Experience," in *William James: Writings 1902–1910* (New York: Library of America, 1987), 21.

4. Mark Solms, "Dreaming and REM Sleep Are Controlled by Different Brain Mechanisms," in *Sleep and Dreaming: Scientific Advances and Reconsiderations*, ed. Edward F. Pace-Schott, Mark Solms, Mark Blagrove, and Stevan Harnad (Cambridge: Cambridge University Press, 2003), 54.

5. Jacques Lusseyran, *And There Was Light* (Boston: Little, Brown, 1965).

Playing, Wild Thoughts, and a Novel's Underground

1. Wilfred Bion, *Taming Wild Thoughts* (London: Karnac Books, 1997), 27.

Sleeping/Not Sleeping

1. Geoffrey Chaucer, *The Book of the Duchess,* line 34.

2. Vladimir Nabokov, *Speak Memory: An Autobiography Revisited* (New York: Pyramid Books, 1967), 24–25.

3. Jorge Luis Borges, "Insomnia," in *Poems of the Night*, ed. Efrain Kristal, trans. Christopher Maurer (New York: Penguin, 2010), 37.

4. Chaucer, *The Book of the Duchess*, lines 28–29.

5. Aristotle, *On the Generation of Animals*, Loeb Classical Library 366, trans. A. L. Peck (Cambridge, MA: Harvard University Press, 1963), 1.1.778b28–33.

6. *The Complete Works of Aristotle: The Revised Oxford Translation*, vol. 1, *On Sleep*, trans. J. I. Beare (Princeton, NJ: Princeton University Press, 1984), p. 722, 1.1.451b7–8.

7. "The Meditations," in *Essential Works of Descartes*, trans. Lowell Bair (New York: Bantam Books, 1961), 60.

8. Maurice Merleau-Ponty, *The Phenomenology of Perception*, trans. Colin Smith (London: Routledge and Kegan Paul, 1962), 164.

9. *Standard Edition of the Complete Psychological Works of Sigmund Freud*, ed. and trans. James Strachey, vol. 14 (1917), *Metapsychological Supplement to the Theory of Dreams* (London: The Hogarth Press, 1957), 222.

10. Jaak Panksepp, *Affective Neuroscience* (Oxford: Oxford University Press, 1998), 266.

11. D. W. Winnicott, "The Deprived Child and How He Can Be Compensated for the Loss of Family Life," in *Deprivation and Delinquency* (London: Tavistock, 1984), 186.

My Father/Myself

1. Jessica Benjamin, *The Bonds of Love: Psychoanalysis, Feminism, and the Problem of Domination* (New York: Pantheon Books, 1988), 102.

2. Charles Dickens, *Little Dorrit* (Oxford: Oxford University Press, 1953), 540.

3. George Oppen, *Collected Poems* (New York: New Directions, 1975), 109.

4. *Henry James: Novels 1881–1886* (New York: Library of America, 1985), 109.

5. D. W. Winnicott, *The Child, the Family, and the Outside World* (London: Penguin, 1991), 117.

6. Paul Auster, *The Invention of Solitude* (New York: Penguin, 1982), 19.

7. Ibid., 81–82.

8. Mary Douglas, *Purity and Danger: An Analysis of the Concepts of Pollution and Taboo* (London: Routledge and Kegan Paul, 1966), 102.

9. Ibid., 103.

10. *The Standard Edition of the Complete Works of Sigmund Freud*, ed. and trans. James Strachey, vol. 19 (1924), *The Dissolution of the Oedipus Complex* (London: Hogarth Press, 1961), 178.

11. Benjamin, *The Bonds of Love,* 100.

12. Quoted in Julia Brigg, introduction to *To the Lighthouse,* by Virginia Woolf (New York: Everyman Library, 1938), xvi.

13. Allan N. Schore, *Affect Regulation and the Origin of the Self: The Neurobiology of Emotional Development* (Hillsdale, NJ: Lawrence Erlbaum, 1994), 97–108.

14. Franz Kafka, *Letter to His Father/Brief an den Vater,* trans. Ernst Kaiser and Eithne Wilkens (New York: Schocken Books, 1953), 19 and 21.

15. "Of Friendship," in *The Complete Essays of Montaigne,* trans. Donald M. Frame (Stanford: Stanford University Press: 1957), 136.

16. Susan Howe, *My Emily Dickinson* (New York: New Directions, 2007), 18–19.

17. Ibid., 19.

18. Ibid., 19.

19. Harold Bloom, *The Anxiety of Influence: A Theory of Poetry* (New York: Oxford University Press, 1997), 11.

20. Howe, *My Emily Dickinson,* 24.

21. Ibid., 25.

The Real Story

1. James Atlas, "Confessing for Voyeurs: The Age of the Literary Memoir Is Now," *The New York Times Magazine*, May 12, 1996, 26.

2. Michael A. Stone, *Abnormalities of Personality: Within and Beyond the Realm of Treatment* (New York: Norton, 1993), 285.

3. Daniel Defoe, *Moll Flanders* (New York: New American Library, 1981), v.

4. Henry Fielding, *Tom Jones* (Oxford: Oxford University Press, 1996), 361.

5. John Cleland, *Fanny Hill or The Memoirs of a Woman of Pleasure* (London: Penguin, 1985), 39.

6. Vicessimus Knox, "On Novel Reading," in *Novel and Romance 1700–1800: A Documentary Record,* ed. Ioan Williams (London: Routledge, 1970), 228.

7. Jean-Jacques Rousseau, *The Confessions,* trans. J. M. Cohen (London: Penguin, 1953), 17.

8. Leopold Damrosch, *Jean-Jacques Rousseau: Restless Genius* (New York: Houghton Mifflin, 2005), 30.

9. Ibid., 15.

10. William James, *The Principles of Psychology* (Chicago: Encyclopaedia Britannica, 1952), 288.

11. David Hume, *A Treatise on Human Nature* (Cleveland: Meridian Books, 1962), 311.

12. Siri Hustvedt, "Yonder," in *A Plea for Eros* (New York: Picador, 2006), 41.

13. Giambattista Vico, *The New Science,* trans. Thomas Goddard Bergin and Max Harold Fisch (Ithaca: Cornell University Press, 1968), 313.

14. Wilhelm Wundt, *Outlines of Psychology,* trans. Charles Hubbard Judd (London: Williams and Norgate, 1902), 261.

15. *The Vygotsky Reader,* ed. Rene van der Veer and Jaan Valsiner (London: Blackwell, 1994), 284.

16. Randy Buckner and Daniel Carroll, "Self-Projection and the Brain," *Trends in Cognitive Science* 11, no. 2 (2006): 50.

17. Ibid., 55

18. Julia Kristeva, *Time and Sense* (New York. Columbia University Press, 1994), 238.

19. Julia Kristeva, *Time and Sense* 239.

20. Marcel Proust, *Remembrance of Things Past,* trans. C. K. Scott Moncrieff and Terence Kilmartin (New York: Vintage, 1982), 3:843.

21. Maurice Merleau-Ponty, *The Phenomenology of Perception*, trans. Colin Smith (London: Routledge and Kegan Paul, 1962), 104–5.

22. Vladimir Nabokov, *Speak Memory*: *An Autobiography Revisited* (New York: Pyramid Books, 1967), 70.

23. Julia Kristeva, *Time and Sense,* 243.

24. Søren Kierkegaard, *Either/Or,* trans. David F. Swensen and Lillian Marvin Swenson (Garden City, NY: Anchor, 1959), 399.

Excursions to the Islands of the Happy Few

1. Benjamin H. D. Buchloh, *Neo-Avantgarde and Culture Industry: Essays on European and American Art from 1955 to 1975* (Cambridge: MIT Press, 2000), 329.

2. R. Llinás, U. Ribrary, D. Contreras, and C. Pedroarena, "The Neuronal Basis for Consciousness," *Philosophical Transactions of the Royal Society B* 353, no. 1377 (1998): 1841–49.

3. Hans Kohut, "Forms and Transformations of Narcissism," *Journal of the American Psychoanalytic Association* 14 (1966): 246.

4. D. W. Winnicott, *Deprivation and Delinquency* (London and New York: Routledge, 1984).

5. John Bowlby, *Attachment and Loss* (New York: Basic Books, 1969).

6. Thomas Kuhn, *The Structure of Scientific Revolutions* (Chicago: University of Chicago Press, 1970).

7. Jürgen Habermas, *The Philosophical Discourse of Modernity: Twelve Lectures*, trans. F. G. Lawrence (Cambridge: MIT Press, 1990), 113.

8. Samuel Beckett, *Waiting for Godot: A Tragicomedy in Two Acts* (New York: Grove Press, 1954), 28.

9. Stafford Beer, preface to *Autopoiesis and Cognition: The Realization of the Living*, by H. R. Maturana and F. J. Varela (Dordrecht, Netherlands: D. Riedel Publishing, 1980), 64.

10. Mignon Nixon, *Fantastic Reality: Louise Bourgeois and a Story of Modern Art* (Cambridge: MIT Press, 2005).

11. Daniel Dennett, *Consciousness Explained* (Boston: Little, Brown, 1991).

12. Antonio Damasio, *Descartes' Error: Emotion, Reason and the Human Brain* (New York: HarperCollins, 1994).

13. V. S. Ramachandran, *A Brief Tour of Human Consciousness: From Imposter Poodles to Purple Numbers* (New York: Pi Press, 2004).

14. David Freedberg, *The Power of Images: Studies in the History and Theory of Response* (Chicago: University of Chicago Press, 1989).

15. A. R. Luria, *The Man with a Shattered World: The History of a Brain Wound*, trans. L. Solotaroff (Cambridge, MA: Harvard University Press, 1972).

16. Maurice Merleau-Ponty, *The Visible and the Invisible*, trans. C. Lefort and A. Lingis (Evanston, IL: Northwestern University Press, 1969), 27.

17. American Psychiatric Association, *Diagnostic and Statistical Manual of Mental Disorders*, 4th ed. (Arlington, VA: American Psychiatric Association, 2000), xxxi.

18. Robert Musil, *The Man Without Qualities*, trans. Sophie Wilkins (New York: Alfred A. Knopf, 1995), 502.

19. Ibid., 503.

20. Ibid., 503.

On Reading

1. Danilo Kis, *A Tomb for Boris Davidovich*, trans. D. Mikic-Mitchell (New York: Penguin, 1980).

2. *The Passions of the Soul*, in *Essential Works of Descartes* (New York: Bantam, 1961).

3. Gottfried Leibniz, *Monadology* in *Discourse on Metaphysics and the Monadology*, trans. George R. Montgomery (Buffalo, NY: Prometheus, 1992).

4. There are many studies on change and inattentional blindness. See R. Rensink, "When Good Observers Go Bad: Change Blindness, Inattentional Blindness, and Visual Experience," *Psyche* 6 (2000): 9; A. Ariga, H. Yokasawa, and H. Ogawa, "Object-Based Attentional Selection and Awareness of Objects," *Visual Cognition* 15 (2007): 685–709. For the broader philosophical implications, see Eric Switzgebel, "Do You Have Constant Tactile Experience of Your Feet in Your Shoes? Or Is Experience Limited to What's in Attention?" *Journal of Consciousness Studies* 14 (2007): 5–35.

Stig Dagerman

1. Stig Dagerman, *The Snake*, trans. Laurie Thompson (London: Quartet Books, 1995).

2. *The Standard Edition of the Complete Works of Sigmund Freud*, ed. and trans. James Strachey, vol. 20 (1926), *Inhibitions, Symptoms, and Anxiety* (London: Hogarth Press, 1959), 132.

3. Søren Kierkegaard, *The Concept of Anxiety*, trans. Edna Hong and Howard Hong (Princeton, NJ: Princeton University Press, 1981), 61.

4. Jean-Paul Sartre, *Being and Nothingness: An Essay on Phenomenological Ontology*, trans. H. E. Barnes (New York: Washington Square Press, 1966).

The Analyst in Fiction: Reflections on a More or Less Hidden Being

1. Sigmund Freud, *On Aphasia: A Critical Study* (1891), trans. E. Stengel (New York: International Universities Press, 1953), 55.
2. Italo Svevo, *Zeno's Conscience*, trans. William Weaver (New York: Everyman's Library, 2001), 3.
3. Vladimir Nabokov, *Lolita* (New York: Charles Putnam and Sons, 1955), 7.
4. Philip Roth, *Portnoy's Complaint* (New York: Vintage, 1994), 274.
5. George Makari, *Revolution in Mind: The Creation of Psychoanalysis* (New York: HarperCollins, 2008), 334.
6. Otto Kernberg, *Borderline Conditions and Pathological Narcissism* (Lanham, MD: Aronson, 1985).
7. Lisa Appignanesi, "All in the Mind," *The Guardian,* February 16, 2008, http://www.guardian.co.uk/books/2008/feb/16/features reviews.guardianreview2.
8. F. Scott Fitzgerald, *Tender Is the Night* (New York: Charles Scribner's Sons, 1961), 208–9.
9. Ibid., 208.
10. Simone de Beauvoir, *The Mandarins*, trans. L. M. Friedman (New York: Norton, 1991), 184–85.
11. D. W. Winnicott, "Counter-Transference," in *The Maturational Processes and the Facilitating Environment* (London: Karnac Books, 1990), 160–61.

Critical Notes on the Verbal Climate

1. Immanuel Kant, *What Is Enlightenment?* trans. H. B. Nisbet (New York: Penguin, 2009), 1.
2. *New York Daily Plebeian*, April 20, 1844, http://www.history teacher.net/USProjects/DBQs2002/DBQ2002_Immigration.htm.

3. Thomas Frank, *What's the Matter with Kansas? How Conservatives Won the Heart of America* (New York: Henry Holt, 2004).

Three Emotional Stories

1. Siri Hustvedt, "Yonder," in *A Plea for Eros* (New York: Picador, 2006), 41.

2. Augustine, *Confessions,* trans. H. Chadwick (Oxford: Oxford University Press, 1988), 10:220–21.

3. Sandra Rudnick Luft, *Vico's Uncanny Humanism: Reading the New Science Between Modern and Post Modern* (Ithaca: Cornell University Press, 2003), 143.

4. Endel Tulving, "How Many Memory Systems Are There?" *American Psychologist* 40, no. 4 (1984): 385–98; Tulving, "What Is Episodic Memory?" *Current Directions in Psychological Science* 2, no. 3 (1993): 67–70; Henry L. Roediger and Fergus I. M. Craik, eds., *Varieties of Memory and Consciousness: Essays in Honour of Endel Tulving* (Hillsdale, NJ: Lawrence Erlbaum, 1989).

5. Jacek Debiec and Joseph E. LeDoux, "The Amygdala and the Neural Pathways of Fear," in *Post-Traumatic Stress Disorder: Basic Science and Clinical Practice,* ed. Priyattam Shiromani, Terence Keane, and Joseph LeDoux (New York: Humana, 2009), 23–39; LeDoux, *Synaptic Self: How Our Brains Become Who We Are* (New York: Viking, 2002); Karim Nader, Glenn E. Schafe, and Joseph LeDoux, "Fear Memories Require Protein Synthesis in the Amygdala for Reconsolidation after Retrieval," *Nature* 406, no. 6797 (2000): 722–26.

6. "Brute and Human Intellect," in *William James: Writings 1878–1889* (New York: Library of America, 1992), 911.

7. Jerome Bruner, *Actual Minds, Possible Worlds* (Cambridge, MA: Harvard University Press, 1986), 3–10.

8. Thomas Kuhn, *The Structure of Scientific Revolutions* (Chicago: University of Chicago Press, 1962).

9. Emile Benveniste, *Problems in General Linguistics,* trans. M. E. Meek (Coral Gables: University of Miami Press, 1971), 217–22.

10. A. R. Luria, *Higher Cortical Functions in Man,* trans. B. Haigh (New York: Basic Books, 1966), 31–35.

11. Maurice Merleau-Ponty, *The Phenomenology of Perception,* trans. C. Smith (London: Routledge and Kegan Paul, 1962), 43.

12. Ibid., 43.

13. Paul Ricoeur, *Time and Narrative,* trans. K. McLaughlin and D. Pellauer (Chicago: University of Chicago Press, 1984), 1:68.

14. Gregory A. Kimble, Michael Wertheimer, and Charlotte L. White, eds., *Portraits of Pioneers in Psychology* (Hillsdale, NJ: Lawrence Erlbaum, 1998), 3:75.

15. D. Hassabis, D. Kumaran, S. D. Vann, and E. Maguire, "Patients with Hippocampal Lesions Cannot Imagine New Experiences," *Proceedings of the National Academy of Sciences* 104 (2007): 1726–31; D. Hassabis, S. D. Kumaran, and E. Maguire, "Using Imagination to Understand the Neural Basis of Episodic Memory," *The Journal of Neuroscience* 27, no. 52 (2007): 14365–74.

16. Dorothée Legrand and Perrine Ruby, "What Is Self-Specific?: Theoretical Investigations and Critical Review of Neuroimaging," *Psychological Review* 116, no. 1 (2009): 258.

17. F. Frassinetti, F. Ferri, M. Maini, and V. Gallese, "Bodily Self: An Implicit Knowledge of What Is Explicitly Unknown," *Experimental Brain Research,* 12 (2011): 159.

18. Shaun Gallagher, *How the Body Shapes the Mind* (Oxford: Oxford University Press, 2005), 24.

19. Ibid., 11–12.

20. William James, *The Principles of Psychology* (Chicago: Encyclopaedia Britannica, 1952), 299.

21. *The Standard Edition of the Complete Works of Sigmund Freud,* ed. and trans. James Strachey, vol. 4–5 (1900), *The Interpretation of Dreams* (London: Hogarth Press, 1953), 460.

22. Marcel Proust, *Remembrance of Things Past*, trans. S. Moncreif and T. Kilmartin (New York: Vintage, 1982), 1:48.

23. Quoted in Dan Zahavi, *Subjectivity and Selfhood* (Cambridge, MA: MIT Press, 2008), 57.

24. Joseph Jaffe, Beatrice Beebe, Stanley Feldstein, Cynthia Crown, and Michael Jasnow, *Rhythms of Dialogue in Infancy* (Boston, MA: Blackwell, 2001), 2.

25. Jaak Panksepp, *Affective Neuroscience: The Foundations of Human and Animal Emotions* (Oxford: Oxford University Press, 1998), 55.

26. Zahavi, *Subjectivity and Selfhood,* 112.

27. Jaak Panksepp, "Neural Nature of the Core SELF: Implications for Understanding Schizophrenia," in *The Self in Neuroscience and Psychiatry*, ed. T. Kircher and A. David (Cambridge: Cambridge University Press, 2003), 204.

28. Antonio Damasio, *Self Comes to Mind: Constructing the Conscious Brain* (New York: Pantheon, 2010), 21.

29. Freud, *The Standard Edition,* vol. 14 (1915), *Instincts and Their Vicissitudes*, 118.

30. Gallagher, *How the Body Shapes the Mind,* 78–79.

31. A. N. Meltzoff and R. Brooks, "Intersubjectivity Before Language: Three Windows on Preverbal Sharing," in *On Being Moved: From Mirror Neurons to Empathy*, ed. S. Braten (Amsterdam: John Benjamins, 2007), 150.

32. L. S. Vygotsky, *Thought and Language*, trans. A. Kosulin (Cambridge, MA: MIT Press, 1986), 84–89.

33. Katherine Nelson, ed., *Narratives from the Crib* (Cambridge MA: Harvard University Press, 1989), 158.

34. Ibid., 163.

35. Françoise Davoine and Jean-Max Gaudillière, *History Beyond Trauma,* trans. S. Fairfield (New York: Other Press, 2004).

36. Quoted in D. Brown, A. W. Sheflin, and D. C. Hammond, eds., *Memory, Trauma, Treatment, and the Law* (New York: Norton, 1998), 94.

37. Freud, *The Standard Edition*, vol. 18 (1920), *Beyond the Pleasure Principle*, 31–32.

38. Brewster Ghiselin, *The Creative Process: Reflections in the Arts and Sciences* (Berkeley, CA: University of California Press, 1952), 32.

39. Ibid., 28.

40. Bruner, *Actual Minds*, 3.

41. Edward F. Kelly and Emily Williams Kelly, *Irreducible Mind: Toward a Psychology for the 21st Century* (with CD of F. W. M. Myers, *Human Personality,* 1903) (Lanham, MD: Rowman and Littlefield, 2007), 445.

42. Ernst Bertram and R. E. Norton, *Nietzsche: Attempt at a Mythology* (Champaign: University of Illinois Press, 2009), 198.

43. F. W. H. Myers, *Human Personality and Its Survival of Bodily Death* (London: Longmans, Green, 1903).

44. R. Jung, C. Gasparovic, R. S. Chaves, R. A. Flores, S. M. Smith, A. Caprihan, et al., "Biochemical Support for the Threshold Theory of Creativity," *Journal of Neuroscience* 29, no. 16 (2009): 5319; R. Jung, J. M. Segal, H. J. Bockholt, R. A. Flores, S. M. Smith, R. S. Chavez, et al., "Neuroanatomy of Creativity," *Human Brain Mapping* 31, no. 3 (2010): 398; C. R. Aldous, "Creativity, Problem Solving and Innovation in Science: Insights from History, Cognitive Psychology and Neuroscience," *International Education Journal* 8, no. 2 (2007): 177.

Freud's Playground

1. *The Standard Edition of the Complete Works of Sigmund Freud,* ed. and trans. James Strachey, vol. 12 (1914), *Remembering, Repeating, and Working Through* (London: Hogarth Press, 1958), 154.

2. Anna Freud, *The Ego and Mechanisms of Defense* (London: Karnac, 1995).

3. Sigmund Freud, *The Standard Edition,* vol. 22 (1932–33), *New Introductory Lectures on Psychoanalysis*, 95.

4. Sigmund Freud, *The Standard Edition,* vol. 21 (1930), *Civilization and Its Discontents,* 117.

5. Sigmund Freud, *New Introductory Lectures,* 95–97.

6. Jaak Panksepp, *Affective Neuroscience* (Oxford: Oxford University Press, 1998), 262.

7. Sigmund Freud, *New Introductory Lectures,* 97.

8. Sigmund Freud, *The Standard Edition,* vol. 2 (1893–1895), *Studies on Hysteria,* 302.

9. Sigmund Freud, *The Standard Edition,* vol. 7 (1905), *Fragment of an Analysis of a Case of Hysteria,* 116.

10. Sigmund Freud, *Remembering, Repeating,* 154. Transference as an "artifical illness" borrows directly from Jean Martin Charcot's notion that while under hypnosis, hysterical patients reproduced their symptoms in "artificial" hysteria.

11. *The Freud/Jung Letters: The Correspondence Between Sigmund Freud and C. G. Jung,* ed. William McGuire (Princeton: Princeton University Press, 1974), 12–13.

12. *The Clinical Diary of Sándor Ferenczi,* ed. Judith Dupont, trans. Michael Balint and Nicola Zarday Jackson (Cambridge, MA: Harvard University Press, 1985).

13. Sigmund Freud, *The Standard Edition,* vol. 4–5 (1900), *The Interpretation of Dreams,* 460.

14. D. W. Winnicott, "Transitional Objects and Transitional Phenomena—A Study in the First Not-Me Possessions," *International Journal of Psychoanalysis* 34 (1953): 90.

15. D. W. Winnicott, "Playing: A Theoretical Statement," in *Playing and Reality* (London: Routledge, 1971), 51.

16. Ibid., 51.

17. Johan Huizinga, *Homo Ludens: A Study of the Play Element in Culture* (Boston: The Beacon Press, 1950), 11.

18. L. S. Vygotsky, "The Role of Play in Development," in *Mind in Society: The Development of Higher Psychological Processes,* ed. Michael

Cole, Vera John-Steiner, Sylvia Scribner, and Ellen Souberman (Cambridge, MA: Harvard University Press, 1978), 99.

19. Martin Buber, *Between Man and Man* (London: Routledge, 1965), 6.

20. Friedrich Schiller, *On the Aesthetic Education of Man,* trans. Reginald Snell (Mineola, NY: Dover, 2004), 77–81.

21. Sigmund Freud, *The Standard Edition,* vol. 7 (1905), *Three Essays on the Theory of Sexuality,* 168.

22. Sigmund Freud, *The Standard Edition,* vol. 20 (1926), *Inhibitions, Symptoms, and Anxiety,* 133.

23. V. Gallese, L. Fadiga, L. Fogassi, and G. Rizzolatti, "Action Recognition in the Premotor Cortex," *Brain* 119 (1996): 593–609.

24. William Preyer, *The Mind of the Child/The Senses and the Will: Observations Concerning the Development of the Human Being in the First Years of Life,* trans. H. W. Brown (New York: Appleton, 1905).

25. Jacques Lacan, "The Mirror Stage as Formative of the *I* Function," in *Ecrits,* trans. Bruce Fink (New York: Norton, 2006), 75–81.

26. Jessica Benjamin, *The Bonds of Love: Psychoanalysis, Feminism and the Problem of Domination* (New York: Pantheon Books, 1988), 49.

27. Sigmund Freud, *The Standard Edition,* vol. 12 (1912), *Papers on Technique,* 118.

28. B. Beebe, J. Rustin, D. Sorter, and S. Knoblauch, "An Expanded View of Intersubjectivity and Its Application to Psychoanalysis," *Psychoanalytic Dialogues* 13 (2003): 777–803.

29. Andrew Meltzoff and M. Keith Moore, "Imitation of Facial and Manual Gestures by Human Neonates," *Science* 198, no. 4312 (1977): 74–78; Giannis Kugiumutzakis, "Neonatal Imitation in the Intersubjective Companion Space," in *Intersubjective Communication and Emotion in Early Ontogeny,* ed. Stein Bråten (Cambridge: Cambridge University Press, 1998), 63–88.

30. Colwyn Trevarthen, "The Concept and Foundations of Infant Intersubjectivity," in *Intersubjective Communication* (ibid.), 17.

31. Maurice Merleau-Ponty, *The Phenomenology of Perception,* trans. Colin Smith (London: Routledge and Kegan Paul, 1962), 352.

32. Allan Schore, *Affect Regulation and the Origin of the Self: The Neurobiology of Emotional Development* (Hillsdale, NJ: Lawrence Erlbaum, 1994).

33. Mirella Dapretto et al., "Understanding Emotions in Others: Mirror Neuron Dysfunction In Children with Autism Spectrum Disorders," *Nature Neuroscience* 9 (2006): 28–30.

34. R. Joseph, "The Neuropsychology of Development: Hemispheric Laterality, Limbic Language, and the Origin of Thought," *Journal of Clinical Psychology* 38 (1982): 243; G. L. Risse and M. S. Gazzaniga, "Well-Kept Secrets of the Right Hemisphere: A Carotid Amytal Study of Restricted Memory Transfer," *Neurology* 28 (1979): 950–53.

35. Endel Tulving, "What Is Episodic Memory?" *Current Directions in Psychological Science* 2, no. 3 (1993): 67–70.

36. Sigmund Freud, *The Standard Edition,* vol. 19 (1923), *The Ego and the Id,* 20.

37. M. M. Bakhtin, *The Dialogic Imagination,* ed. Michael Holquist, trans. Caryl Emerson and Michael Holquist (Austin: University of Texas Press, 1981).

38. Sigmund Freud, *The Standard Edition*, vol. 18 (1920), *Beyond the Pleasure Principle,* 14–17.

39. *The Seminar of Jacques Lacan,* vol. 11, *The Four Fundamental Concepts of Psychoanalysis,* ed. Jacques-Alain Miller, trans. Alan Sheridan (New York: Norton, 1981), 60–64 and 239.

40. Vygotsky, "The Role of Play," 97.

41. Panksepp, *Affective Neuroscience,* 282.

42. Sigmund Freud, *Studies on Hysteria,* 148.

43. Siri Hustvedt, *The Shaking Woman or A History of My Nerves* (New York: Picador, 2009).

44. Marjorie Taylor, *Imaginary Companions and the Children Who Create Them* (Oxford: Oxford University Press, 1999), 15.

45. *Annual Progress in Child Psychiatry and Development 2000–2001,* ed.

Margaret E. Hertzig and Ellen Farber (London: Routledge, 2002), 110.

46. Somogy Varga, "Explaining Impaired Play in Autism," *Journal für Philosophie und Psychiatrie* 3, no. 1 (2010): 7.

47. D. W. Winnicott, "Primitive Emotional Development," *International Journal of Psychoanalysis* 26 (1945): 140.

48. Taylor, *Imaginary Companions*, 34–61.

49. Todd Feinberg, *From Axons to Identity: Neurological Explorations of the Nature of the Self* (New York: Norton, 2009), 90–91.

50. Ibid., 85.

51. Sigmund Freud, *Interpretation of Dreams*, 590.

52. Ibid., 596.

53. Ibid., 103.

54. Quoted in Elizabeth Young-Bruehl, *Anna Freud: A Biography* (New Haven: Yale University Press, 2004), 286.

The Drama of Perception: Looking at Morandi

1. Quoted in Karen Wilken, *Giorgio Morandi: Works, Writings, Interviews* (Barcelona: Ediciones Poligrafa, 2007), 146.

2. Quoted in Laura Mottioli Rossi, ed., *The Later Morandi: Still Lifes, 1950–1964* (Venice: Mazzota, 1999), 13. Catalogue for the exhibition at the Peggy Guggenheim Gallery, Venice, April 30–September 13, 1999.

3. Maurice Merleau-Ponty, "Eye and Mind," trans. Carleton Dallery, in *The Primacy of Perception*, ed. John Wild (Chicago: Northwestern University Press, 1964), 164.

4. Eric R. Kandel, James H. Schwartz, and Thomas M. Jessel, eds, *Principles of Neural Science*, 4th ed. (New York: McGraw-Hill, 2000), 502–3.

5. Quoted in Gottfried Boehm, "Giorgio Morandi's Artistic Concept," in *Morandi*, ed. Ernst Gerhard Güse and Franz Armin Morat (Munich: Prestel, 2008), 15.

6. "Perception, Spatiality, and the Body," in *The Essential Husserl: Basic Writings in Transcendental Philosophy,* ed. Donn Welton (Bloomington. Indiana University Press, 1999), 165.

7. Boehm, "Morandi's Artistic Concept," 19

8. Ibid., 20

9. Siri Hustvedt, "Not Just Bottles," in *Mysteries of the Rectangle* (New York: Princeton Architectural Press, 2005), 131–32.

10. Antonio Damasio, *The Feeling of What Happens* (San Diego: Harcourt, 1999), 285–87.

11. Quoted in Leon Edel, *Henry James: A Life* (New York: Harper and Row, 1985), 250.

12. Kym Maclaren, "Embodied Perception of Others as a Condition of Selfhood: Empirical and Phenomenological Considerations," *Journal of Consciousness Studies* 15, no. 8 (2008): 75–76.

13. Janet Abramowicz, *Giorgio Morandi: The Art of Silence* (New Haven: Yale University Press, 2004), 216.

14. Ibid., 197.

15. Shaun Gallagher and Dan Zahavi, *The Phenomenological Mind: An Introduction to Philosophy of Mind and Cognitive Science* (London: Routledge, 2008), 145.

16. Merleau-Ponty, "Eye and Mind," 167.

Louise Bourgeois

1. Louise Bourgeois, *Destruction of the Father/Reconstruction of the Father: Writings and Interviews 1923–1997,* ed. Marie-Laure Bernadac and Hans-Ulrich Obrist (Cambridge, MA: The MIT Press, 2005), 1.

2. Ibid., 21.

3. Bourgeois, "Child Abuse," *Artforum* 20, no. 4 (1982): 40–47.

4. Robert Storr, "Abstraction: L'Esprit Géométrique," in *Louise Bourgeois,* ed. Frances Morris (London: Rizzoli, 2008), 26.

Old Pictures

1. Mark Solms and Oliver Turnbull, *The Brain and the Inner World: An Introduction to the Neuroscience of Subjective Experience* (New York: Other Press, 2002), 82.

2. John Berger, "Uses of Photography," in *About Looking* (New York: Pantheon, 1980), 54.

3. Georges Didi-Huberman, *Invention of Hysteria: Charcot and the Photographic Iconography of the Salpêtrière,* trans. Aliza Hartz (Cambridge, MA: MIT Press, 2004), 29.

4. Ibid., 32.

5. Roland Barthes, *Camera Lucida: Reflections on Photography,* trans. Richard Howard (New York: Farrar, Straus and Giroux, 1980), 99.

6. John Berger, *Ways of Seeing* (London: Penguin, 1972), 47.

7. Quoted in Frances A. Yates, *The Art of Memory* (London: Penguin, 1966), 17.

8. Antonio Damasio, *The Feeling of What Happens* (San Diego: Harcourt, 1999), 120–22.

9. David Levi-Strauss, *Between the Eyes: Essays on Photography and Politics* (New York: Aperture, 2004), 74.

10. Susan Sontag, *On Photography* (New York: Picador, 1977), 160.

11. Quoted in Daniel Brown, Alan W. Scheflin, and D. Corydon Hammond, *Memory, Trauma Treatment, and the Law* (New York: Norton, 1998), 440.

12. Jean Baudrillard, *Simulacra and Simulation* The Body in Theory: Histories of Cultural Materialism, trans. Sheila Faria Glaser (Ann Arbor, MI: University of Michigan Press, 1994), 12.

13. Paul Virilio, *The Aesthetics of Disappearance*, trans. Philip Beitschman (New York: Semiotext(e), 1991).

14. Quoted in Ralph Harrington, "The Railway Accident: Trains, Trauma and Technological Crisis in Nineteenth-Century England," http/www.york.ac.uk/insti/irs/irshome/papers/rlyacc.htm.

Kiki Smith: Bound and Unbound

1. Mary Douglas, *Purity and Danger: An Analysis of the Concepts of Pollution and Taboo* (London: Routledge and Kegan Paul, 1966), 150.
2. Deborah Solomon, "How to Succeed in Art," *New York Times Sunday Magazine*, June 27, 1999, 30–41.

Truth and Rightness: Gerhard Richter

1. Maurice Merleau-Ponty, "Eye and Mind," trans. Carleton Dallery, in *The Primacy of Perception,* ed. John Wild (Chicago: Northwestern University Press, 1964), 162.
2. Dietmar Elger, "Landscape as Model," *Gerhard Richter: Landscapes,* ed. Elger (Ostfldern-Ruit: Hatje Cantz, 2011), 16.
3. Claire Petitmengin, "Toward the Source of Thoughts: The Gestural and Transmodal Dimension of Lived Experience," *Journal of Consciousness Studies* 14, no. 3 (2007): 58.
4. Ibid., 58.
5. Robert Storr, "Interview with Gerhard Richter," in *Gerhard Richter: Forty Years of Painting* (New York: Museum of Modern Art, 2002), 289.

Why Goya?

1. *The Mirror of Art: Critical Studies by Baudelaire,* trans. Jonathan Mayne (Garden City, NY: Doubleday Anchor Books, 1956), 183.
2. Ibid., 184.
3. Quoted in Philip Hofer, introduction to *Francisco Goya y Lucientes, The Disasters of War* (New York: Dover, 1967), 1.
4. David Sylvester, "Goya," in *About Modern Art: Critical Essays 1948–1997* (New York: Henry Holt, 1997), 253–58.
5. Fred Licht, *Goya* (New York, London: Abbeville Press, 2001), 174–93.

6. Robert Hughes, *Goya* (New York: Alfred A. Knopf, 2003), 307.

7. Michael Nyman, *Facing Goya*, libretto by Victoria Hardie, Warner Classics, CD 0927-45342-2, 2002.

8. Goya is referred to in connection with McCullin in almost every article written about him, and he himself has mentioned Goya in interviews: "When I took pictures in war I couldn't help thinking of Goya." See "The Images and Memories of War," *Open Country*, BBC Radio 4, April 1, 2005, http://lan... ...content/images -and-memories-war.

9. John Berger, "The Honesty of Goya," *Selected Essays*, ed. Geoff Dyer (New York: Pantheon, 2001), 57.

10. Gregory Paschalidis, "Images of War and the War of Images," Aristotle University of Thessaloniki, 2006, http://genesis.ee.auth .gr/dimakis/Gramma/7/06-paschalidis.htm.

11. Susan Sontag, *On Photography* (New York: Farrar, Straus and Giroux, 1973), 19.

12. See Jean Baudrillard, *Simulacra and Simulation* (Ann Arbor: University of Michigan Press, 1995).

13. See *The Paul Virilio Reader*, ed. Steve Redhead (New York: Columbia University Press, 2004).

14. Susan Sontag, *Regarding the Pain of Others* (New York: Farrar, Straus and Giroux, 2003), 45.

15. Hughes, *Goya*, 314.

16. See Antonio Damasio's discussion of his patient Eliot, whose frontal lobe damage creates an emotional detachment and lack of empathy that is debilitating. Damasio, *Descartes' Error: Emotion, Reason and the Human Brain* (New York: Quill: HarperCollins, 2000), 34–79.

17. Nelson Goodman, *Languages of Art: An Approach to a Theory of Symbols* (Indianapolis and Cambridge: Hackett, 1976), 248.

18. D. O. Hebb, *The Organization of Behavior* (New York: Wiley, 1949).

19. Margaret M. Bradley, Maurizio Codispoti, Bruce N. Cuthbert, and Peter J. Lang, "Emotion and Motivation I: Defensive and

Appetitive Reactions in Picture Processing," *Emotion* 1, no. 3 (2001): 276–98.

20. Giacomo Rizzolatti and Michael A. Arbib, "Language Within Our Grasp," *Trends in Neuroscience* 21, no. 5: 188–94.

21. Battaglia and Freedberg presented their findings at a small seminar "Art and the Brain" at Columbia University on June 13, 2006. I was present that day and have summarized their findings as I remember them, but have no further information about publication of the paper.

22. Matthew Botvinick, Amishi P. Jha, Lauren M. Bylsma, Sara A. Fabian, Patricia E. Solomon, and Kenneth M. Prkachin, "Viewing Facial Expressions of Pain Engages Cortical Areas Involved in Direct Expression of Pain," *NeuroImage* 25 (2005): 312–19.

23. It is obvious that I am among those who accept that Goya is the artist of the Black Paintings. For a discussion of the controversy, see my essay, "More Goya: There Are No Rules in Painting," in *Mysteries of the Rectangle: Essays on Painting* (New York: Princeton Architectural Press, 2005), 113–18.

24. Siri Hustvedt, *What I Loved* (New York: Henry Holt, 2003), 202.

25. There is a single precedent I know of for altering a work of art. Robert Rauschenberg asked Willem de Kooning for a drawing to erase, which he got. See Mark Stevens and Annalyn Swan, *De Kooning: An American Master* (New York: Knopf, 2004), 358–60.

26. Maia Damianovic, "Dinos and Jake Chapman," *Journal of Contemporary Art*, 1997, http://www.jca-online.com/chapman.html. It is notable that here the brothers are quoted as if they were a single being with one voice.

27. Siri Hustvedt, "Narratives in the Body: Goya's *Los Caprichos*," in *Mysteries of the Rectangle,* 62–91.

28. More interesting than the rather obvious references to medical technologies in this work is the idea of fusion, which refers back to the brothers themselves as sibling collaborators.

29. Quoted in Jonathan Jones, "Look What We Did," *The Guardian*, March 31, 2003.

30. Baudelaire, *The Mirror of Art*, 186.

31. Hustvedt, *What I Loved*, 167.

32. Joseph E. LeDoux, "Emotion as Memory: Anatomical Systems Underlying Indelible Neural Traces," in *Handbook of Emotion and Memory*, ed. S. A. Christensen (Hillsdale, NJ: Lawrence Erlbaum, 1992), 380-111.

33. J. H. Krystal, S. M. Southwick, and D. S. Charney, "Post-Traumatic Stress Disorder: Psychobiological Mechanisms of Traumatic Remembrance," *Memory Distortion: How Minds, Brains, and Societies Reconstruct the Past* (Cambridge, MA: Harvard University Press, 1995), 150-72.

34. See Hustvedt on trauma: "More Goya," 105-7.

35. Quoted in Daniel Brown, Alan W. Scheflin, and D. Corydon Hammond, *Memory, Trauma Treatment, and the Law* (New York: W. W. Norton, 1998), 95-96.

36. Neurologist V. S. Ramachandran has argued that "the need to isolate a single visual modality before you amplify the signal in that modality" is an organizing principle of art in general, which, he says, explains "why an outline drawing or sketch is more effective as 'art' than a full colour photograph." Ramachandran and William Hirstein, "The Science of Art: A Neurological Theory of Aesthetic Experience," *Journal of Consciousness Studies* 6, no. 6-7 (1999): 24. This argument, however, seems too pat. Less isn't always more, and the camera, like the paintbrush, is a tool for making art. Such a principle cannot explain the fascination of a Jackson Pollock or the great triptychs of Hieronymus Bosch, for example, works that overwhelm the viewer with visual detail.

37. Lawrence Ferlinghetti, "In Goya's Greatest Scenes We Seem to See," *A Coney Island of the Mind* (New York: New Directions, 1958), 9-10.

38. Ivo Andric, *Conversation with Goya: Bridges, Signs,* trans. Celia Hawkesworth and Andrew Harvey (London: The Menard Press, 1992), 10–11.

39. Ibid., 16.

40. Janis Tomlinson, *Francisco Goya y Lucientes: 1746–1828* (London: Phaidon Press, 1994), 247–48.

41. Konstantin Pavlov, "Capriccio for/about Goya," in *Capriccio for Goya,* trans. Ludmilla G. Popova-Wightman (Princeton, NJ: Ivy Press, 2003), 61.

42. Debora Greger, "Musée des Beaux Arts," *Western Art* (New York: Penguin, 2004), 105.

43. It seems to me that the effect of the proliferation of photographs and films from war zones and disaster areas all over the world may be the very opposite of "derealization." Goya's images have come to seem more rather than less relevant to contemporary artists who are inundated with documentary evidence of slaughter around the globe.

Embodied Visions: What Does It Mean to Look at a Work of Art?

1. William James, *The Principles of Psychology* (Chicago: Encyclopaedia Britannica, 1952), 191.

2. Quoted in Dan Zahavi, "Inner Time Consciousness and Pre-Reflective Awareness," *The New Husserl: A Critical Reader,* ed. D. Walton (Bloomington: Indiana University Press, 2003), 158.

3. Jacques Lacan, "The Mirror Stage as Formative of the *I* Function," in *Ecrits,* trans. Bruce Fink (New York: Norton, 2006), 75–81.

4. William Preyer, *The Mind of the Child,* trans. H. Brown (New York: D. Appleton, 1888–1889), 195–99.

5. Andrew Meltzoff and M. Keith Moore, "Explaining Facial Imitation: A Theoretical Model," in *Early Development and Parenting* 6 (1997): 179–92.

6. G. W. F. Hegel, *The Phenomenology of Mind*, 2nd ed., trans. J. B. Baille (London: George A. Allen and Unwin Ltd., 1949), 83.

7. D. W. Winnicott, "Mirror-Role of the Mother and Family in Child Development," in *The Predicament of the Family: A Psychoanalytical Symposium*, ed. P. Lomas (London: Hogarth Press, 1967), 26–33.

8. See Allan Schore, *Affect Regulation and the Origin of the Self: The Neurobiology of Emotional Development* (Hillsdale, NJ: Lawrence Erlbaum, 1994).

9. V. Gallese, L. Fadiga, L. Fogassi, and G. Rizzolatti, "Action Recognition in the Premotor Cortex," *Brain* 119 (1996), 593–609.

10. See Andrew Bowie, *Schelling and Modern European Philosophy: An Introduction* (London: Routledge, 1993), 45–54.

11. Franz Brentano, *Psychology from an Empirical Standpoint*, trans. Antos C. Rancurello, ed. D. B. Terrell and Linda McAllister (London: Routledge, 1995), 88.

12. Maurice Merleau-Ponty, *Phenomenology of Perception,* trans. Colin Smith (London: Routledge and Kegan Paul, 1962).

13. Thomas S. Kuhn, "Revolutions as Changes of World View," chapter 10 in *The Structure of Scientific Revolutions*, 2nd ed. (Chicago: University of Chicago Press, 1970).

14. See Eric R. Kandel, James Schwartz, Thomas M. Jessell, eds., *Principles of Neural Science*, 4th ed. (New York: McGraw-Hill, 2000), 492–505.

15. Merleau-Ponty, *Phenomenology of Perception*, 104.

16. L. F. Barrett and Moshe Bar, "See It with Feeling: Affective Predictions during Object Perception," *Philosophical Transactions of the Royal Society* 364 (2009): 1325–34.

17. Paul Auster, *The Book of Illusions* (New York: Henry Holt, 2002), 286.

18. H. R. Maturana and F. J. Varela, *Autopoiesis and Cognition: The Realization of the Living* (Boston: D. Reidel, 1980).

19. Shaun Gallagher, *How the Body Shapes the Mind* (Oxford: Oxford University Press, 2005).

20. Claire Petitmengin, "Toward the Source of Thoughts: The Gestural and Transmodal Dimension of Lived Experience," *Journal of Consciousness Studies* 14, no. 3 (2007).

21. Alva Noë, *Action in Perception* (Cambridge, Mass. MIT Press, 2004).

22. J. J. Gibson, *The Ecological Approach to Visual Perception* (Hillsdale, NJ: Lawrence Erlbaum, 1979).

23. Andreas Engel and Peter König, "Paradigm Shifts in Neurobiology: Towards a New Theory of Perception," in *Philosophy and the Cognitive Sciences,* ed. R. Casati Barry Smith, and G. White (Wein and Leipzig: Hölder-Pichler-Tempsky, 1994), 131–38.

24. James C. Anderson, "Aesthetic Concepts of Art," *Theories of Art Today*, ed. Noel Carroll (Madison: University of Wisconsin Press, 2000), 65–92.

25. Ibid., 86.

26. L. S. Vygotsky, *Mind in Society: The Development of Higher Psychological Processes*, ed. Michael Cole, Vera John-Steiner, Sylvia Scribner, and Ellen Souberman (Cambridge, Mass: Harvard University Press), 96.

27. Merleau-Ponty, *Phenomenology of Perception,* 109.

28. Vygotsky, *Mind in Society,* 99.

29. *Standard Edition of the Complete Psychological Works of Sigmund Freud*, ed. and trans. James Strachey, vol. 12 (1914), *Remembering, Repeating, and Working Through* (London: Hogarth Press, 1953), 154.

30. D. W. Winnicott, *Playing and Reality* (London: Routledge, 1975), 51.

31. Ibid., 53.

ACKNOWLEDGMENTS

I gratefully acknowledge the museums and institutions that invited me to speak as part of their lecture series, which inspired the writing of several essays in this collection, as well as the magazines and journals where a number of others were originally published.

"Variations on Desire: A Mouse, a Dog, Buber and Bovary," *Conjunctions*: 48 (2007).

"My Strange Head: Notes on Migraine," *New York Times* migraine blogs: migraine.blogs.nytimes.com/author/siri-hustvedt (2007).

"Search for a Definition," *Assises Du Roman 2009: Lexique Nomade, Le Monde, Villa Gillet,* Christian Bourgois, Paris (2009).

"Playing, Wild Thoughts, and a Novel's Underground." Delivered in Lyon at the Villa Gillet Writer Festival (2009).

"Sleeping/Not Sleeping," *New York Times* insomnia blogs: opinionator.blogs.nytimes.com/2010/03/all-nighters (2010).

"Outside the Mirror," *Allure* (May 2011).

"Some Musings on the Word *Scandinavia*," *Lettre Internationale,* Denmark: 08 (2005).

"My Inger Christensen," *Jyllands Posten* [Danish newspaper] (Jan. 8, 2009); reprinted in *Poetry* (May 2009).

"My Father/Myself," *Granta*: 104 (2008).

"The Real Story," *Salmagundi:* Spring/Summer (2011).

"Excursions to the Islands of the Happy Few," *Salmagundi*: Fall/ Winter (2010).

"On Reading," *Columbia:* 49 (2011).

"Stig Dagerman." Foreword to *The Snake, Ormen,* Norstedts Forlag, Sweden (2010).

"The Analyst in Fiction: Reflections on a More or Less Hidden Being," *Contemporary Psychoanalysis*: 46, no. 2 (2010).

"Three Emotional Stories." Delivered as a lecture as part of Pain, Poetry, and Perception: A Symposium on the Convergence of Neuroscience, Literature, and Psychoanalysis at Georgetown University, Oct. 30, 2010. Sponsored by the Baltimore Washington Center for Psychoanalysis and the Department of Psychiatry Georgetown University Hospital. *Neuropsychoanalysis:* 13, no. 2 (Dec. 2011).

"Freud's Playground." Delivered as the thirty-ninth annual Sigmund Freud Lecture for the Sigmund Freud Foundation in

Vienna (May 6, 2011); published in *Salmagundi:* Spring/Summer (2012).

"Notes on Seeing," *Nomadikon: The Bergen Center of Visual Culture*: www.nomadikon.net/contentjtem.aspx?ci=125.

"The Drama of Perception: Looking at Morandi." Delivered as a lecture at the Metropolitan Museum of New York in the series Sunday Lectures at the Met (Sept. 21, 2008); published in *The Yale Review:* 97, no. 4 (2009).

"Louise Bourgeois" published as "The Places That Scare You" in *The Guardian* (Oct. 6, 2007).

"Duccio di Buoninsegna at the Met." "La Vierge et l'Enfant" in *Nouvel Observateur* (Aug. 18, 2005).

"Kiki Smith: Bound and Unbound," catalogue essay for Kiki Smith: *Wellspring,* Repères, Cahiers d' art contemporain, no. 139, Galerie Lelong, Paris (2007).

"This Living Hand" as "The Writer Siri Hustvedt on the Experience of Drawing" in *The Guardian* (Sept. 19, 2009).

"Truth and Rightness: Gerhard Richter," catalogue essay for *Gerhard Richter: Overpainted Photographs*. Museum Morsbrich, Leverkusen, Centre de la photographie Genève (2009).

"Annette Messager: Hers and Mine," published as "Puppet Master" in *The Guardian* (Feb. 21, 2009).

"Necessary Leaps: Richard Allen Morris," catalogue essay for Richard Allen Morris Retrospective: 1958–2004 at the Museum

Haus Lange, Krefeld, Germany, and Museum of Contemporary Art, San Diego (2005).

"Margaret Bowland's *Theatrum Mundi*," catalogue essay for *Excerpts from the Great American Songbook*, Babcock Galleries, New York, and the Greenville County Museum of Art (2011).

"Why Goya?" Delivered as a lecture at the Prado Museum in Madrid for Lecture Series sponsored by Fundacion Amigos Museo del Prado (Feb. 20, 2007); published in Spanish as "Francisco de Goya o los equivos," by Fundacion Amigos Museo del Prado (2008).

"Embodied Visions: What Does It Mean to Look at a Work of Art?" Delivered as the third annual Schelling Lecture at the Academie der Bildenen Künste in Munich (Feb. 27, 2010); published as a bilingual book by Deutscher Kunst Verlag (2010); published in *The Yale Review*: 98, no. 4 (2010).

SIRI HUSTVEDT

The Shaking Woman or A History of My Nerves

'Provocative but often funny, encyclopaedic but down to earth . . . an extraordinary double story' Oliver Sacks

While speaking at a memorial event for her father, the novelist Siri Hustvedt suffered a violent seizure from the neck down. Was it triggered by nerves, emotion – or something else entirely?

In this profound, thought-provoking and revealing book, Hustvedt takes the reader on her journey through psychiatry, philosophy, neuroscience and medical history in search of a diagnosis.

'Fascinating . . . she leaves the reader thinking about his or her bouts of illness in a thoroughly fresh way'
Lorna Bradbury, *Daily Telegraph*

'As with Sacks, scientific knowledge and a powerful capacity for empathy are closely linked . . . It is Hustvedt's gift to write with exemplary clarity of what is by necessity unclear.'
Hilary Mantel, *Guardian*

'A short book with an encyclopaedic breadth, one that recognises the "terrible strangeness" of the inner life'
Lisa Appignanesi, *Independent*

SIRI HUSTVEDT
The Summer Without Men

'By turns funny, moving and erudite, playfully
reminding us of a contemporary Jane Austen'
Daily Mail

After Mia Fredriksen's husband of thirty years asks for a
pause – to indulge his infatuation with a young French
colleague – she cracks up (briefly), rages (deeply), then
decamps to the prairie town of her childhood to consider
her position. It's a familiar scenario, though what tran-
spires in this provocative, mordant and vivacious
tragicomedy is anything but predictable.

'A rich and intelligent meditation on female identity,
written in beguiling lyrical prose ... heady and
intoxicating'
The Sunday Times

'It's an astonishingly joyful read ... a book that
shines with intellectual curiosity and emotional
integrity ... every page reminds us that, as Mia's doctor
tells her, "tolerating cracks is part of being alive".'
Guardian

'A warm, affecting tale about love, loss and finding
consolation in female friendship ... I, for one, would
prefer Hustvedt's name on the cover to that of many
male novelists.
Tatler